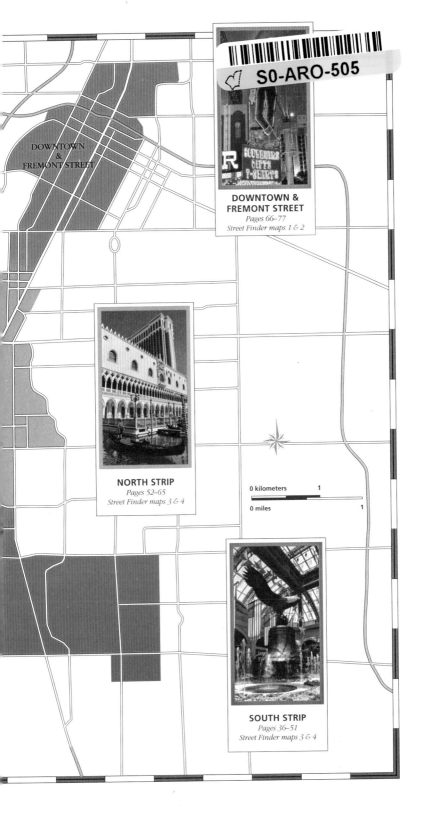

DOWNTOWN
&
FREMONT STREET

S0-ARO-505

**DOWNTOWN &
FREMONT STREET**
*Pages 66–77
Street Finder maps 1 & 2*

NORTH STRIP
*Pages 52–65
Street Finder maps 3 & 4*

0 kilometers   1

0 miles   1

SOUTH STRIP
*Pages 36–51
Street Finder maps 3 & 4*

EYEWITNESS TRAVEL

LAS VEGAS

EYEWITNESS TRAVEL

LAS VEGAS

MAIN CONTRIBUTOR: DAVID STRATTON

LONDON, NEW YORK,
MELBOURNE, MUNICH AND DELHI
www.dk.com

MANAGING EDITOR Aruna Ghose
ART EDITOR Benu Joshi
PROJECT EDITOR Shahnaaz Bakshi
PROJECT DESIGNER Kavita Saha
PICTURE RESEARCH Taiyaba Khatoon
SENIOR CARTOGRAPHER Uma Bhattacharya
CARTOGRAPHER Alok Pathak
DTP COORDINATOR Shailesh Sharma
DTP DESIGNER Vinod Harish

MAIN CONTRIBUTOR
David Stratton

PHOTOGRAPHER
Nigel Hicks

ILLUSTRATORS
Pramod Negi, Arun Pottirayil, Madhav Raman, Ashok Sukumaran

Reproduced by Colourscan (Singapore)
Printed and bound by South China Printing Co. Ltd., China

First American Edition 2005

10 11 12 13 10 9 8 7 6 5 4 3 2 1

Published in the United States by
DK Publishing, 375 Hudson Street,
New York, New York 10014

Reprinted with revisions 2007, 2008, 2009, 2010

Published in Great Britain by Dorling Kindersley Limited.

A CATALOGING IN PUBLICATION RECORD IS AVAILABLE FROM THE
LIBRARY OF CONGRESS.

ISSN: 1542-1554
ISBN: 978-0-75666-151-9

Front cover main image: view of Las Vegas Strip at dusk

MIX
Paper from
responsible sources
FSC
www.fsc.org FSC™ C018179

Lucky the Clown outside Circus
Circus *(see pp64–5)*

CONTENTS

HOW TO USE
THIS GUIDE **6**

INTRODUCING
LAS VEGAS

FOUR GREAT DAYS IN
LAS VEGAS **10**

PUTTING LAS VEGAS
ON THE MAP **12**

THE HISTORY OF
LAS VEGAS **16**

LAS VEGAS AT A
GLANCE **24**

LAS VEGAS THROUGH
THE YEAR **30**

Mesmerizing light shows, Fremont
Street Experience *(see p73)*

◁ The colorful, kaleidoscopic lights of the Strip at night

The luxurious Venetian, overlooking the Strip *(see pp58–9)*

Poker chips

Red Rock Canyon

Bellagio
(see pp48–9)

HOW TO USE THIS GUIDE

This Dorling Kindersley travel guide helps you to get the most from your visit to Las Vegas by providing detailed practical information and expert recommendations. *Introducing Las Vegas* maps the city and region, setting it in its historical and cultural context, and describes events through the entire year. *Las Vegas at a Glance* is an overview of the city's main attractions. *Las Vegas Area by Area* starts on page 34. This is the main sightseeing section, which covers all the important sights, with maps, photographs, and illustrations. *Farther Afield* looks at sights just outside the city, while *Beyond Las Vegas* explores other inviting locations within easy reach of the city. Information about hotels, restaurants, shops, entertainment, and sports is found in *Travelers' Needs*. The *Survival Guide* has advice on everything from using the postal service and the telephone system to Las Vegas's medical services and public transport system.

FINDING YOUR WAY AROUND THE SIGHTSEEING SECTION

Each of the three sightseeing areas in Las Vegas is color-coded for easy reference. Every chapter opens with an introduction to the area of the city it covers, describing its history and character, and has a *Street-by-Street* map illustrating typical parts of that area. Finding your way around the chapter is made simple by the numbering system used throughout. The most important sights are covered in detail in two or more full pages.

Each area has color-coded thumb tabs.

1 Introduction to the area
For easy reference, the sights in each area are numbered and plotted on an area map. This map also shows monorail stations. The area's key sights are listed by category, such as Museums and Galleries and are also shown on the Street Finder on pages 190–195.

Locator map

A locator map shows where you are in relation to other areas in the city centre.

2 Street-by-Street map
This gives a bird's-eye view of interesting and important parts of each sightseeing area. The numbering of the sights ties up with the area map and the fuller description of the entries on the pages that follow.

Stars indicate the sights that no visitor should miss.

LAS VEGAS AREA MAP

The colored areas shown on this map *(see inside front cover)* are the three main sightseeing areas used in this guide. Each is covered in a full chapter in *Las Vegas Area by Area (see pp34–91)*. They are highlighted on other maps throughout the book. In *Las Vegas at a Glance*, for example, they help you locate the top sights. They are also used to help you find the position of two walks and a drive *(see pp84–91)*.

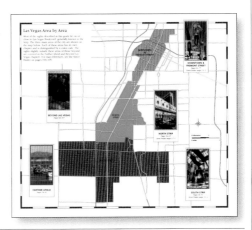

Numbers refer to each sight's position on the area map and its place in the chapter.

Story boxes provide information about historical or cultural topics relating to the sights.

3 Detailed information
All the important sights in Las Vegas are described individually. They are listed in order following the numbering on the area map at the start of the section. Practical information includes a map reference, opening hours, and telephone numbers. The key to the symbols is on the back flap.

The visitors' checklist gives all the practical information needed to plan your visit.

Practical information provides everything you need to know to visit each sight. Map references pinpoint the sight's location on the *Street Finder* map *(see pp190–195)*.

4 Las Vegas's major sights
Important buildings are dissected to reveal their interiors; museums and galleries have color-coded floorplans to help you find the most important exhibits.

The list of star features recommends the places that no visitor should miss.

INTRODUCING
LAS VEGAS

FOUR GREAT DAYS IN LAS VEGAS

As one of the world's busiest tourist destinations, the city of Las Vegas offers just about everything – grand hotels, spectacular shows, excellent shops and restaurants, theme park attractions, and the natural beauty of the surrounding lakes, parks, and canyons. Most visitors, however, are here for a short period and need to plan their visit efficiently so as to sample the best of all that is available.

A Cirque du Soleil artist, Bellagio

The following itineraries present suggestions for four distinct days of sightseeing, exploring, and amusement, and offer ideas on where to eat, what to see, and what to do for entertainment. However, these suggestions are just that and can be modified to suit your requirements. The price guides are indicative of the cost of transport and admission (if any) for two adults or for a family of two adults and two children.

Classical setting of Grand Canal Shoppes at the Venetian

SHOPPING AND SIGHTSEEING

- **Shop at Via Bellagio**
- **Lunch at Grand Canal Shoppes**
- **Light-and-sound shows at Fremont Street Experience**
- **"O" at the Bellagio**

TWO ADULTS allow at least $300

Morning
Start at **Via Bellagio** *(see p137)*, an upscale shopping promenade that consists of some of the world's most exclusive shops, such as Giorgio Armani, Gucci, Prada, Tiffany & Co., Hermès, and Fred Leighton. Farther north on the Strip is **Forum Shops at Caesars Palace** *(see p136)*, an eclectic mix of designer shops. Walk across the street, and head for the **Venetian** *(see pp58–9)*. Take some time to admire the magnificent architecture that re-creates

famous sights of Venice. After a brief photography session, head for **Grand Canal Shoppes** *(see p137)*, a chic shopping arcade set along a canal. The complex also has several eateries to stop at for a quick lunch.

Afternoon
A short distance from here is **Fashion Show Mall** *(see p136)*, the city's largest mall, which is anchored by high-end department stores. For shoppers who prefer to rummage, head downtown and check out **The Attic** *(see p141)* for vintage clothing from the 1950s to the 1970s. Also see the light-and-sound shows at **Fremont Street Experience** *(see p73)*. In the evening, put your feet up and take in the Cirque du Soleil production of **"O"** *(see p144)* at Bellagio. Reservations are required for this spectacular, fantastical, water-themed show.

WILD, WEIRD, AND WONDERFUL

- **Visit the Lion Habitat**
- **Try the thrilling rides at Stratosphere Tower**
- **See Masquerade Show in the Sky**

TWO ADULTS allow at least $175

Morning
Begin at **MGM Grand** *(see p44)*, and see wild cats at the **Lion Habitat**. Then head to the **Liberace Museum** *(see p45)*, which features the famous entertainer's striking cars and outrageous outfits. Head back to the Strip and take the monorail to Harrah's. Across the street is **Mirage** *(see p56)*. Then end the morning with a visit to see the white tigers and the playful dolphins at **Siegfried & Roy's Secret Garden and Dolphin Habitat** *(see p56)*.

Atlantic bottlenose dolphins at play, Dolphin Habitat, Mirage

Afternoon

Head to **Sahara** *(see p62)* for lunch at **NASCAR Café** *(see p129)*. Walk to **Stratosphere Tower** *(see p63)* and try the thrill rides, situated nearly 1,000 ft (305 m) high above the ground. Nearby is the **Viva Las Vegas Wedding Chapel** *(see p168)* that performs themed weddings, and the **Little White Chapel** *(see p168)* with its drive-up window for quick weddings. In the evening, catch **Show in the Sky** at **Rio** *(see p50)*, which features floats and exotic dancers. The dining choices at Rio are eclectic, and many restaurants nearby – such as **Buzio's Seafood Restaurant** *(see p125)* – are also superb.

Sheer red sandstone cliffs at Red Rock Canyon

GREAT OUTDOORS

- **Enjoy a hike at Red Rock Canyon**
- **Picnic at Willow Springs**
- **Drive up Mount Charleston**

TWO ADULTS allow at least $50

Morning

Head out on a 20-minute drive from the Strip to **Red Rock Canyon** *(see p80)*. Take the 13-mile (21-km) scenic loop drive and view the majestic red sandstone rock formations. Allow time for a hike – a minimum 60-minute walk – into one of the many canyons here. **Willow Springs** *(see p80)* is a good picnicking spot, or visit **Bonnie Springs'** *(see p81)* coffee shop for lunch.

Afternoon

After lunch, make your way northwest along Highway 95 to **Toiyabe National Forest** *(see p81)*. Drive up **Mount Charleston** *(see p81)*, which is located within the forest and is a popular year-round destination for hiking, backpacking, picnicking, and overnight camping, as well as skiing and snowboarding during winter. Stop at the **Mount Charleston Ranger Station** *(see p154)* for maps and any information on the area's ecology and history. On the way down the mountain, pay a visit to the **Mount Charleston Hotel** *(see p120)*. The **Canyon Dining Room** *(see p133)* here offers a variety of satisfying meat and fish dishes in comfortable rustic surroundings along with sweeping views of the mountains and trees.

A FAMILY DAY

- Rides at Adventuredome
- Eat candy at M&M's World
- Visit Bodies: the Exhibition
- Watch the Tournament of Kings show

FAMILY OF FOUR allow at least $430

Morning

It is a good idea to get an early start at **Circus Circus's Adventuredome** *(see pp64–5)*, the most popular children's attraction in Las Vegas. This indoor amusement park features many

Riders being spun around on Chaos at Adventuredome

rides, fast-paced as well as toddler-friendly, and a variety of arcade games. Also stop at **Carnival Midway** *(see p64)* to enjoy free circus acts such as clowns and trapeze and high-wire artists. Go south on the Strip and savor the chocolates at **M&M's World** *(see p44)*. Next door, **GameWorks** *(see p44)* is the ultimate video game arcade.

Afternoon

Stop at **New York-New York** *(see p43)* for a quick lunch of great burgers and sandwiches at **ESPN Zone** *(see p124)*. Take a free monorail ride from **Excalibur** *(see p42)* down to **Mandalay Bay's Shark Reef** *(see pp40–41)*, a huge aquarium with sharks, reptiles, and other marine life. Get back on the monorail for a short ride to **Luxor** *(see p42)* and learn all about the human anatomy at **Bodies: the Exhibition** *(see p42)*. In the evening, walk back to **Excalibur** and dine while watching racing chariots, jousting knights, and sword fights at the **Tournament of Kings** *(see p172)* show.

Visitors watching the marine life at Shark Reef, Mandalay Bay

Putting Las Vegas on the Map

Renowned as the Entertainment Capital of the
World, Las Vegas covers 113 sq miles (292 sq km) of
the Nevada desert in Southwest USA. Located
270 miles (434 km) northeast of Los Angeles, the
population of this city is constantly growing. More
than 38 million visitors come to Las Vegas each
year, lured by its casinos and other attractions. An
international airport and interstate highways connect
the city to the rest of the country and the world.
Within easy driving distance are lakes, canyons, and
vast desert plateaus.

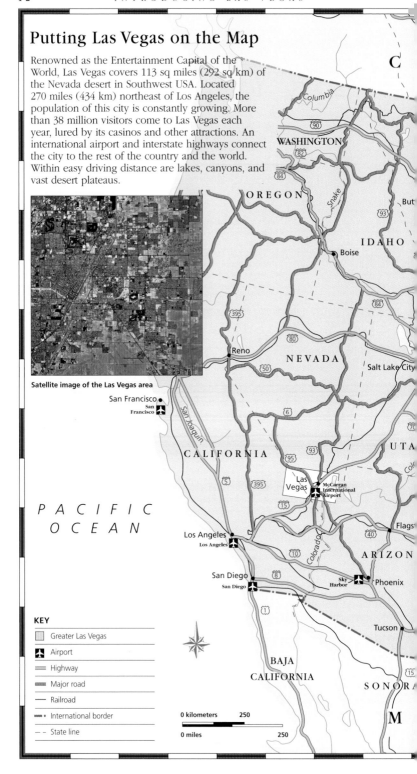

Satellite image of the Las Vegas area

KEY

▦	Greater Las Vegas
✈	Airport
▬	Highway
▬	Major road
—	Railroad
—·—	International border
– –	State line

0 kilometers   250

0 miles   250

C

Columbia

WASHINGTON

OREGON

Snake

IDAHO

Boise

But

Reno

NEVADA

Salt Lake City

San Francisco
San Francisco

San Joaquin

CALIFORNIA

UTA

PACIFIC
OCEAN

Las Vegas

McCarran International Airport

Los Angeles
Los Angeles

Flags

Colorado

ARIZON

San Diego
San Diego

Sky Harbor

Phoenix

Tucson

BAJA
CALIFORNIA

SONORA

M

NORTH AMERICA

CANADA

UNITED STATES
OF
AMERICA

• Las Vegas

ATLANTIC
OCEAN

PACIFIC
OCEAN

MEXICO

Gulf of
Mexico

Caribbean Sea

SOUTH AMERICA

A D A

Missouri

MONTANA

NORTH
DAKOTA

WYOMING

Casper

UNITED NEBRASKA
STATES OF AMERICA

SOUTH
DAKOTA

Sioux Falls

IOWA

Des Moines

Lincoln

Omaha

Platte

St Paul

Minneapolis
Minneapolis-
St Paul

Denver

Denver

COLORADO

Colorado Springs

KANSAS

Arkansas

Wichita

Kansas City

Topeka

OKLAHOMA

Tulsa

Albuquerque

Oklahoma City

Rio Grande

NEW
MEXICO

El Paso

I C O

CHIHUAHUA

GREATER LAS VEGAS

Desert
National
Wildlife Range

0 kilometers 5

0 miles   5

Mt. Charleston
3632m

North
Las
Vegas

Red Rock
Canyon

Las
Vegas

Lake
Mead

Blue
Diamond

Henderson

Hoover Dam

Mountain
Springs

Boulder
City

Central Las Vegas

The Las Vegas valley is split into east and west sections with the Las Vegas Boulevard or the Strip serving as the central divider. The Strip also often acts as a starting point for visitors who want to explore the city's attractions, many of which are located along the boulevard or within a few blocks of it. These include luxurious and grand mega resorts, museums, fantastic shows, massive shopping malls, theme parks, and much more. Towards the north end of the Strip is the downtown area, home to the entertaining Fremont Street Experience and Neonopolis center.

Neon Signs, Downtown Las Vegas
The downtown area and Fremont Street (see pp66–77) feature an interesting collection of restored neon signs, including the old Hacienda's horse and rider.

Fashion Show Mall
The jewel of the city's shopping malls, Fashion Show is home to upscale department stores such as Nordstrom, Saks Fifth Avenue, and Neiman Marcus, as well as more than 225 shops, boutiques, and restaurants (see p57).

Flamingo Las Vegas
The glittering pink-and-orange feather sign outside this hotel is one of Las Vegas's most recognized icons (see p51). Nothing remains of Bugsy Siegel's original resort except a stone pillar and a small plaque in the casino's garden.

KEY

▢	Major sights
🚊	City monorail
🚊	Free monorail
🚌	Greyhound bus terminal
P	Parking
ℹ	Tourist information
🚔	Police station
⊠	Post office
—	Monorail route

Showgirl from Jubilee!, Ballys
The longest-running show on the Strip, Jubilee! at Bally's (see p47) is an extravaganza celebrating classic Las Vegas glitz and glitter.

Map labels: INDUSTRIAL ROAD, CIRCUS CIRCUS DR, Circus Circus, STARDUST ROAD, CONV DRIVE, FASHION SHOW DRIVE, NORTH ST, Wynn Las Vegas, SPRING MOUNTAIN RD, BURBANK, SANDS, Venetian, AVENU, VIKING ROAD, ALBERT AVE, WEST FLAMINGO ROAD, NEVSO DRIVE, Bellagio, EA, S VALLEY VIEW BLVD, ARVILLE STREET, UNIVERSITY AVE, CAMERON STREET, WEST HARMON AVENUE, POLARIS AVENUE, FRANK SINATRA DRIVE, AUDRIE, KOVAL, LAS VEGAS BOULEVARD SOUTH, EAST ST, HARF, LANE, SOUTH ST, TOMPKINS AVE, WEST TROPICANA AVENUE, RENO AVE, EA, EAST HACIENDA AVENUE, Mandalay Bay

Fremont Street Experience
Night turns into day as hundreds of visitors stroll under this brightly-lit canopy to watch the amazing light-and-sound shows (see p73).

Madame Tussaud's
The Vegas branch of this famous wax exhibition in London is located at the Venetian (see pp58–9). More than 100 celebrities, including Hollywood personalities, rock stars, and sports figures are displayed here. A special exhibit features "Las Vegas Legends," such as Elvis Presley, Frank Sinatra, and Liberace.

Mystère at Treasure Island
The longest running Cirque du Soleil show in Las Vegas, this spectacular production showcases fantastic circus acts, and is a surrealistic celebration of music, dance, acrobatics, mime, and comedy (see pp56–7).

The Orleans
This hotel and casino boasts an impressive array of facilities. These include an 18-screen cinema complex, bowling alley, spa, and a large arena used for concerts and special events (see pp56–7).

THE HISTORY OF LAS VEGAS

*O*ne of America's most modern cities, Las Vegas did not exist before the 20th century. Initially an oasis for desert travelers, many people say that it was only after Bugsy Siegel built the Flamingo hotel in 1946 that the town shed its frontier image in favor of ultra-modern neon. Since then, Las Vegas's growth has centered around its image as the world's entertainment capital.

Most of the Southwest and the area today known as Las Vegas was once submerged by a huge lake fed by waters from the retreating glaciers of the last Ice Age, 25,000 years ago. The earliest signs of human activity in this region date back 11,000 years to the Paleo Indian period. Skilled hunters of mammoths and other large animals, the Paleo-Indians roamed the area in small groups between 10,000 and 8,000 BC.

Gradually, the climate began to change and became increasingly warm. As a result, the lake slowly dried up, and the area around today's Las Vegas turned to desert. In order to survive in this new environment, the Paleo-Indians underwent long period of adaptation. As the large mammals died out, they began hunting small game and gathering roots and berries. These hunters-and-gatherers came to be known as Archaic Indians. Though the area they occupied was arid, spring waters were plentiful in places. Anthropologists believe that as the population grew, settled farming

Anasazi Indian bowl

societies began to appear. By about AD 800, Anasazi Indians, or Ancient Ones, had settled along the washes, dry beds of inter-mittent streams, and in the valleys to the north and east of what is now Las Vegas. A highly advanced Native civilization, they grew corn, beans, and squash; hunted with bows and arrows; made baskets; and lived in pit houses. By 1050 however, the area was inexplicably abandoned, possibly due to drought.

EARLY EXPLORERS

As time passed, the peaceful and semi-nomadic Southern Paiute tribe came to the region, and occupied it for the next seven centuries. They grew corn and squash, and hunted wild animals. Petroglyphs indicate the Paiute had settlements at Red Rock Canyon *(see p80)*, and Valley of Fire *(see p81)*. One of the first Europeans they met was in 1776, when Francisco Garces, a Franciscan friar, traveled along the Old Spanish Trail, which connected the Catholic-Spanish missions between New Mexico and California.

TIMELINE

800 Anasazi Indians settled in Southern Nevada

Anasazi earrings

1776 Spanish missionaries "discover" the area

AD 500	750	1000	1250	1500	1750

1050 Native peoples abandon the region

Petroglyphs found in the Valley of Fire

◁ **Painting depicting the early days of gambling in Las Vegas**

Mormon pioneers on the great trek westward

Garces was followed 50 years later by fur trader and explorer Jedediah Smith, who passed through present-day Southern Nevada and blazed a route that would traverse the Sierra Nevada Mountains. In 1829, Spanish trader Antonio Armijo and his scout Rafael Rivera traveled along the Spanish Trail and found a path that led them through an area with oasis-like springs. They named it Las Vegas, or "The Meadows."

By the mid-1800s, the area had become a popular camping spot because of its source of water. In 1845, John C. Fremont, a cartographer with the US Topographical Corps, led an expedition through the region, and drew accurate maps of the Nevada landscape.

Exploration eventually ended in exploitation with the Paiutes losing control of their land as the Las Vegas Valley's popularity finally resulted in its colonization. In 1855, the Mormon president, Brigham Young *(see p105)*, sent a group led by William Bringhurst to set up a mission in Las Vegas, where they built a fort and

Helen Stewart, local ranch owner

developed farmlands. The discovery of lead at nearby Mount Potosi attracted miners from Salt Lake City and led the Mormons to launch a mining operation. Their lack of experience and growing dissension between the missionaries and the miners, coupled with crop failures and harsh summers, forced the Mormons to abandon their mission in 1858. Mining continued, however, and in 1861, the discovery of silver at Potosi led to a fresh influx of prospectors. Among them was Octavius Gass, a failed gold prospector.

THE CITY'S BEGINNINGS

A permanent settlement developed in 1865, when Gass seized the opportunity to take ownership of the Old Mormon Fort and set up a ranch – the Las Vegas Ranch – and supply station. Gass succeeded in growing crops by digging irrigation channels on the land. By 1872, he owned most of the land in Las Vegas. However, he eventually slid into debt and was forced to sell his land to Archibald Stewart, a wealthy rancher.

TIMELINE

Mormon pioneers

1826 Explorer Jedediah Smith passes through Southern Nevada

1845 John C. Fremont leads an expedition to Las Vegas

1855–58 Mormons establish a settlement in Las Vegas Valley

1864 Nevada admitted to the Union as the 36th state

1884 Helen Stewart becomes owner of the Las Vegas Ranch

1825	1840	1855	1870	188

Following Stewart's death in 1884, his wife Helen took charge of the land. Over the next 20 years, she acquired more land and ran the ranch as a profitable resort. In 1903, she sold the Las Vegas Ranch to William A. Clark, proprietor of the San Pedro, Los Angeles, and Salt Lake Railroad, who planned to take advantage of its strategic location, as an ideal stopping point for trains. By 1905, the railroad was completed and a train service had begun. In January of the same year, a golden spike was driven in just south of Las Vegas, attracting yet more speculators to the area. The publicity generated by the railroad created a huge demand for land, and on May 15, 1905, the railroad company auctioned 1,200 lots of land. Almost overnight, the city was transformed as buildings sprang up and businesses were established.

Roulette session in progress at a casino in Las Vegas

DEVELOPMENT

The city of Las Vegas, with a population of about 1,500, was officially incorporated as a municipality in 1911. The same year, the railroad built a locomotive repair yard here. The resulting jobs doubled the population. But it was not a model town. There was no sewage system, prostitution was rife in the city's red-light district, Block 16, and gambling, though illegal, was widespread. Some modernization, however, did take place. By 1915, residents had 24-hour electricity, and the Las Vegas Land and Water Company began graveling streets and laying water pipes.

In 1931, Nevada legislators legalized quick divorces and gambling, the latter in attempts to gain tax revenues.

The Great Depression did not affect Las Vegas much. Building work on the Hoover Dam project *(see p83)*, originally known as Boulder Dam, began in 1931 and employed about 5,100 workers, funnelling millions of dollars into the economy. It even led to the creation of Boulder City *(see p82)* to house the dam's workers. Completed in 1937, the dam provided the first reliable source of water, along with cheap electricity, to meet the city's demands. It also formed Lake Mead *(see p82)*.

During this period, new casinos were emerging in downtown and spreading south on Las Vegas Boulevard. El Rancho opened in 1941 followed by Last Frontier in 1942. Around this time, the US military set up base in Las Vegas. In a strange turn of events, this led to the closure of Block 16 as the War Department threatened to bar service personnel from the town until "Sin City" cleaned up its act.

The Hoover Dam under construction

The Rise and Fall of the Mob

Although gambling was legalized in Las Vegas in 1931, it was not until almost a decade later that it attracted the attention of criminal elements who recognized the full potential of the city's growing gambling industry. The appearance of Bugsy Siegel, a New York mobster, on the city's horizon marked the emergence of the Mafia in Las Vegas, and for several years from the 1940s onward, organized crime and Las Vegas walked hand in hand. The tide began to turn in the 1960s as Nevada state authorities passed new laws in attempts to weaken the mob's hold on the city. However, it was the arrival of billionaire Howard Hughes, and the subsequent advent of legitimate corporations, that finally signaled the end of the mob.

Arrival of the Mob
Bugsy Siegel (left) *opened the Flamingo hotel (see p51) in 1946 using funds provided by New York mobsters.*

Flamingo's Second Opening
After Bugsy's death, Phoenix mobster Gus Greenbaum took over the Flamingo, and the second opening of the $5 million casino and resort was a big success. Many other casino-resorts, bankrolled by organized crime, sprang up during the 1950s.

Casino Operator Moe Dalitz
Through the 1950s and 60s, mobster Moe Dalitz opened several casinos along the Strip with the help of Jimmy Hoffa, head of the Teamsters labor union. The union's $269 million fund was used to purchase Circus Circus, Dunes, and Stardust among others.

GAMBLING HALLS AND CLUBS ALONG FREMONT STREET
Bright lights and neon signs of several casinos and clubs illuminate the sidewalks of Fremont Street (1948). Located in the heart of downtown, this street was the city's most visited and popular area until the rise of the Strip.

Casinos Funded by "the Boys"
By 1959, Americans started getting wise to how involved the mob was in running Las Vegas. A Reader's Digest article told of how casinos such as Desert Inn, Flamingo, Frontier, Sands, Riviera, Sahara, and many others had been funded by "the boys" in Detroit, Minneapolis, Cleveland, Miami, New York, and New Jersey.

The Rat Pack

Frank Sinatra, Dean Martin, Sammy Davis Jr., and other members of the Rat Pack were regular performers at the Sands and Desert Inn, and sealed Las Vegas's reputation as an entertainment mecca. Sinatra's links to Mafia chieftain Sam Giancana soon brought him under the notice of federal agencies aiming to rid the city of its mob affiliations in the 1960s.

The Apache hotel was bought by Texas bootlegger and gambler Benny Binion, who changed its name to Binion's Horseshoe.

HOWARD HUGHES (1905–76)

Billionaire Howard Hughes arrived in Las Vegas in November 1966, moving into a luxurious suite on the ninth floor of the Desert Inn hotel. When the hotel's management tried to move him out a few months later, Hughes bought the place for $13.25 million. Although he never left his room in four years, he spent some $300 million buying Vegas properties. These included the Silver Slipper hotel and casino across the Strip, whose blinking neon slipper disturbed him. As owner he had it switched off.

Hughes is credited with bringing legitimate business and a sanitized image to Vegas, sounding the death knell of mob investment in the city. However, as recently as the 1970s and 80s mobsters were caught skimming profits from some Vegas hotels.

Billionaire entrepreneur Howard Hughes

Anthony Spilotro and Wife

Mob figure Anthony "the Ant" Spilotro and his wife, Nancy, leave the federal building in Las Vegas after a session in court on racketeering charges (1986). Charges of corruption and tax evasion were filed against many Vegas mobsters in the 1970s and 80s.

Public Corporations

In 1967, a new law in Nevada allowed public corporations to obtain gambling licenses. This paved the way for companies such as Hilton, MGM, and Holiday Inn to begin legitimate building programs in Las Vegas. Eventually, the influence of corporate America loosened the mob's grip on casinos.

LAS VEGAS'S CHANGING FACE

In 1950, the newly created Nevada Proving Ground, later named the Nevada Test Site, brought the atomic age to Vegas. The periodic nuclear test explosions added to the city's entertainment value. Las Vegans celebrated the tests by holding the Miss Atomic Bomb beauty pageant, as well as picnics at points that afforded a bird's-eye view of the explosions.

At the same time, a construction frenzy, which lasted for more than a decade, seemed to grip the city. Soon, downtown and Las Vegas Boulevard, which later came to be known as the Strip, were packed with casino-resorts that had been built at an incredible pace. Each tried to outdo the other in terms of scale and extravagance. Entertainers such as Frank Sinatra (see p27) and the Rat

Movie stars and celebrities throng to Las Vegas

Pack held sold-out shows at the Sands hotel, which opened in 1952. The nine-story Riviera hotel (see p62), which opened in 1955, was the city's first high-rise resort. This was followed by the 15-story Fremont Hotel (see p72) in downtown Las Vegas.

By 1960, the city's population had grown to 65,000. With the advent of air conditioning, interstate highways, and transcontinental travel, Las Vegas was fast becoming a leading tourist destination and a favorite haunt of movie stars, millionaires, and other celebrities.

Las Vegas's gambling industry was also going through an overhaul. In the 1980s, corporate entities implemented tighter cash accounting rules in their casinos. This gave state regulators the impetus to insist on the same statewide. The remaining traces of the mob's influence were gradually being erased. Slowly, but surely, the city's image was changing. Amid the bright lights and the hordes of tourists, Las Vegas was becoming a family destination.

NEVADA TEST SITE

Originally a gunnery range for the US Army Air Corps during World War II, the site became a testing range for nuclear weapons at the end of the war. Located 90 miles (145 km) north of Vegas, the site conducted its first test in January 1951 on a stretch of desert called Frenchman Flat. Over the next 11 years, 126 atomic bombs were detonated above ground. Open-air testing was banned under the First Nuclear Test Ban Treaty, but underground testing went on for the next 30 years. In 1996, President Bill Clinton signed the Comprehensive Test Ban Treaty, which ended all nuclear testing.

Radioactive cloud at the Nevada Test Site

BOOMTOWN

Las Vegas experienced a period of mixed fortunes in the 1970s. MGM Grand – today Bally's (see p47) –

TIMELINE

1950	1955	1960	1965	1970	1975	1980

1951 First atomic bomb detonated at Nevada Test Site

1955 Gaming Control Board created to regulate gaming industry

Howard Hughes

1966 Howard Hughes arrives in Las Vegas

1968 Vegas's first family-friendly hotel, Circus Circus, launched

1975 Nevada's gaming earnings cross $1 billion mark

1955 Riviera opens as the city's first "high-rise"

1960 The Rat Pack take the stage at the Sands hotel

1966 Caesars Palace opens as first major, themed resort

Marble Statue, Caesars Palace

opened in 1973 and heralded the age of the mega resort. With 2,100 rooms the hotel earned the title of "world's largest resort." However in 1975, flash floods wreaked havoc on the Strip, and in 1978, gambling was legalized in Atlantic City. Both these events had an adverse effect on the city's tourism industry. But it was not long before Las Vegas recovered and entered a phase of large-scale expansion. In 1989, entrepreneur and hotelier Steve Wynn *(see p26)* opened the $620 million Mirage *(see p56)*, the costliest and grandest resort the city had ever seen. Its phenomenal success spurred the construction of many theme-based mega resorts, such as Excalibur *(see p42)*, Luxor *(see p42)*, Treasure Island *(see pp56–7)*, and a new MGM Grand *(see p44)*, which had over 5,000 rooms. Wynn struck gold again in 1998 when he launched the $1.6 billion Bellagio *(see pp48–9)*, which along with the Venetian *(see pp58–9)*, is considered to be one of the most opulent and lavish resorts in the world.

A lion statue at MGM Grand

Unencumbered by the slow-growth ordinances enacted by its neighbor Reno, the Las Vegas boom has continued unabated. While burnishing its reputation as an entertainment capital, it has become home to a growing legion of full-time residents. In 2007 the New Frontier, the second hotel and casino to open on the Strip, was demolished to make way for a new resort resembling The Plaza, New York.

Today, Las Vegas is one of the fastest growing cities in the country. Sunny skies, casinos, inexpensive food, thrill rides, and a range of entertainment options attract millions of visitors each year. New projects – shopping malls, mega resorts – continue to unfold at a rapid pace. In 2008 The Palazzo *(see p56)* opened at a cost of $2.7 billion, and in 2009 the 2,304-suite Encore connected to the incredible Wynn Las Vegas *(see pp60–61)*.

Amid this amazing ever-changing scenario, just two things remain constant: the way the city looks and the type of people who live here.

The glittering and shimmering vista of Las Vegas in its centennial year

Steve opens Mirage

1993 MGM Grand, the world's largest hotel, is built

1996 Stratosphere Tower, The country's tallest observation tower, is built

1999 The lavish Venetian is built

Campanile Tower, Venetian

2005 Wynn Las Vegas opens

2007 New Frontier demolished

1990 | **1995** | **2000** | **2005** | **2010** | **2015**

5 The National als Rodeo held

Fremont Street Experience

1994 Construction begins on the Fremont Street Experience

1998 Bellagio is built for $1.6 billion, the most at the time

2004 Las Vegas Monorail opens to the public

2005 Las Vegas celebrates its centennial year

2008 The Palazzo opens

LAS VEGAS AT A GLANCE

A city like no other in the world, spectacular Las Vegas shimmers amid the Nevada desert. Only Vegas can take the best and the most recognized landmarks of other cities, and re-create them grander and flashier than the originals. Fueled by tourism, the city is best known for its hotels: huge flamboyant resorts with their own museums, shows, rides, and casinos. The range of attractions extends beyond Las Vegas as well and includes the natural splendor of the surrounding area, such as the Grand Canyon *(see pp96–101)*. To make your visit as rewarding as possible, the following pages are a quick guide to the best Las Vegas has to offer, highlighting the city's best wedding chapels and its most celebrated residents and visitors. Below is a selection of the top ten tourist attractions that no visitor should miss.

LAS VEGAS'S TOP TEN TOURIST ATTRACTIONS

Bellagio Fountains
See p49

Cirque du Soleil Shows
See pp144 & 147

Gondola Rides at the Venetian
See pp58–9

Death Valley
See pp106–7

Shark Reef
See p41

Red Rock Canyon
See p80

Fremont Street Experience
See p73

Hoover Dam
See p83

Grand Canyon
See pp96–101

◁ The replica Statue of Liberty outside New York-New York dominates this night-time view of the South Strip

Famous Visitors and Residents

As one of the world's most popular entertainment destinations, Las Vegas is associated with many glamorous personalities. These include movie stars such as Mickey Rooney, Lana Turner, and Leonardo DiCaprio; famous singers such as Frank Sinatra and Elvis Presley; eccentric billionaires such as Howard Hughes; and mobsters such as Benjamin "Bugsy" Siegel. Some have been drawn to Las Vegas from other parts of the country, while others call it home. All have left their mark on the city and, indeed, on the world.

Welcome sign for Howard Hughes, near Landmark hotel, Las Vegas

ENTREPRENEURS AND BILLIONAIRES

The famous Las Vegas Strip came into being when Los Angeles hotelier Thomas Hull (1893–1964) decided to build the El Rancho on the dusty highway, a few miles south of Fremont Street. The idea came to him as he counted the number of cars that passed by on the highway as he once waited for his flat tire to be fixed. The hotel was an instant hit, especially with the Los Angeles celebrity crowd. Eccentric billionaire Howard Hughes (1905–76) arrived in Las Vegas in 1966, and moved into a lavish suite at Desert Inn. When the hotel management asked him to move out a few months later, Hughes bought the hotel for $13.25 million. This led to a buying spree of several hotel properties, and an era of corporate ownership of casinos that marked the end of mob investment in the city.

Steve Wynn,
Chairman and CEO
of Wynn Resorts

The father of the Las Vegas mega resorts, Kirk Kerkorian, built the world's largest resort hotel three times. The first was in 1969, when he built the 1,500-room International, which later became Las Vegas Hilton (see p62). However, his crowning achievement was the 5,000-room MGM Grand (see p44) that he built in 1993. In true pioneering spirit, Kerkorian is currently planning the construction of a huge, multi-billion dollar "urban metropolis" between the Monte Carlo and Bellagio hotels. The City Center project is likely to include a 4,000-room resort and casino, three 400-room hotels, 1,650 luxury condominiums, and an extensive retail, entertainment, and dining space.

Billionaire businessman and hotelier Steve Wynn is credited with building some of the most expensive and most opulent hotels in Las Vegas, such as Bellagio, (see pp48–9) and the Wynn Las Vegas (see pp60–61).

GANGSTERS AND CRIMINALS

Infamous New York Mobster Benjamin Siegel (1905–47) brought Hollywood celebrity status to Las Vegas, even though most of the spotlight shone after his violent death in 1947. On one of his many cross-country trips he stopped in Las Vegas and came up with the idea of building a Miami-modern type of casino-resort in the middle of the desert, on what is now the Strip. Built at a huge cost of $6 million, the Flamingo opened in 1946 with posh amenities never before seen in the city. Today, Flamingo Las Vegas (see p51) is among the city's most archetypal resorts.

Underworld crime boss Morris "Moe" Dalitz (1899–1989) came to Las Vegas in the 1940s and soon became a major player in the city's casino business. In 1950, he opened the lavish Desert Inn, which raised the standard of Vegas casinos by offering the best and the most extravagant of all amenities and services. In the following years, Dalitz purchased a string of casinos along the Strip, including Stardust, Dunes, and Sahara, and turned them into highly successful business ventures.

Texan gambler and bootlegger Benny Binion (1904–89) opened Binion's Horseshoe casino (see p71) in 1951 and transformed the sawdust-floored casinos into carpeted gambling halls where players were encouraged to place huge bets. By the 1970s, he

Benjamin "Bugsy" Siegel, gangster turned Vegas hotelier

Andre Agassi, the world-class tennis player, who was born in Las Vegas

had raised the betting limit to $10,000. For gamblers with bigger bankrolls, he would gladly remove the limits. At its peak in the late 1980s, Horseshoe was the most profitable casino in town. Binion also established the World Series of Poker (see p31) in 1970, which is one of Vegas's most famed annual events.

SPORTS PERSONALITIES

World-class tennis player Andre Agassi is a native of Las Vegas and was born here in 1970. He was recognized as a tennis prodigy at the age of three and he turned pro at the age of 16. Agassi has won virtually every major tennis tournament, and was ranked number one in the mid-1990s. In 2001, he married acclaimed tennis player Steffi Graf, who has won 22 major championships. The couple, who are now both retired from professional tennis, currently reside in Las Vegas with their two children, a boy and a girl.

French figure skater Surya Bonaly has won nine French national championships and silver medals at three world championships. She became a US citizen in 2004, and is now a resident of Las Vegas.

Former baseball star pitcher Greg Maddux, who won an unprecedented four straight Cy Young Awards in the mid-1990s and a record 18 Gold Gloves, is also a resident of Las Vegas.

Golfing legend Tiger Woods is a frequent visitor and can often be seen playing high-stakes games at MGM Grand. The same was true of former basketball player, Charles Barkley, forced to quite the habit due to large debts.

ENTERTAINERS

Glitz became a part of Las Vegas's persona when Wladziu Liberace (1919–87) made his debut here in 1944. An accomplished pianist, he was one of Las Vegas's most flamboyant performers, who wowed crowds with his showmanship and portrayal of outlandish "characters." Liberace soon became famous for his multicolored and sequined apparel, as well as his endearing wit.

He later became a Las Vegas resident and even opened his own museum (see p45). But, it was pop music legend Frank Sinatra (1915–98) who gave Las Vegas its ultra-hip, cool image. In 1953, he performed at the now-demolished Sands hotel

Britney Spears, a regular in Vegas

Frank Sinatra receives the "Pied Piper Award" at Caesars Palace

and was an instant success. Sinatra, Dean Martin, Sammy Davis Jr., and Joey Bishop made up the Rat Pack, and sealed Las Vegas's reputation as an adult playground.

More than a decade later, the undisputed King of Rock 'n' Roll, Elvis Presley (1935–77), arrived in Las Vegas. His debut performance in 1969 at the International Hotel, now the Las Vegas Hilton, was a runaway success. Elvis appeared for a record 837 sold-out shows there.

Other entertainers associated with Las Vegas include renowned comedian Jerry Lewis, singers Celine Dion, Wayne Newton, and Barbra Streisand, and the illusionists Siegfried and Roy. Other performers, such as Elton John, sign up for a certain number of shows over a specified period of time.

CELEBRITIES

Las Vegas's close proximity to Southern California has made it a popular getaway and entertainment mecca for the Hollywood crowd since the early 1940s. Even when it was just a Western-style resort town, many of the movie world's elite enjoyed taking refuge in the solitude of the Southern Nevada desert. Some of the regular visitors were Mickey Rooney, Humphrey Bogart, Rosemary Clooney, Maurice Chevalier, Gary Cooper, and Lana Turner, just to name a few.

Today, a new generation of Hollywood celebrities has made Vegas a kind of extension of Los Angeles – a place to jet to for a weekend rock concert, golf tournament, or championship prize fight. Paris Hilton, Britney Spears, Tara Reid, Leonardo DiCaprio, and Eminem make frequent visits to the city's many nightclubs. And some, such as singer Gladys Knight, have established residence here.

Las Vegas's Best: Wedding Chapels

Weddings are big business in Las Vegas with more than 120,000 marriage licenses issued annually. Celebrities such as Elvis Presley, Richard Gere, Paul Newman, Bruce Willis, Michael Jordan, Clint Eastwood, and Britney Spears all got married in Vegas. With an extensive selection of wedding chapels to choose from, ceremonies can range from drive-through affairs to lavish extravaganzas with helicopter rides over the city's skyline, and from simple civil proceedings to themed events amid singing Elvis impersonators *(see pp166–9)*. Most of the resorts also have at least one wedding chapel, and offer elaborate wedding packages as well.

Guardian Angel Cathedral
This Catholic church holds services and the collection plate often receives casino chips as offerings (see p57).

Paradise Falls
This tropical garden chapel is located at Flamingo Las Vegas (see p51). *Beautiful waterfalls, palm trees, and lush surroundings create a romantic setting for weddings.*

Bellagio's Wedding Chapel
Stained-glass windows, and fresh flowers form part of the decor at this elegant chapel. Couples can spend up to $18,000 for a lavish ceremony that includes a wide variety of services (see pp166–7).

Little Church of the West
The Little Church opened in 1942, making it the city's oldest wedding chapel. This famous redwood-sided chapel has a colorful flower garden, and more than 100 couples get married here each week.

Graceland Wedding Chapel

This tiny Cape Cod-style chapel stages a ceremony with an Elvis impersonator handling the service, ending with a 15-minute musical tribute to the King of Rock 'n' Roll (see p76).

Hartland Mansion

Once visited by Elvis Presley, this expansive mansion is located in a quiet residential neighborhood. The banquet hall can accommodate weddings and receptions of up to 700 people (see p90).

Chapel of the Flowers

This picturesque chapel has a charming outdoor setting with waterfalls, lush greenery, fragrant flowers, a quaint wooden bridge, and garden gazebo. People from all over the world come here to tie the knot.

Chapel of the Bells

In service since the 1960s, this intimate chapel has performed marriage ceremonies for many celebrities, including South American soccer champion Pele, Mickey Rooney, Ernest Borgnine, Kelly Ripa, and Beverly DeAngelo.

0 kilometers 1

0 miles 1

LAS VEGAS THROUGH THE YEAR

Las Vegas enjoys an average of more than 312 days of sunshine each year, allowing for the enjoyment of various outdoor activities almost every day of the year. Spring and fall are the most comfortable seasons as visitors and residents alike revel in the pleasantly warm days, filled with several sporting events, including golf and boxing championships, baseball tournaments, and NASCAR races. June ushers in four, hot months of summer, with daytime temperatures averaging

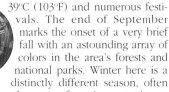

World Series of Poker chip

39°C (103°F) and numerous festivals. The end of September marks the onset of a very brief fall with an astounding array of colors in the area's forests and national parks. Winter here is a distinctly different season, often close to freezing at times. However, in December the National Finals Rodeo, and Christmas and New Year's celebrations draw huge crowds and make this one of the busiest times of the year. The city is also a premier destination for conventions.

SPRING

The spring months are usually very mild. The days are virtually cloud-free, and outdoor enthusiasts can enjoy the parades, carnivals, and numerous sporting activities that take place during these months.

MARCH

NASCAR Weekend *(early Mar)*, Las Vegas Motor Speedway. The Busch Series and the Nextel Cup races are held over three days. This is the largest sporting event of the year, and attracts more than 150,000 racing fans.
ShoWest Convention *(mid-Mar)*. This huge, motion picture industry event lures several celebrities to town.
March Madness *(mid-Mar–early April)*. College basketball season takes off as teams compete in a lead up to the

Actress Gwyneth Paltrow at ShoWest Convention

Racing cars at the UAW-Daimler Chrysler 400 Series, Nextel Cup, Las Vegas

NCAA (National Collegiate Athletic Association) Championship finals.
St. Patrick's Day Parade *(Mar 17)*. More than 100 entrants and colorful floats set off on the city's biggest parade. Resorts use the occasion to run specials on corned beef and cabbage and green beer.
Big League Weekend *(late Mar or early April)*, Cashman Field. Baseball season swings into action with gusto as six major league teams compete against each other.

APRIL

Native American Arts Festival *(first weekend)*, Clark County Heritage Museum. Presents dance, drama, and musical performances. An outdoor craft market features over 40 vendors with Native American arts, crafts, and food.
Mardi Gras *(early Apr)*. The Fremont Street Experience

and several hotels gear up for special Mardi Gras festivities with live Dixieland jazz, street carnivals, and Cajun cuisine.

MAY

Cinco de Mayo *(Sun closest to May 5)*. Annual Mexican celebration with fun-filled activities at parks throughout the city. Casinos and hotels offer food and drink specials, as well as free giveaways.
Helldorado Days *(early May)*. This event has developed into a charity fundraiser, featuring a golf tournament, poker championship, trap shooting contest, and two rodeos. There is also a parade with floats and a fireworks show.
Memorial Day Weekend *(last weekend)*. The city comes alive during three days of parties, outdoor concerts by international performers, sizzling shows, sports events, and appetizing cuisines.

AVERAGE DAILY HOURS OF SUNSHINE

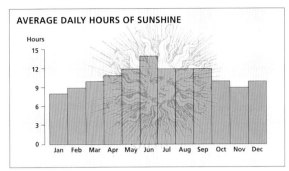

Hours

15
12
9
6
3
0

Jan Feb Mar Apr May Jun Jul Aug Sep Oct Nov Dec

Sunshine Chart

A sunny climate is one of Las Vegas's main attractions. There are very few days with no sunshine at all, even in the winter. However, the summer sun can be very fierce and adequate precautions against sunburn and sunstroke should be taken. Sunscreens, a hat, and sunglasses are highly recommended as is drinking plenty of water.

SUMMER

Summer begins in earnest in mid to late June as temperatures climb steadily beyond the 32°C (90°F) mark. This is also festival time for Las Vegas with two food and one film festival to look forward to. For racing enthusiasts, the NASCAR Craftsman Truck Series is a treat, while gaming lovers enjoy the annual World Series of Poker tournament.

JUNE

World Series of Poker *(Jun 2–Jul 15)*, Rio. More than 20,000 players match wits in this annual tournament. Buy-ins range from $1,000 for the ladies' game to $10,000 for the No-limit Texas Hold 'em World Championship.

Cine Vegas Film Festival *(second week)*. An exciting and hugely popular film festival, with the chance to see great movies as well as many Hollywood stars. Several seminars are held for budding screenwriters and producers.

JULY

Fourth of July *(Jul 4)*. Fireworks, drinking, gambling, barbecues, and outdoor concerts, as well as high temperatures mark the celebration. Local parks sponsor sports contests, pancake breakfasts, and other events.

AUGUST

Men's Apparel Guild in California (MAGIC) *(third week)*. The latest in men's and women's fashion apparel is showcased twice a year – in February and August. Some celebrities also display their own latest lines of clothing.

SEPTEMBER

San Gennaro Feast and Street Fair *(mid-Sept)*. The centerpiece of this famous festival is the Italian cuisine feast with over 60 ethnic food vendors. The four-day event also features a carnival midway, Miss San Gennaro beauty pageant, rides, games,

live bands, and several stalls of arts and craft.

Greek Food Festival *(mid-Sept)*, St. John's Orthodox Church. Luscious pastries and lip-smacking Greek foods and specialties are available at this festival, which is held in celebration of the Greek Independence Day. Events include authentic Greek music, folk dancing, a huge shopping bazaar, and many other forms of entertainment that take place on the lush grounds of this massive church, which is located near Hacienda Road and Jones Boulevard.

Loaf of bread at the Greek Food Festival

NASCAR Craftsman Truck Series *(late Sept)*, Las Vegas Motor Speedway. This special NASCAR event is held for trucks. More than 70 Chevy, Ford, and Dodge pick-ups race at speeds of up to 160 mph (257 km/h) in this exciting competition.

Guests enjoy a MAGIC opening night party at the Hard Rock Hotel and Casino

AVERAGE MONTHLY RAINFALL

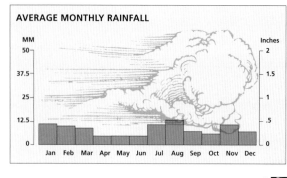

MM | Inches
50 — | — 2
37.5 — | — 1.5
25 — | — 1
12.5 — | — .5
0 — | — 0

Jan Feb Mar Apr May Jun Jul Aug Sep Oct Nov Dec

Rainfall Chart
Las Vegas receives an average rainfall of about four inches each year. Nearly half of the total annual rainfall occurs during January, February, and August, which are the wettest months of the year. Some rainfall also takes place in late summer and early fall, when Southern Nevada experiences scattered electrical storms.

FALL

Although this is probably the shortest season in Las Vegas, it is also one of the most pleasant. The period from mid-October to mid-November is filled with warm days and cool nights, and the ground is covered with leaves in striking colors. The atmosphere is festive with Halloween and Thanksgiving just around the corner. An ideal time for golfing and other outdoor activities.

Brightly colored fall leaves

OCTOBER

Art in the Park *(early Oct)*, Bicentennial Park, downtown Boulder City. This is one of the biggest festivals of the year, as hundreds of craftsmen and artists display their works.
Justin Timberlake Shriners Hospitals for Children Open

Justin Timberlake Shriners Hospitals for Children Open

(mid-Oct), Summerlin. Top professional golfers from around the world team up with amateur players for this week-long championship, held at the Tournament Players Club.
Halloween *(Oct 31)*. Thousands of revelers fill the streets of Las Vegas and celebrate this eerie holiday by dressing up in scary costumes. Casinos, hotels, and clubs host night-long parties with music, food, and a lot of drinking and dancing.

NOVEMBER

Pro Bull Riders Final *(early Nov)*, Thomas & Mack Center on the campus of University of Nevada, Las Vegas *(see pp86–7)*. This thrilling four-day event features the top bull riders of the country as they compete for a million dollar cash prize.
Thanksgiving *(Nov 24)*. Visitors and local residents get into the holiday spirit with a long weekend of delicious food, beverages, and general merriment.

WINTER

Like many desert resorts, Las Vegas has winters that are usually mild with bright, sunny days, while the nights are literally freezing. The city is covered in sparkling and glittery decorations as everybody prepares for the Christmas and New Year celebrations, and football fans get ready for the Super Bowl weekend.

Dangerous antics at the National Finals Rodeo

DECEMBER

National Finals Rodeo *(early Dec)*, Thomas & Mack Center. This 13-day event is the nation's richest rodeo, and features the top 15 competitors in seven different events – bareback riding, steer wrestling, team roping, saddle bronc riding, calf roping, bull riding, and barrel racing.
Parade of Lights *(mid-Dec)*, Lake Mead marina *(see p82)*. Fifty boats show-off their special lights at this luminous lake event. Trophies are awarded, including a Best of Show award for the most brilliant display. Past parades have drawn up to 20,000 shoreline spectators.
Las Vegas Bowl *(third Sat)*, Sam Boyd Stadium. College football season kicks off as top teams from Pac-10 Conference and Mountain West Conference compete.
Christmas *(Dec 25)*. Like Thanksgiving, this is another holiday when a large number of families visit Las Vegas, and the city is literally bursting at the seams. Malls

AVERAGE MONTHLY TEMPERATURE

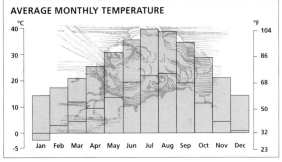

°C: 40, 30, 20, 10, 0, -5
°F: 104, 86, 68, 50, 32, 23

Jan Feb Mar Apr May Jun Jul Aug Sep Oct Nov Dec

Temperature Chart
As befitting a land of extremes, temperatures in Vegas can range from below freezing on many nights from December through February to an uncomfortable high of 40°C (105°F) during July and August. On rare occasions, Vegas also experiences snowfall. Spring and fall offer the most comfortable weather.

and shopping centers are overflowing, restaurants host elaborate Christmas dinners, and hotels throw lavish, night-long parties.

New Year's Eve *(Dec 31)*. There is hardly any standing room at the busiest holiday of the year. Casinos stage huge and extravagant New Year's Eve bashes, though many of them are by invitation only for their best customers. One of the biggest parties is on Fremont Street as the block comes alive with fireworks, laser displays, and live bands.

JANUARY

Consumer Electronic Show (CES) *(early Jan)*. More than 2,500 vendors and manufacturers from all over the world convene at this gathering and display the latest high-tech electronic gadgets, including digital cameras, audio and video systems, home theaters, satellite systems, wireless communications, and more.

The show is expected to attract approximately 140,000 visitors each year.

Chinese New Year *(late Jan or first half of Feb)*. Celebrate the New Year, Oriental style. The occasion is marked by festivities that include entertainers from Asia, with authentic dance performances, including the Lion Dance, which is believed to chase out evil spirits. It also features cultural exhibits, Asian cuisines, and mahjong tournaments. Dates vary from year to year.

Chinese New Year, Bellagio

Las Vegas International Marathon *(late Jan)*. More than 10,000 athletes from around the globe participate in this annual race. The event includes the Marathon, Half Marathon, and an International Friendship 5k Run.

FEBRUARY

Super Bowl Weekend *(last weekend in Jan or first weekend in Feb)*. Football frenzy

A heart-shaped decoration for Valentine's Day, Chapel of Love

hits the city during the Super Bowl weekend, which determines the National Football League champion. Several casinos and resorts celebrate with special football parties.

Valentine's Day *(14 Feb)*. Couples flock to any of the hundreds of wedding chapels *(see pp28–9)* in Las Vegas on this day to tie the nuptial knot or renew their vows. Those planning to wed on this day should make chapel and other reservations in advance.

PUBLIC HOLIDAYS

New Year's Day (Jan 1)
Martin Luther King Jr. Day (3rd Mon in Jan)
President's Day (3rd Mon in Feb)
Memorial Day (last Mon in May)
Independence Day (Jul 4)
Labor Day (1st Mon in Sep)
Columbus Day (2nd Mon in Oct)
Veteran's Day (Nov 11)
Thanksgiving Day (4th Thu in Nov)
Christmas Day (Dec 25)

New Year celebrations light up the sky in Las Vegas

New York-New York (see p43) and its re-created Manhattan skyline as seen from the Strip ▷

LAS VEGAS AREA BY AREA

SOUTH STRIP

The southern section of the famous Las Vegas Strip is a Mecca of sights and sounds that vary from the sublime to the exotic, from the outrageous to the bewildering. The area that stretches from Flamingo Road down to Mandalay Bay Drive contains some of the newest and most lavish of Las Vegas's famed casino resorts. Among the landmarks are Bellagio, one of the city's most expensive and opulent casino hotels, and MGM Grand. Several of the resorts trace their roots to Las Vegas's

Liberace's Rolls Royce, Liberace Museum

earliest days. These include Flamingo Las Vegas, built by the infamous mobster Benjamin Siegel in 1946, and Caesars Palace, which opened in 1966. Many others have managed to re-create not just the appearance, but also the ambience of great cities, such as Paris, New York, Rome, and Monte Carlo, through remarkably meticulous reproductions. Located just a short distance from the Strip is the University of Nevada, Las Vegas (UNLV) – the city's educational center.

SIGHTS AT A GLANCE

Hotels and Casinos

Bally's ⑮
Bill's Gamblin' Hall & Saloon ㉑
Bellagio pp48–9 ⑯
Caesars Palace ⑳
Excalibur ③
Flamingo Las Vegas ㉒
Gold Coast ⑱
Hard Rock Hotel & Casino ⑫
Luxor ②
Mandalay Bay pp40–41 ①
MGM Grand ⑧
Monte Carlo ⑥
New York-New York ⑤
The Orleans ④

Palms Casino Resort ⑰
Paris Las Vegas ⑭
Planet Hollywood Resort & Casino ⑬
Rio ⑲
Tropicana Resort & Casino ⑨

Museums and Galleries

Auto Collections at the Imperial Palace ㉓
Liberace Museum ⑩
UNLV Marjorie Barrick Museum ⑪

Malls

Showcase Mall ⑦

GETTING THERE

The entire length of South Strip can be accessed by CAT bus The Deuce. The Las Vegas Monorail makes limited stops along the Strip. Free monorails connect Mandalay Bay to Luxor and Excalibur.

KEY

	Street-by-Street map *See pp38–9*
	Las Vegas Monorail
	Free monorail
	Tourist information

0 kilometers 1

0 mile 1

◁ Colorful and patriotic theme at the ever-changing Bellagio Conservatory *(see pp48–9)*

A View of South Strip

This southern stretch of the Strip is home to a cluster of vast, lavishly-themed hotels, including Mandalay Bay, Luxor, New York-New York, Paris Las Vegas, Monte Carlo, and Bellagio. Aiming to satisfy all the needs of a visitor in one location, with restaurants, shops, theaters, and casinos, these mega resorts are best appreciated at night when the lights, fountains, and other special effects come to life. It is in the evening that these hotels become a fantasyland of riotous design and architecture, such as the illuminated sphinx that fronts the Luxor hotel's striking pyramid and the delightful, flawlessly choreographed dancing fountains at the classy and chic Bellagio.

View of South Strip from Mandalay Bay

New York-New York
A replica of the Statue of Liberty forms part of the façade of this hotel, which is composed of a host of Manhattan landmarks ❺

Luxor
The casino is home to two fascinating and interactive exhibits: Bodies and Titanic ❷

Excalibur
The towers at this resort are a kitsch fantasy of medieval England ❸

Monte Carlo
Renaissance-style architecture comes to life at this hotel ❻

★ **Mandalay Bay**
One of the most popular attractions here is the Shark Reef ❶

TROPICANA AVE

LAS VEGAS BLVD

Showcase Mall
This striking building has a giant neon Coca-Cola bottle near the entrance. A huge games arcade makes the mall popular with families ❼

Tropicana Resort & Casino
This casino was rebuilt in the late 1970s, with a stunning Art Nouveau-style stained-glass ceiling and glass lamps ❾

MGM Grand
This famous statue of Leo, symbol of the Hollywood film studio, MGM, rises 45 ft (15 m) above the corner of Tropicana Avenue ❽

Caesars Palace

Reproduction Roman statuary adorns the grounds of Caesars Palace. One of the Strip's oldest and most glamorous hotels, Caesars was built in 1966. Inside, the lavish Forum Shops mall features moving statues **20**

LOCATOR MAP
See Street Finder maps 3 & 4

Imperial Palace

A pagoda fronts this Asian-themed hotel, famous for its classic car collection that is open to visitors **23**

★ Bellagio

Lighting the ceiling of the hotel's elegant lobby, this colorful glass installation was designed by famous glass artist Dale Chihuly **16**

Paris Las Vegas

A half-scale replica of the Eiffel Tower stands tall at this resort's entrance **14**

0 meters 300
0 yards 300

FLAMINGO ROAD

THE STRIP

FLAMINGO ROAD

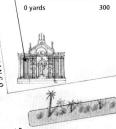

Bill's Gamblin' Hall & Saloon

This resort's refined decor has carved oak and the world's largest stained-glass mural **21**

Flamingo Las Vegas

The flaming pink-and-orange neon flower of the Flamingo hotel's façade is a famous Strip icon. Redesigned in the 1970s and 80s, the original 1946 building was the beloved project of gangster turned hotelier, Bugsy Seigel (see p26) **22**

Bally's

This hotel's colorful entryway is lined with neon columns, palm trees, and cascading fountains, and gives a futuristic look to this mega resort **15**

Planet Hollywood Resort & Casino

Located at the center of the Strip, featuring 100,000 sq ft (9,300 sq m) of gaming, restaurants, nightclubs, and encircled by Miracle Mile Shops **13**

STAR SIGHTS

★ Mandalay Bay

★ Bellagio

Mandalay Bay ❶

Las Vegas may be located in the middle of a desert, but visitors can still get a taste of the tropics at this island-themed mega resort. The hotel is built around an expansive lagoon, surrounded by lush ferns and other tropical plants, and features a sand-and-surf beach with a wave-generating machine. During the summer months, the beach is the venue for outdoor concerts by well-known bands, including the Beach Boys and the B-52's. Mandalay Bay is also home to one of the city's most popular attractions – Shark Reef, an aquarium specializing in sharks and other aquatic predators.

Elephant head fountain

Aureole
This famous restaurant serves Continental specialties, and hosts a four-story-tall wine vault (see p127).

★ **Mandalay Bay Beach**
Beach-goers enjoy the sun, sand, and surf, courtesy of a wave-making machine. In addition to the deck chairs, guests can use the luxurious private bungalows and cabanas, or lounge on a day bed.

Convention Center

Shark Reef

Lazy River
This winding river offers swimmers a chance to float through the lagoon while sipping a tropical drink.

Waterfalls at Faux Ruins
Cascading waterfalls set among palm trees and mystical architecture create a soothing and tranquil ambience.

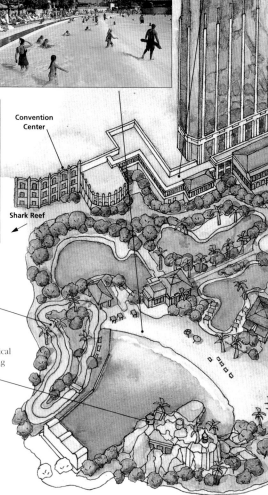

STAR FEATURES

★ Mandalay Beach

★ Pedestrian's Entrance

★ Pedestrian's Entrance

The hotel's exterior showcases Asian architectural elements such as pagodas. Stone sculptures of winged dragons stand guard at the sidewalk leading from the Strip to the resort's entrance.

VISITORS' CHECKLIST

3950 Las Vegas Blvd S. **Map** 3 C5. **Tel** (702) 632-7777. CAT bus The Deuce. MGM Grand Station; free monorail from Excalibur. hotel: 24 hrs; Shark Reef: 10am–8pm daily (10pm Fri & Sat). for Shark Reef. www.mandalaybay.com

House of Blues

This concert venue presents an intimate setting and is an excellent place to enjoy live music by top music artists (see p151).

Façade

The hotel's golden, Y-shaped towers glisten brightly in the sunlight and present an attractive backdrop to the tropical-themed landscape out front.

SHARK REEF

This massive aquarium and sea life exhibit contains over 1,200 species of aquatic life, including sharks, exotic fish, sea turtles, crocodiles, and more. The attraction begins with an outdoor exhibit of deadly Amazon predators, including the red tail catfish, monkey fish, and black piranha, along with the komodo dragon. Visitors descend through tunnels into the aquarium section where they can observe a variety of sharks, eels, and other tropical fish. A favorite among kids is the petting pond where they can touch rays and Port Jackson sharks.

Visitors enjoying a closer look at the marine life, Shark Reef

Four Seasons Hotel occupies four floors in Mandalay Bay. Its restaurants and health club are located here.

An impressive replica of the Great Sphinx at the entrance of Luxor

Luxor ②

3900 Las Vegas Blvd S. **Map** 3 C5.
Tel (702) 262-4000; (800) 288-1000. ◯ 24 hours (see p114). ☐
🖥 www.luxor.com

With its pyramid design and Egyptian theme, Luxor is undoubtedly the most unique and most recognizable hotel in Las Vegas. The magnificent entrance is marked by a huge sandstone obelisk and the resort's porte-cochere is a ten-story towering replica of the Great Sphinx.

Built in 1993, the 350-ft (106-m) high pyramid is covered in dark glass. Its apex features a 40-billion-candlepower beacon – the world's strongest – emitting a shaft of light more than 10 miles (16 km) high into space each night. Inside, the pyramid's atrium is large enough to stack nine Boeing 747s, and hosts three levels of lavish dining, gambling, and entertainment.

The guest rooms of the hotel are built into the pyramid's sloping walls and are reached by "inclinators" – elevators that rise at a 39-degree angle, and make passengers feel as if they are riding an enclosed ski lift.

The interior of the pyramid is tastefully decorated with Egyptian-themed furnishings, including statues and

hieroglyphic-inscribed tapestry and faux trees.

Among the hotel's many attractions is **Bodies: The Exhibition**. This showcases real specimens of the human body including 13 whole-body specimens and more than 260 organs and partial body specimens. The innovative display allows the visitor a detailed, three-dimensional look at the human form – something not often seen outside of the medical profession.

Features include organs that illustrate the damage caused by over-eating and lack of exercise, along with analysis of the respiratory, skeletal, muscular and circulatory systems. The comparison of a healthy lung and a black lung ravaged by smoking is very powerful.

Another exhibition, Titanic, gives visitors an insight into life aboard the doomed ship. Luxor is also home to the Cirque du Soleil production, **CRISS ANGEL Believe**. This playful magic show pays homage to Harry Houdini.

🎭 **CRISS ANGEL Believe**
Luxor. ◯ 7pm & 9:30pm Tue–Sat.
📷 ☐

🏛 **Bodies: The Exhibition**
Luxor. ◯ 10am–10pm daily. 📷 ☐

Excalibur ③

3850 Las Vegas Blvd S. **Map** 3 C4.
Tel (702) 597-7777; (800) 937-7777.
◯ 24 hours (see p115) ☐
www.excalibur.com

Built to resemble a medieval castle, Excalibur's entrance features white towers, turrets, and a 265-ft (81-m) high bell tower that stands guard over the moat. Inside, the medieval theme is further reflected in the cobblestone foyer and rock-walled atrium with a three-story-high fountain. The massive registration desk is flanked by suits of armor, and decorated with red-on-red wall coverings.

One of the Strip's larger hotels, Excalibur caters mostly to families and is usually packed. The 100,000-sq ft (9,300-sq m) casino is one of the city's biggest, and the action is usually fast, frenzied, and fairly noisy.

The Octane Bar on walk level is the perfect place for a drink before dinner or a show. The bartenders and waiters perform high-energy dance routines throughout the evening, which seem to be thoroughly enjoyed by the bar's clientele.

The level below the casino has a dungeon "fun zone" for kids, with a video arcade, games, and the Fantasy Faire Midway's thrilling and simulated Magic Motion Machine adventure rides.

Colorful towers of the medieval fantasy castle at Excalibur

The Orleans ❹

4500 W Tropicana Ave. **Map** 3 A4.
Tel (702) 365-7111; (800) 675-3267.
⬤ 24 hours (see p113). ♿
www.orleanscasino.com

This Cajun-themed hotel and casino opened in 1996 and was initially a clone of its more popular cousin, Gold Coast *(see p47)*. However, since then its popularity with local gamblers has flourished, and the property has undergone expansion three times.

In 2004, The Orleans completed a third hotel tower that increased the resort's room count to 1,886. Moreover, the casino was expanded and presently covers an area of about 135,000 sq ft (12,542 sq m). An 8,500-seat arena has also been added, which is now the winter home of the Wranglers, a professional hockey team. The Orleans Arena is the venue for various concerts and other sporting events that take place throughout the year as well.

Like the other "locals-oriented" resorts in town, The Orleans offers a variety of attractions for the Vegas resident. Among them are an 18-screen movie theater and 70-lane bowling alley. The hotel also features an 827-seat headliner showroom that often hosts rock stars from the 1960s and 1970s, as well as ten restaurants that serve an eclectic range of cuisines to choose from, including American, Japanese, and Mexican.

The glittering neon sign of The Orleans

New York-New York ❺

3790 Las Vegas Blvd S. **Map** 3 C4.
Tel (702) 740-6969; (800) 693-6763.
⬤ 24 hours. (see p112). ♿
www.nynyhotelcasino.com

This hotel's re-creation of the Manhattan skyline dominates the Tropicana Avenue corner of the Strip – a no mean feat in a street of such impressive façades. At

The thrilling The Roller Coaster, New York-New York

the core of the hotel's towers are replicas of some of New York City's most famous landmarks, such as the New York Public Library, the Empire State, Chrysler, and Seagram Buildings, and a 150-ft (46-m) high Statue of Liberty. Roaring around the complex is the thrilling The Roller Coaster – a Coney Island-style roller coaster – that twists and dives at speeds of 65 mph (105 kph) and passes through the casino itself. Every detail of the hotel's interior is designed to reflect a part of New York City, from the 1930s style wood-paneled lobby to the areas around the casino floor, which feature many of the city's most famous landmarks including Times Square. This striking

casino is entered from the Strip via a replica of Brooklyn Bridge, which is one-fifth the size of the original.

Adding to the Manhattan flavor are versions of many popular New York eateries. Set among Greenwich Village brownstones is a wide selection of cafés, restaurants, and bars offering a choice of live music from swing and jazz to Motown and rock.

Monte Carlo ❻

3770 Las Vegas Blvd S. **Map** 3 C4.
Tel (702) 730-7777; (800) 311-8999.
⬤ 24 hours (see p115). ♿
www.montecarlo.com

European refinement and Vegas glitz come together in a unique blend at Monte Carlo. The architecture features stately columns, Renaissance-style statues, and cascading fountains, yet it resists lapsing into overstated Baroque.

Some of the best attractions in town can be found at Monte Carlo. Lance Burton's magic show *(see p146)*, performed in a 1,200-seat theater, is one of the most popular shows in Vegas.

On the top floor of the Monte Carlo an exclusive concept in hotels has been developed – an elegant and unpretentious hotel within a hotel. HOTEL32 has 50 rooms and suites and is designed to make every guest feel as though they are rich and famous. There is 24-hour service, the finest amenities, and personal suite assistants,

Lance Burton's magic show at Monte Carlo

An enormous Coca-Cola bottle dominates the entrance to Showcase Mall

Showcase Mall ❼

3785 Las Vegas Blvd S. **Map** 3 C4.
Tel (702) 597-3117. ☐ varies for
each attraction. &

This neon-clad building,
which showcases an
unmissable 100-ft (33-m) high
neon Coca-Cola bottle, is an
excellent place to take
children and also offers
enough to satisfy adults who
need a break from the casinos.

There are two main
attractions here: **GameWorks**
and **M&M's World**.

GameWorks, which is the
brainchild of movie mogul
Steven Spielberg, offers
visitors hands-on entertainment
with virtual dance stations,
Harley-Davidson racing, and
traditional arcade games. The
company was purchased in
2005 by Sega Entertainment
USA, the North American arm
of the giant SEGA Corpo-
ration, a worldwide leader
of amusement facilities and
software. SEGA has developed
the site with over 60 new
spectacular, state-of-the-art
games, as well as excellent
food and beverage outlets,
the GameWorks Grill, Glacier
Bar, and the Lost Bar.

M&M's World is little more
than a promotional exhibit for
the company's products, but
it does provide fun elements
and plentiful chocolate
samples on the M&M's Tour.

There are also reasonably
priced restaurants and cafés
throughout the mall.

🎮 GameWorks
Showcase Mall. **Tel** (702) 432-
4263. ☐ 10am–midnight Sun–Thu,
10–1am Fri & Sat. 📷 &
www.gameworks.com

🍫 M&M's World
Showcase Mall.
Tel (702) 736-7611; (800) 848-
3606. ☐ 9am–11pm Sun–Thu,
9am–midnight Fri & Sat. &

MGM Grand ❽

3799 Las Vegas Blvd S. **Map** 3 C4.
Tel (702) 891-1111; (800) 929-1111.
☐ 24 hours (see p115). & 📷
www.mgmgrand.com

The emerald-green MGM
Grand building is fronted by
the famous Leo, a 45-ft (15-m)
tall bronze lion used as the
symbol of the MGM
Hollywood film studio. The
original MGM hotel was built
in the 1970s farther down the
Strip on the site of the present
Bally's hotel (see p47), and

was named after the 1930s
film, *Grand Hotel*.

Today, the MGM Grand has
a massive 5,044 rooms and is
home to a huge casino, which
sprawls over 171,000 sq ft
(15,886 sq m), and is bigger
than the playing field at Yan-
kee Stadium.

Proclaiming itself as Vegas's
"City of Entertainment," MGM
Grand has an exhilarating
variety of bars and restaurants
including fine dining at
L'Atelier de Joel Robuchon, and
Centrifuge, a bustling bar with
good pop music and fun live
entertainment. The hotel's
expansive lobby has a brass
registration desk, behind which
sits an 80-panel video screen
that flashes advertisements.
MGMGrand is also home to a
luxurious spa and salon.

The **MGM Grand Lion
Habitat** offers the chance to
see these magnificent animals
at close quarters.

The Grand Garden Arena is
a 17,000-seat venue famous
for hosting special events,
and mega concerts for big
names such as the Rolling
Stones, Barbra Streisand and
Elton John, as well as major
sports events and world
championship boxing. The
750-seat Hollywood Theater
attracts many top entertainers,
including David Copperfield,
Howie Mandel, and Tom
Jones. At night, a re-creation
of New York's somewhat
notorious nightclub Studio 54
beckons those who want to
dance the night away.

🦁 MGM Grand Lion Habitat
MGMGrand. ☐ 11am–10pm
daily. &

Lioness at the Lion Habitat, MGM Grand

The striking stained-glass ceiling of the casino at the Tropicana Resort & Casino

Tropicana Resort & Casino 9

3801 Las Vegas Blvd S. **Map** 3 C4. **Tel** (702) 739-2222; (800) 634-4000. ◯ 24 hours (see p114). ♿ **www**.tropicanalv.com

A tropical island paradise would be an apt description of the Tropicana hotel. The entrance of this resort features two 35-ft (10.5-m) tall Maori gods, palm trees, a lagoon, and a Polynesian longhouse, which hosts various forms of Hawaiian entertainment. The tropical theme continues inside with wood-and-bamboo furnishings.

A delightful 5-acre (2-ha) water park is home to three pools, three spas, and a water slide. Waterfalls and exotic foliage provide a habitat for flamingoes, black swans, and Brazilian parrots. In addition to the main casino, the pool provides swim-up blackjack tables that have a waterproof surface and money dryers.

Other attractions include the Beatles tribute act Penny Lane in the Bobby Slayton Room.

Liberace Museum 10

1775 E Tropicana Ave. **Map** 4 F4. **Tel** (702) 798-5595. ◯ 10am–5pm Mon–Sat, noon–4pm Sun. ♿ **www**.liberace.org

The serene Spanish-style façade of the Liberace Museum is a vivid contrast to its glittering contents. Founded in 1979, the museum

celebrates the life and work of one of Las Vegas's best-loved and most glamorous performers, Liberace (see p27). The cars, pianos, and bejeweled costumes of this flamboyant personality are exhibited in three sections. The main area houses 18 of Liberace's 39 pianos. The cars include a rare Rolls Royce covered with shimmering mirror tiles and beautifully etched galloping horses in which Liberace would arrive for many of his Las Vegas shows.

Lavishly rhinestoned costumes and sparkling stage jewelry are also on show. The costumes worn at his final 1986 performance took six seamstresses, wearing protective sunglasses against the glare of the stones, several months to make.

One of the world's largest Austrian rhinestone, which weighs more than 50 lb (23 kg), is also displayed here, near Liberace's personal memorabilia, which includes several precious jewel-encrusted, tiny music boxes.

A US bicentennial Rolls Royce at Liberace Museum

UNLV Marjorie Barrick Museum 11

4505 S Maryland Pkwy, University of Nevada, Las Vegas. **Map** 4 E4. **Tel** (702) 895-3381. ◯ 8am–4:45pm Mon–Fri, 10am–2pm Sat. ● public hols. ♿ **www**.hrc.nevada.edu/museum

Located at the University of Nevada, Las Vegas (see pp86–7), this museum showcases exhibits relating to the state's flora and fauna, and some anthropological displays. The Southwestern collection features mammals and fossils from the Mojave Desert (see p105). The highlight is the collection of Native American and Meso-American artifacts, Guatemalan

Exhibit at Barrick Museum

textiles, and Mexican dance masks. The museum also displays several works by students and faculty, as well as traveling exhibitions. In front of the museum is the Xeric Garden, which displays drought-tolerant indigenous plants and uses efficient irrigation methods to create an attractive desert landscape. Shaded benches lining the paths provide a peaceful refuge just steps away from the college quad.

The rock 'n' roll-themed exterior of Hard Rock Hotel & Casino

Hard Rock Hotel & Casino ⓬

4455 Paradise Rd. **Map** 4 D4.
Tel (702) 693-5000; (800) 473-7625
◯ 24 hours (see p115). ♿
www.hardrockhotel.com

As the name suggests, the rock 'n' roll theme reigns supreme at this hotel. The theme extends well beyond just the resort's decor, as the Hard Rock Hotel & Casino presents itself as a shrine to rock and its unforgettable superstars.

The circular-shaped casino showcases various priceless treasures, such as Elton John's piano, Elvis Presley's jumpsuit, and a gold-plated, 32-saxophone chandelier. The casino also features several museum-like displays of rock memorabilia, which includes Beatles collectibles, vintage records, guitars, drum sets, and much more.

Reflecting a Southern California influence, the hotel's pool area has a sandy beach lagoon, gardens, and a row of tent cabanas. Whirlpools and spas are also available here. Moreover, the hotel's 4,000-seat venue, the Joint (see p148) is an excellent place to experience a rock concert.

The resort underwent an expansion in 2009, including the opening of 860 guest rooms, restaurants, and retail outlets.

Planet Hollywood Resort & Casino ⓭

3667 Las Vegas Blvd S. **Map** 3 C4.
Tel (702) 785-5555; (877) 333-9474.
◯ 24 hours (see p114). ♿
www.planethollywoodresort.com

This resort, at the center of the Strip, features over 100,000 sq ft (9,300 sq m) of gaming, fine dining, lounges, nightclubs, a full-service spa, celebrity-themed suites, and is home to the production *Peepshow (see p145)*.

The 52-story PH Towers, which opened in 2009, boast a tropical pool, an ultramodern fitness center, and luxurious guest rooms.

A major attraction of the resort is the **Miracle Mile** shopping center *(see p137)*. This meandering collection of shops and restaurants set among North African backdrops has been transformed into a streamlined and modern "experiental" shopping center with an interactive directional system to help shoppers get around, a water feature and state-of-the-art video imagery.

The hotel's Theater for the Performing Arts *(see p148)* is currently one of the best venues in town for shows and concerts. The London Club casino is for "high rollers".

The Crazy Shirts shop logo from Miracle Mile

Paris Las Vegas ⓮

3655 Las Vegas Blvd S. **Map** 3 C3.
Tel (702) 946-7000. ◯ 24 hours
(see p114). ♿ 🅿
www.parislasvegas.com

Paris Las Vegas welcomes guests into a miniature version of France's City of Lights. The resort showcases replicas of famous Paris landmarks, such as the Louvre, Hôtel de Ville, Opera House, Arc de Triomphe, and a 50-story high Eiffel Tower.

The authenticity extends to parking valets yelling "*allez-allez*" to one another and the casino employees spouting phrases such as "*bonjour*" and "*comment allez vous?*" to guests who are often amused if not surprised to hear French expressions from a Pacific Rim bellhop. The architectural details of the casino meticulously re-create Parisian street life, including cast-iron street lamps, and everything is set beneath a fabulous painted sky.

Cobblestone streets wind along the edge of the casino and are filled with shops selling an array of expensive French goods, including clothes, wine, cheese, and chocolate.

The resort also boasts five lounges, a spa, and two wedding chapels.

A remarkably meticulous re-creation of the Eiffel Tower, Paris Las Vegas

The neon-lit entrance of Bally's, as seen from the Strip at night

Bally's 🅕

3645 Las Vegas Blvd S. **Map** 3 C3.
Tel (702) 739-4111.
☐ 24 hours (see p113). ♿
www.ballyslasvegas.com

Located next to Paris Las
Vegas, Bally's was originally
built as the MGM Grand in
1973. However, in 1980, the
hotel was the site of a terrible
fire. In 1986, Bally Gaming
Corporation, a slot manufac-
turing company, bought the
property and named it Bally's.

The resort's 2,814 guest
rooms are among the largest
in the city, and are mostly
decorated with upscale contemporary furniture.

Expansion in the 1990s led
to the addition of the Colorful
Plaza – a space-age entryway
of huge neon columns, palm
trees, and cascading fountains,
surrounded by lush, land-
scaped gardens. It also has
four, 200-ft (61-m) long, moving sidewalks, which bring
customers in from the Strip.

Bally's long-running show,
Jubilee! (see p145), is the
quintessential Vegas production with its lengthy and
extravagant opening number,
feathered showgirls, pyrotech-
nic effects, and variety acts.

Another highlight is the
resort's spa – a full-service
health club, which features
state-of-the-art fitness equipment, whirlpool spas, and
steam and sauna rooms, as
well as hydrotherapy tubs.

The hotel also has a good
collection of shops and a
large outdoor pool area.
A monorail links the hotel
with MGM Grand farther
up the street.

Bellagio 🅖

See pp48–9.

Palms Casino Resort 🅗

4321 W Flamingo Rd. **Map** 3 A3.
Tel (702) 942-7777. ☐ 24 hours
(see p114). ♿ **www**.palms.com

In 2005, the Palms added the
40-story Fantasy Tower and in
2008 added the 47-story
Palms Place, which increased
the number of guest rooms at
the complex to 1,300. The
amenities on offer here have
made the resort a favorite of
many, especially 20- and 30-
something partygoers who are
attracted by the Palms' nightlife scene.

One of the hotel's nightclubs,
Rain, attracts international
headline acts. The nightclub
is surrounded by a computer-
programmed river of water
flanked by dancing jets and
fountains. The dance floor is
accented by pyrotechnics and
other special effects and lighting. Other exciting venues
here are the ghostbar

(*see p150*), a penthouse
nightspot that seems to "float"
high above the city and offers
stunning views, the Pearl, a
state-of-the-art concert theater
which accommodates up to
2,500 guests, and the Playboy
Club, the only one of its kind
in the world.

Gold Coast 🅘

4000 W Flamingo Rd. **Map** 3 B3.
Tel (702) 367-7111.
☐ 24 hours (see p112). ♿
www.goldcoastcasino.com

One of the most popular
neighborhood hotels is the
Gold Coast. The complex has
a tasteful, understated – a
rarity in Las Vegas – Spanish
flair with a white adobe
exterior and red-tile roof.
The registration area features
an arched entry, carved-
wood doors, stained-glass
windows, and tiled floors.
The rooms are elegantly decorated, in keeping with the
overall style of the complex.

The list of hotel amenities
are of the something-for-
everyone variety, and include
six restaurants, five bars, a
large casino, a 70-lane bowling alley, and a cabaret
lounge for live bands.

The mezzanine level offers
bingo sessions and hundreds
of serious bingo players
gather eight times a day for
games that resemble the rush
at the after-Christmas sales.

The hotel has a landscaped
pool area where guests can
relax, as well as a tiny shopping arcade. The highlight is
a wine-and-spirits shop with
more than 200 collectible
miniatures available.

Crowds gather at the bingo room, Gold Coast

Bellagio ⑯

Decoration in the Conservatory

The crown jewel of South Strip, the luxurious Bellagio resort opened in 1998 at a cost of $1.6 billion. The goal of Steve Wynn, who conceived this monument to leisure, was to create a hotel "that would exemplify absolute quality while emphasizing romance and elegance." Facing a large pristine lake, the resort has been built to resemble an idyllic village on the shores of Italy's Lake Como. Inside, beautiful carpets and delicate Carrara marble mosaics adorn the floors. Bellagio is also home to Cirque du Soleil's mesmerizing and awe-inspiring water spectacular, "O".

Cirque du Soleil's "O"
Swimmers perform flawlessly choreographed musical acts at this water-based show.

Bellagio Gallery of Fine Art
As the Strip's only art venue to hold exhibitions, this gallery hosts temporary shows of paintings, sculptures, and other masterpieces by internationally-acclaimed artists such as Claude Monet.

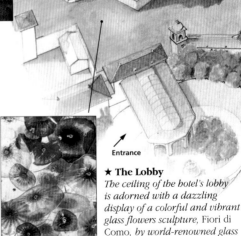

The Conservatory
This massive greenhouse has picturesque floral displays, exquisitely arranged in theatrical presentations. The colors and themes of these natural displays change from season to season.

Entrance

STAR FEATURES

★ The Lobby

★ Front Façade

★ Via Bellagio

★ Dancing Fountains

★ **The Lobby**
The ceiling of the hotel's lobby is adorned with a dazzling display of a colorful and vibrant glass flowers sculpture, Fiori di Como, *by world-renowned glass artist Dale Chihuly.*

VISITORS' CHECKLIST

3600 Las Vegas Blvd S.
Map 3 C3. **Tel** (702) 693-7111.
CAT bus The Deuce.
Bally's Station. 24 hours.
www.bellagio.com

★ Front Façade

The classical elegance of Italian architecture comes to life with ocher- and terra-cotta-colored Mediterranean-style buildings and cobblestone pathways that overlook an expansive lake.

★ Via Bellagio

This upscale shopping promenade is a glass-enclosed version of Beverly Hills' famed Rodeo Drive, and presents an eclectic selection of designer shops and boutiques, such as Hermès, Prada, Giorgio Armani, Tiffany, Chanel, Dior, and Fred Leighton (see p137).

Restaurants Facing the Lake

Spectacular views and a romantic ambience are on offer along with a range of cuisines at some of the city's best eateries, such as Olives and Yellowtail.

★ Dancing Fountains

Each evening the lake features a magnificent ballet of dancing fountains choreographed to music and lights. More than 1,000 streams of water shoot up to 250 ft (76 m) in the air with music by Luciano Pavarotti, Andrea Bocelli, Frank Sinatra, and Lionel Ritchie.

Rio ❶⑨

3700 W Flamingo Rd. **Map** 3 B3.
Tel *(702) 777-7777, (800) 752-9746.*
⏲ *24 hours (see p115).* ♿
www.playrio.com

The Brazilian theme runs strong at this upbeat and fast-paced all-suite hotel. Located just about half a mile west of the Strip, the hotel is easily identified by the red-and-purple neon accented towers and its brightly lit sign.

The Mardi Gras atmosphere is nowhere more evident than at the Masquerade Village – a dining, shopping, gambling, and entertainment complex. The highlight here is the production of the *Show in the Sky!* (hourly 7pm–midnight, Thursday to Sunday). A unique show with stunning dancers performing on stage in eye-popping costumes designed by DKNY and Victoria's Secret and fantasy floats gliding above the crowd.

One of the major attractions at this hotel is the annual World Series of Poker competition *(see p31)*. The Rio is also known for its eclectic collection of restaurant choices, and, for its after-hours fun. The Penn & Teller illusionist duo are a regular fixture.

Catering to outdoor relaxation, the hotel offers a sandy beach at the edge of a tropical lagoon, with waterfalls, four swimming pools, and an entertainment gazebo. The Rio is one of Vegas's most popular venues for a wedding, with a choice of indoor and outdoor locations.

The exclusive Forum Shops, Caesars Palace

Caesars Palace ❷⓿

3570 Las Vegas Blvd S. **Map** 3 B3.
Tel *(702) 731-7110; (800) 634-6661.*
⏲ *24 hours (see p114).* ♿
www.caesarspalace.com

The grandeur that once defined Rome now exists at Caesars Palace. Marble statues, fountains, imported cypress trees, and toga-clad cocktail waitresses help the mega resort realize its theme of Roman opulence. The hotel's Roman Plaza – an excellent example of Roman statuary and architecture – greets patrons entering from the Strip. The Plaza also hosts a number of shops and The Spanish Steps Bar.

Outside the palatial entrance and to the right of the main fountain is the Brahma Shrine, a replica of a popular Buddhist shrine in Thailand, where visitors can pray and leave offerings of fruit and flowers. This classic Vegas casino was the first themed hotel on the Strip and soon established a reputation for attracting top artists, from singer Andy Williams to magician David Copperfield. The tradition continues in the Colosseum *(see p148)*, with visiting artists such as Elton John, Bette Midler, and Cher. Caesars Palace has also been the venue for international sports events, including championship tennis with stars such as John McEnroe and Andre Agassi.

The hotel presently houses three casinos, four lounges, and 5-acre (2-ha) Garden of the Gods – a landscaped area with fountains, three swimming pools, and an outdoor wedding chapel. The Qua Baths and Spa include Roman-style baths, waterfalls, a fitness center, and arctic ice room. The casinos have all been refurbished. Olympian wall-art, coffered ceilings, and light decor create an elegant atmosphere.

Marble statue, Caesars Palace

The Forum Shops *(see p136)* at Caesars Palace is home to more than 160 designer shops and chic eateries, and is a tourist attraction in its own right. The entrance to the shops is directly connected to the pedestrian sidewalk on Las Vegas Boulevard. Replicas of the exquisite Trevi and Triton Fountains in Rome adorn a sweeping plaza, which has a large reflective pool at its center. Guests can also ride a majestic spiral escalator.

The hotel's guest rooms are considered among the finest in the city. Recent developments include the Octavius Tower, three luxurious pool-villa suites, and an outdoor whirlpool spa retreat.

Carnivals and colorful floats at the *Show in the Sky*, Rio

Brilliantly illuminated pink-and-orange feather sign, Flamingo Las Vegas

Bill's Gamblin' Hall & Saloon ㉑

3595 Las Vegas Blvd S. **Map** 3 C3.
Tel (702) 737-2100. ☐ 24 hours
(see p114). ♿
www.billslasvegas.com

The motif at Bill's Gamblin' Hall & Saloon is strongly reminiscent of 19th-century San Francisco. The Nob Hill-theme, based on one of San Francisco's most celebrated neighborhoods, is evident throughout the resort with crystal globe chandeliers, carved oak, and a stained-glass mural depicting, *The Garden of Earthly Delights.* Measuring 30 ft (9 m) long and 5 ft (1.5 m) high, it is the world's largest stained-glass mural, and it took more than 8,000 hours to complete. The hotel's 200 rooms are charmingly decorated with Victorian wallpaper and paintings, floral carpeting, etched mirrors, white-lace curtains, and four-poster brass beds.

Previously named Barbary Coast, the resort was opened in 1979 by the longtime casino operator Jackie Gaughan and his son Michael. Since then it has undergone three renovations in attempts at modernization. Although smaller in scale to the other resorts along the Strip, the casino is usually crowded and is known to have a friendly atmosphere.

Flamingo Las Vegas ㉒

3555 Las Vegas Blvd S. **Map** 3 C3.
Tel (702) 733-3111; (800) 732-2111.
☐ 24 hours (see p113). ♿
www.flamingolasvegas.com

The bright pink-and-orange neon feather sign of the Flamingo hotel's façade is, to many, the archetypal

An example of the celebrity-owned cars on show at Imperial Palace

Las Vegas icon. However, most are unaware that this sign was never a part of the original 1946 hotel and was added much later. Nothing remains of the first Flamingo resort: the last vestiges of this building, which includes notorious mobster Bugsy Siegel's *(see p26)* private suite, were bulldozed in 1996. A stone pillar and a plaque in the garden behind the casino pay tribute to the mobster.

In the 1990s, a $130-million renovation created one of the most elegant pool areas in Vegas. Set among landscaped gardens, two Olympic-sized pools are veiled by tropical plants and palm trees, flanked by islands that provide a

home to pink flamingoes. The hotel also has a kids' pool, two Jacuzzis, and a water slide that leads to three additional pools. Flamingo's wedding chapel is also set in the pool area. Both guests and visitors may use the renowned tennis club, which has four floodlit night courts, a practice court, and a tennis shop.

Auto Collections at the Imperial Palace ㉓

3535 Las Vegas Blvd S.
Map 3 C3 **Tel** (702) 731-3311.
☐ 10am–6pm daily (see p114). 🅿
♿ www.autocollections.com

Located on the fifth floor of the Imperial Palace hotel's parking lot, this multi-million-dollar collection of classic cars from around the world will impress even the most auto-phobic of visitors. The late Ralph Engelstad, owner of the Imperial Palace, began his collection with a 1929 Ford Model A roadster in 1979. Two years later, the museum was opened with space for 200 cars. As well as vintage Fords, the exhibition includes such classics as Mercedes, Chevrolets, Cadillacs, and a range of military vehicles. Today, many of the cars are for sale, with some of them sporting steep price tags of more than a million dollars.

The collection is constantly changing as cars are sold and new ones replace them. At various times the exhibits have included a Duesenberg Murphy Roadster owned by Howard Hughes. More recent are the Cadillacs, Lincolns, and Chevrolets of the 1950s and 1960s with their elongated tail fins and leather seats, such as Jacqueline Kennedy's 1961 Lincoln Continental. A 1976 Cadillac, which once belonged to Elvis Presley, is another former exhibit.

Neon-lit signs of Bill's Gamblin' Hall & Saloon, plus its nightclub, Drai's

NORTH STRIP

At one time, the northern end of the Las Vegas Strip was known for its aging and oftentimes "working-class" casinos. Hotels such as the Sahara, and Circus Circus were popular with travel agents and tour operators, but never held the star billing which the elite resorts south of Flamingo Road commanded. That has all changed with the opening of the Venetian in 1999, Wynn Las Vegas (2005), The Palazzo (2008), and Encore (2009). These mega resorts leveled the field with their southern counterparts, and set the standard for not just the future developments, but also for older resorts that underwent large-scale modifications and renovations. North Strip also hosts the city's premier shopping complex, the Fashion Show Mall. Expansion of the area has made this mall the jewel of Vegas's shopping promenades and one of its most visited destinations.

Lucky the Clown, Circus Circus

SIGHTS AT A GLANCE

Hotels and Casinos
Circus Circus pp64–5 ⑫
Harrah's ①
Las Vegas Hilton ⑪
Mirage ④
The Palazzo ③
Riviera ⑩
Sahara ⑬
Stratosphere ⑭
Treasure Island – TI ⑤

Venetian pp58–9 ②
Wynn Las Vegas pp60–61 ⑨

Malls
Fashion Show Mall ⑥

Cathedrals
Guardian Angel Cathedral ⑧

Walks
Walk of Stars ⑦

GETTING THERE
North Strip can be accessed by CAT bus The Deuce. The Las Vegas Monorail makes limited stops along the Strip. A free monorail connects Mirage to Treasure Island.

KEY

▨	Street-by-Street map *See pp54–5*
🚆	Las Vegas Monorail
🚆	Free monorail
⊠	Post office
ℹ	Tourist information

0 meters 800
0 yards 800

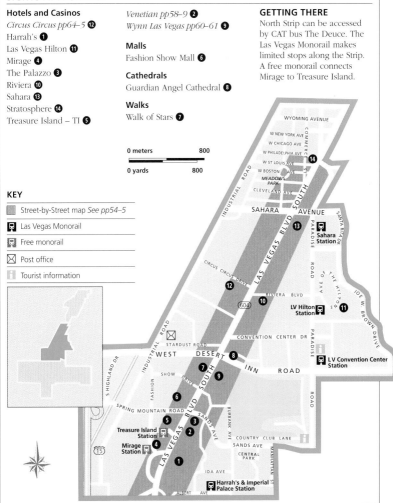

◁ Gondola rides in front of the beautifully re-created Doge's Palace at the Venetian, North Strip *(see pp58–9)*

A View of North Strip

The first casino resort to open on the Las Vegas Strip in 1941 was the El Rancho Vegas Hotel & Casino, which was located on the northern section of the Strip, on the corner of Sahara Avenue. A building boom followed in the 1950s, resulting in a swathe of resorts. The Sands, Desert Inn, Sahara, and Stardust hotels began the process that has transformed the Strip into a high-rise adult theme park. Many of these North Strip resorts remain, but they are now unrecognizable from their earlier incarnations –

View of the Palazzo and the Venetian

thanks to million-dollar rebuilding programs.
   Today, resorts such as the Venetian and Mirage have established the Strip's reputation for upscale quality, and almost nothing remains of the spit-and-sawdust atmosphere the city once had.

Treasure Island – TI
The pirate-themed world of Treasure Island lures passers-by to the spectacular Sirens of TI *show, held each evening on the hotel's Strip-side lagoon* **5**

Mirage
Both stylish and ornate, this resort's beautiful, Strip-facing gardens feature an "erupting" volcano **4**

Fashion Show Mall
Currently the largest shopping center in Vegas, this mall has more than 250 stores, an entertainment complex, and a food court **6**

Walk of Stars
One hundred stars bearing the names of celebrities are embedded in the sidewalk **7**

The Palazzo
This stylish hotel casino opened in 2008, complete with its own theater and 60 luxury boutiques **3**

★ Wynn Las Vegas
This opulent hotel's striking entrance has an impressive mountain surround-ed by a lake **9**

★ Venetian
Acclaimed as one of the world's most luxurious hotels, the Venetian has mock canals flow-ing through its shopping area **2**

Harrah's
A colorful mural adorns the façade of this resort. The hotel also hosts the Carnaval Court – a carnival-themed entertainment, dining, and shopping complex **1**

LOCATOR MAP
See Street Finder maps 3 & 4

Stratosphere
An observation deck at the top of this hotel's 1,149-ft (350-m) tower offers fine views. There are thrill rides too, including the Big Shot (see p63) 14

★ **Circus Circus**
Lucky the Clown beckons visitors to this resort, which offers circus acts and traditional carnival games on the mezzanine floor above the casino 12

W. SAHARA AVE

THE STRIP

0 meters 300
0 yards 300

Sahara
This Moroccan-themed hotel opened in 1952 and is one of the city's oldest hotels. It features two of the most popular attractions on the Strip – the fast-paced Cyber Speedway and the thrilling roller coaster ride, Speed 11

Guardian Angel Cathedral
Located on Desert Inn Road, this chapel has elegant marble floors and imposing buttress support columns 8

Riviera
The colorful, neon-lit, and seemingly jewel-encrusted façade of Riviera highlights the hotel's hit shows, and is one of the most dazzling landmarks along North Strip 10

STAR SIGHTS

★ Circus Circus

★ Venetian

★ Wynn Las Vegas

Singer Clint Holmes show billboard at Harrah's

Harrah's ❶

3475 Las Vegas Blvd S. **Map** 3 C3.
Tel *(702) 369-5000.* ⬭ *24 hours*
(see p116). ♿ www.harrahs.com

Once the world's largest Holiday Inn, Harrah's is now a property of Harrah's Entertainment Inc., which has owned and operated the 2,579-room resort since 1983. However, it was only in 1992 that the name was changed in order to enhance the corporation's image in the gaming industry. Till the mid-1990s, the hotel followed a riverboat theme. But this was scrapped in 1997 in favor of a European carnival theme that features an entertainment and shopping complex – Carnaval Court – strolling performers, and colorful exterior murals.

The casino, which always seems to be in a state of renovation, meanders over nearly 100,000 sq ft (9,290 sq m), and is often crowded and noisy.

A race and sports book is also available for betting purposes.

The hotel's entertainment offerings are anchored by The Improv comedy club *(see p146)* and such artists as the acclaimed comedienne Rita Rudner.

Venetian ❷

See pp58–9.

The Palazzo ❸

3325 Las Vegas Blvd S. **Map** 3 C3.
Tel *(702) 607-7777.* ⬭ *24 hours*
(see p116). ♿
www.palazzolasvegas.com

Following a celebratory opening in January 2008, The Palazzo aims to achieve unparalleled luxury and contemporary chic on the Las Vegas Strip. This resort-hotel-casino combines sophisticated design with home comforts. Together with the Venetian *(see pp58–9)* and Sands Expo and Convention Center, The Palazzo helps create the largest hotel and convention complex in the world.

The Mirage ❹

3400 Las Vegas Blvd S. **Map** 3 C3.
Tel *(702) 791-1111; (800) 627-6667.*
⬭ *24 hours* (see p116). ♿ ▣
www.mirage.com

Perhaps more than any other hotel, The Mirage revolutionized the Strip when it opened

in 1989, setting out to draw visitors with attractions other than just the casino.

The façade introduces the complex's South Sea Island theme with tropical gardens, a blue lagoon, and waterfalls. However, the star of the show is a huge volcano that erupts, every hour from 6pm to midnight.

Inside, there is an atrium filled with exotic plants and, behind the main desk, a 20,000-gallon (90,000-liter) aquarium is filled with brightly colored fish. The hotel also hosts **Siegfried & Roy's Secret Garden and Dolphin Habitat**. This facility is home to several rare breeds and a family of Atlantic bottlenose dolphins. The lush, landscaped area allows a close look at threatened white tigers, lions, and panthers, and is designed to resemble their natural habitat. The 2.5 million-gallon (9.5 million-liter) Dolphin Habitat provides a wonderful and spacious home for the dolphins.

🍴 **Siegfried & Roy's Secret Garden and Dolphin Habitat**
Mirage. ⬭ *Call (702) 791-7188 for opening hours and pricing.* 📷 ♿

Treasure Island – TI ❺

3300 Las Vegas Blvd S. **Map** 3 C2.
Tel *(702) 894-7111; (800) 944-7444.*
⬭ *24 hours* (see p116). ♿
www.treasureisland.com

Located next to its sister hotel The Mirage, Treasure Island offers contemporary style, a high-energy atmosphere, and superb service. Its stunning facilities include eight restaurants, five bars, a salon, outdoor pool, and a cabana.

The hotel's old pirate theme has been completely revamped.The cove now boasts a blue-water lagoon that fronts the Strip and is surrounded by high rock cliffs, shrubs, and palm trees. It is the setting for the spectacular new *Sirens of TI* show, a free 12-minute musical adventure set in the 17th century. The

Waterfall by day, volcano by night – the impressive entrance at the Mirage

action features sultry sirens who lure a band of pirates into their clutches with seductive songs, stir up a storm, and transform the cove into a 21st-century party. The balcony of the resort nightclub, Tangerine, which features a contemporary burlesque, is a great spot from which to view the *Sirens of TI*.

Other nightlife includes *Mystère (see p144)*, a Cirque du Soleil production, which is performed in a specially customized showroom. This stunning contemporary circus is a surrealistic celebration of music, dance, spellbinding acrobatics and gymnastics, mime, and comedy.

Treasure Island's other attractions include a nightclub called Kahunaville.

Fashion Show Mall ❻

3200 Las Vegas Blvd S. **Map** 3 C2.
Tel (702) 369-0704. ☐ *varies* ♿

This sprawling multi-level shopping mall *(see p136)* is spread over 2 million sq ft (185,806 sq m) and is the largest on the Strip. Known as one of Las Vegas's premier shopping destinations, the Fashion Show Mall features more than 250 shops and boutiques, and is anchored by several major department stores, such as Macy's, Saks Fifth Avenue, Dillard's, Neiman Marcus, Bloomingdale's Home,

An explosive battle scene from the *Sirens of TI* show, Treasure Island

and Nordstrom. The mall also has many fine art galleries, restaurants, cafés, and a food court.

Part of the latest expansion includes a Great Hall that has an 80-ft (24-m) long catwalk and is often the venue for fashion shows and demonstrations. One of the newest attractions here is Fashion Show's multimedia – Cloud – which faces the Strip. This huge mushroom-like canopy is lit at night and, when combined with four moving video screens, broadcasts special events, exhibitions, and shows taking place inside.

Walk of Stars ❼

Map 3 C2. ☐ *24 hours.*

Following in the footsteps of Hollywood's Walk of Fame, Las Vegas christened its own Walk of Stars along the famed Strip in 2004. Located on the sidewalks between Sahara Avenue and Russell Road, the Walk honors people who have achieved prominence in a variety of fields such as entertainment, sports, and the military. Each star is embedded in a 3-ft (0.9-m) square slab of polished granite weighing 350 lb (159 kg), and is inlayed with the recipient's name and their area of specialty. The first inductee was Wayne Newton, whose granite star and plaque was placed in the sidewalk close to where the New Frontier hotel once stood, where Newton performed for 15 years. Other names that have

been nominated for the Las Vegas honor include members of the Rat Pack *(see pp20–1)*, Siegfried & Roy, and Liberace *(see p27)*. Eventually, the Walk of Stars could host as many as 3,000 stars.

Guardian Angel Cathedral ❽

336 Cathedral Way. **Map** 3 C2.
Tel (702) 735-5241. ☐ *7:30am–4pm daily.* ♿

Of the many churches in Las Vegas, the one with the largest percentage of visitors is the Guardian Angel Cathedral. One of its most famous worshippers was Danny Thomas, a successful comedian and entertainer, whose charitable donations helped furnish the church.

Located just east of the Strip near Desert Inn Road, the huge A-frame church is paved with beautiful

Guardian Angel Cathedral

marble floors and has flying buttress support columns. An unusual feature of the sanctuary is the stained-glass window, which depicts a harlequin hovering over a hotel and a pair of dice at the foot of a cross.

Nevertheless, services are conventional with several services of mass celebrated on weekends along with two daily ones during the week. Tourists often drop casino chips into the collection plate, and each week an employee (known as the Chipmonk) redeems the tokens.

Stylish and modernist lobby of the Fashion Show Mall

Venetian ❷

One of Las Vegas's most spectacular mega resorts, the Venetian is a meticulous re-creation of the grandeur and beauty of Venice. Much of the architecture includes nearly exact reproductions of well-known landmarks, such as St. Mark's Square, the Doge's Palace, Rialto Bridge, and a 315-ft (96-m) tall Campanile Tower, which overlook the waters of the Grand Canal – complete with gondolas and singing gondoliers. The fantasy continues inside where vast areas of lavish marble flooring, statues, and replicas of famous Venetian paintings are found. A condo tower is under construction between the Venetian and Palazzo.

Entertainer at the Venetian

★ Doge's Palace
The walls of this stately replica have been made by stones from the same marble quarry as the real palace in Italy.

The Grand Canal
This graceful waterway wends its way through shops, boutiques, and restaurants as it sparkles beneath faux Adriatic skies, painted and lit to replicate dusk at all times of the day and night.

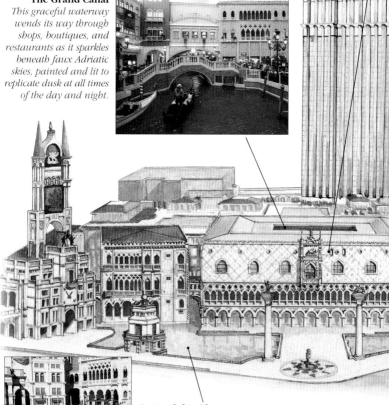

★ Gondola Rides
These romantic rides are one of the main attractions here. The wooden gondolas are authentic, as are the singing gondoliers, many of whom have come to Las Vegas from Italy.

STAR FEATURES

★ Doge's Palace

★ Madame Tussaud's

★ Gondola Rides

Entrance from the Strip
Graceful bridges, brick piazzas, a serpentine canal, and faithful renditions of classical and stylish Italian architecture enthrall those passing by along the Strip.

VISITORS' CHECKLIST

3355 Las Vegas Blvd S. **Map** 3 C3. **Tel** (702) 414-1000; (888) 283-6423. CAT bus The Deuce. Harrah's Station 24 hours.
www.venetian.com

The Lobby
The stunning lobby is decorated with polished marble and glimmering lamps, under a domed ceiling of exquisite gilt and hand-painted frescoes framed in 24-carat gold.

★ Madame Tussaud's
This branch of London's renowned waxworks museum features many Las Vegas legends, including Frank Sinatra.

The Rialto Bridge is a strikingly accurate version of Venice's Ponte di Rialto, the city's oldest bridge. The people-mover sidewalks, however, are a strictly Las Vegas touch.

The Campanile Tower is another excellent replica of a Venetian monument and serves as an entrance to the resort's Grand Canal Shoppes.

Wynn Las Vegas ❾

The opening of Wynn Las Vegas in 2005 saw the addition of one of the city's most dramatic casino resorts to the Strip. The hotel complex is the first element of what will eventually become the ultimate city resort. A stage of development was completed in December 2008 at the opening of Encore, Wynn's new resort. Wynn's luxurious surroundings – a marble-walled casino, award-winning restaurants, dazzling nightspots and entertainment, and an elegant shopping promenade – are open to the public. The spa is available to non-guests during the week and all Strip guests can play on the golf course.

Curved bronze-glass façade of the 50-story hotel tower

DECOR AND DESIGN

Whereas most Strip hotels are designed to show off their attractions, Wynn Las Vegas was fashioned to hide them. The stunning bronze-glass façade of the hotel's gigantic 60-story **tower** and part of the forest-clad mountain are all passers-by see from Las Vegas Boulevard. The fact that its treasures are not on display adds to the resort's reputation for exclusivity and for being the most expensive in town.

Once inside, the extent of Wynn's opulent design and the quality of the workmanship and materials becomes apparent. From the main entrance, visitors arrive at the **Atrium** where they can stroll along its tree-lined walkways tiled with brightly colored floral mosaics and where globes of silk flowers adorn the trees. At the center of the resort is its architectural highlight: the shimmering **Lake of Dreams** and its magnificent backdrop, the **man-made mountain**. Covered with more than 1,500 trees, the 140-ft (43-m) high mountain towers over the lake while curtains of water cascade down its dramatic waterfall. Together they form an amphitheater lined with restaurants and shops, a unique setting for the theatrical performances held here at night.

Unlike the decor in other Las Vegas casino-hotels, which are unified by a theme, Wynn is decorated in a casual chic style. The bedrooms have floor to ceiling windows offering stunning views of Las Vegas' skyline.

GAMBLING AND ENTERTAINMENT

Although its gaming space totals 111,000 sq ft (10,000 sq m), Wynn's **casino** feels intimate. It comprises ten areas, including Baccarat, High Limit, Poker, Private Gaming, Race and Sports Book, plus four gaming rooms containing slot machines and table games. The casino is designed around comfort and the latest technology and there are daily poker tournaments.

The resort features two entertainment venues including the specially designed Wynn Theater, where *Le Rêve (see p147)*, a live aquatic production of aerial acrobatics, gymnastics and dazzling technological effects, is

Spectacular light show projected onto the waterfall at the Lake of Dreams

performed. The stage is surrounded by a pool of water out of which rise the actors and sets. As the theater is in the round, all seats have great, uninterrupted views of the spectacular show.

Wynn's other stage, the **Encore Theater**, is home to an impressive variety of headline, international performers.

One of the most exciting spots to view a performance on the Lake of Dreams is from one of the **Parasol Up/Down** bars with a cocktail. The nightly productions feature 4,000 color-changing lights that project images onto the natural screen created by a wall of water.

DINING AND NIGHTLIFE

Celebrity chefs at Wynn, unlike those at most big-name establishments, are on the premises. A prix-fixe meal at the award-winning signature restaurant **Alex** starts at $145 per person. At **Bartolotta Ristorante di Mare** *(see p130)* the finest seafood is flown in daily from Europe. For a romantic experience, diners can eat in their own private lakeside cabana. At elegant sushi restaurant **Okada** *(see p130)*, you can dine beside one of the resort's dramatic waterfalls or just sip cocktails at their lakeside bar. **Tryst**

Metallic spheres on the lake in front of Bartolotta Ristorante di Mare

(see p150) is located beneath Okada. This stunningly stylish nightclub has as its centerpiece a 94-ft (29-m) waterfall, which descends into a lagoon. With its red velvet walls, dim lighting and a dance floor that extends from inside the club to an outdoor patio right over the lagoon, Tryst is an alluring if pricey night out.

LUXURY SHOPPING

The glass, brass, and chrome storefronts along the **Wynn Esplanade** *(see p137)* glitter with the golden names of the luxury trade – Chanel, Cartier, Christian Dior, Alexander McQueen, Louis Vuitton, Manolo Blahnik, and Oscar de la Renta. There are also seven exclusive Steve Wynn

VISITORS' CHECKLIST

3131 Las Vegas Blvd S.
Map 3 C2. *Tel (702) 770-7000;
(877) 321-WYNN.* CAT bus
The Deuce. Harrah's
Station. 24 hours.
www.wynnlasvegas.com

stores: Wynn & Co. Jewelry, Wynn & Co. Watches, Wynn Signature Shop, Wynn LVNV, Shoe In, Mojitos Resort Wear, and San Georgio. The latter sells beds, chandeliers, and table settings inspired by the designs at the hotel. But the shopping highlight is the **Penske-Wynn Ferrari/Maserati Dealership** located next to the main valet pick-up. The showroom displays some of the world's finest vehicles, including championship Formula One racing cars. The dealership's inventory includes new and previously owned Ferraris and Maseratis.

High-performance cars at the Penske-Wynn showroom

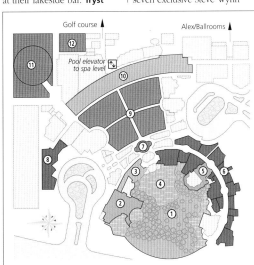

Golf course ▲   Alex/Ballrooms ▲

Pool elevator to spa level

WYNN LAS VEGAS

Bartolotta Ristorante di Mare ⑤
Encore Theater ⑫
Casino ⑨
Atrium ③
Hotel tower ⑩
Lake of Dreams ④
Le Rêve ⑪
Man-made mountain ①
Okada / Tryst ②
Parasol Up/Down bars ⑦
Penske-Wynn Ferrari showroom ⑧
Wynn Esplanade ⑥

KEY

◻ Decor and design
▨ Gambling and entertainment
◻ Dining and nightlife
■ Luxury shopping

Sparkling neon stars light up Riviera's façade at night

Riviera ⑩

2901 Las Vegas Blvd S. **Map** 3 C2.
Tel (702) 734-5110; (800) 634-6753.
◯ 24 hours (see p117). 🚻
www.rivierahotel.com

One of the many hotels
built on the Strip during the
post-World War II building
boom, Riviera opened
in 1955. With its nine-story
tower, the hotel became the
city's first high-rise. Some
of the key characters of the
city's past have featured in
the resort's history. Liberace
(see p27) was the first headliner here, appearing with
legendary Hollywood actress,
Joan Crawford, who was
the official hostess on the
hotel's opening night.

Today, Riviera
occupies 1,000 ft
(300 m) of the Strip, and
boasts more than 2,000
rooms. Several million
dollars have been
spent on refurbishing
the resort in recent
years. While its glamor
is somewhat faded,
Riviera retains
an "old Vegas" atmo-
sphere, symbolized by
its large, brash casino.
This is one of the less
expensive, big Strip
hotels, but still offers
a good range of
facilities, as well as
four shows.

Las Vegas Hilton ⑪

3000 Paradise Rd. **Map** 4 D2.
Tel (702) 732-5111; (800) 732-7117.
◯ 24 hours (see p117). 🚻
www.lvhilton.com

Elvis Presley is the star most
associated with this hotel,
appearing here for a record
837 performances, all of which
were sold out. Today, artists
such as Barry Manilow and
ZZ Top perform here, but
visitors can still pay tribute to
the King at his lifesize statue
just off the lobby.

The hotel's proximity to the
Las Vegas Convention Center
makes it popular with business people. The convenience
of a walkway through the
property and a Las Vegas
Monorail station afford con-
ventioneers easy and quick
access. Luxurious surroundings and a plush 74,000 sq ft

Many stars have performed at the Las Vegas Hilton

casino draw others to the
resort too.

A $100 million renovation
in 2008 added the rooftop
pool with private cabanas,
and a spa. The fitness center
includes championship tennis
courts, where visitors can
have private lessons from a
tennis pro. Gamblers can get
a "casino'ssage", a relaxing
massage, without having to
leave their game.

The 1,600-seat Hilton
Theater features performances
by Barry Manilow most
nights, and hosts other headliners such as Tony Bennett.

Fifteen restaurants offer an
array of dining choices. A
particular highlight is Benihana, a Japanese exhibition-style
eatery enhanced by lush
Japanese gardens, flowing
ponds and exotic statuary.
Both visitors and locals have
voted Benihana one of the
best restaurants in the city
three years in a row in *What's
On* Magazine.

Circus Circus ⑫

See pp64–5.

Sahara ⑬

2535 Las Vegas Blvd S. **Map** 4 D1.
Tel (702) 737-2111. ◯ 24 hours
(see p116). 🚻
www.saharalasvegas.com

This Moroccan-themed hotel
opened in 1952 and soon
became one of the city's most
sought-after entertainment
destinations. Actor Ray Bolger
and singer Lisa Kirk headlined
at the hotel's showroom – the
Congo Room – on its inaugural
night. Over the years, Sahara
has showcased
performances by
countless stars such as
Ann-Margret, Liza Min-
nelli, and Tina Turner,
as well as featuring a
wide variety of Broad-
way musicals, circus
acts, and sports
events. Its most
famous performers
were The Beatles,
who made their Las
Vegas debut at the
casino in 1964. Today,
however, Sahara is

The Big Shot ride shoots visitors 160 ft (49 m) up the Stratosphere Tower

trying to find its niche in the entertainment market after the failure of its large-scale magic shows.

Over the past few years, the hotel has undergone several changes in its attempt to court popularity. Sahara's famous vertical sign – once the world's tallest freestanding one – has been replaced by a 160-ft (49-m) neon marquee and electronic reader board. In a 2008 expansion, worth $100 million, the resort added two new towers, Moroccan-style arches, palm trees, and cascading fountains.

Prominently facing the Strip is the NASCAR Café, which overflows with car-racing enthusiasts when there is a big race in town. Wannabe race car drivers can head for **Cyber Speedway**, where they can test their skills on small-scale replicas of stock cars that "race" over a virtual reality track. A large wraparound screen provides the visual simulation of driving down the Strip or the Las Vegas Motor Speedway. The motion-simulated cars can attain virtual speeds of nearly 200 mph (322 km/hr). Up to eight people can compete at a time.

Moroccan-themed architecture at Sahara

Visitors can also try **Speed – The Ride**, the fastest electromagnetic roller coaster in Las Vegas. The ride reaches a speed of 70 mph (112 km/hr), and is a thrilling, twisting white-knuckler.

Cyber Speedway
Sahara. noon–10pm daily. for observation deck only.

Speed – The Ride
Sahara. noon–10pm daily.

Stratosphere ⑭

2000 Las Vegas Blvd S. **Map** 4 D1. **Tel** (702) 380-7777; (800) 998 6937 24 hours (see p116). www.stratospherehotel.com

Somewhat isolated at the north end of the Strip, away from the main attractions, this resort hotel boasts the 1,149-ft (350-m) high **Stratosphere Tower** – a Las Vegas landmark and the tallest building west of the Mississippi River. The summit has indoor and outdoor observation decks, which offer unparalleled views of the city and the surrounding terrain.

The tower's elevators whisk visitors to the top, where there is a choice of three exciting – not to say alarming – rides: the **Big Shot**, that shoots visitors 160 ft (49 m) up in the air; the **X Scream**, an open vehicle that resembles a huge seesaw and swings riders over the tower's edge; and **Insanity**, which dangles daredevils over the tower's edge with the help of cables.

The casino at Stratosphere is spread over an expansive area of 100,000 sq ft (9,500 sq m), and includes both a poker room and a keno lounge.

Big Shot, X Scream, and Insanity
Stratosphere. 10–1am Sun–Thu, 10–2am Fri & Sat. for observation deck only.

Sculptures of camels and their riders outside Sahara hotel

Stratosphere Tower, one of the Strip's most prominent landmarks

Riders being spun around on Chaos in Adventuredome

Circus Circus ⑫

2800 Las Vegas Blvd S. **Map** 3 C2.
Tel (702) 734-0410; (800) 634-3450.
⭕ *24 hours (see p115).* ♿
www.circuscircus.com

Located at the north end of the Strip, this circus-themed casino opened in 1968 as a complete family destination offering a unique combination of gambling and children's entertainment. However, initially, the property did not offer any accommodation. It was not until 1974, when Circus Circus was purchased by businessman William Bennett, that a hotel was added and the resort became a popular stop for the entire family. Today, the hotel is known for the wide variety of attractions it offers for adults and children alike.

A large colorful clown marquee fronts this hotel, which has three casinos spread over 100,000 sq ft (9,500 m). The main casino resembles a circus tent with a pink-and-white big top. The floor above the casino hosts the Carnival Midway that features a video arcade, fair games, and free circus acts, as well as trapeze artists and other aerialists flying high above the heads of the gamblers below. A good spot to view the action is from the Carousel Bar, a slow-revolving platform bar located next to the circus acts. At the rear of the hotel is the Adventuredome theme park housed in a pink canopy.

Circus Circus:Adventuredome

Merry-go-round at Adventuredome

The largest indoor theme park in the country, Adventuredome is spread over a massive area and has enough rides and attractions to keep visitors fully engaged for an entire afternoon. While some rides are gentle and ideally suited for younger children, the park also has several exciting rides, including a thrilling roller coaster, a stomach-wrenching sling shot, and a water flume ride. A carnival midway and many smaller attractions, such as bumper cars, rock- and net-climbing, and miniature golf, are also available.

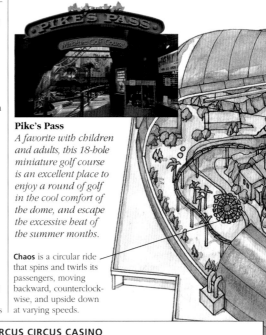

Pike's Pass
A favorite with children and adults, this 18-hole miniature golf course is an excellent place to enjoy a round of golf in the cool comfort of the dome, and escape the excessive heat of the summer months.

Chaos is a circular ride that spins and twirls its passengers, moving backward, counterclockwise, and upside down at varying speeds.

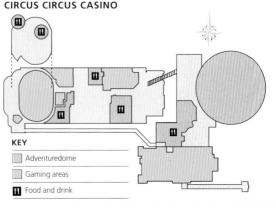

CIRCUS CIRCUS CASINO

KEY

▦	Adventuredome
▦	Gaming areas
🍴	Food and drink

★ Sling Shot
This exciting and spine-chilling tower ride shoots its passengers 100-ft (30-m) up along its pole at an incredible force of acceleration, and then hurls them back down again.

Lazer Blast creates a futuristic world filled with special visual effects, as teams use laser guns in a battle for the highest score.

VISITORS' CHECKLIST

Circus Circus. **Map** 3 C2.
Tel (702) 794-3939. ◯ daily, hours vary. ⌂ ⛭
www.adventuredome.com

Xtreme Zone
Enjoy the physical challenge of rock climbing and rappeling up and down on this formidable mountain face.

★ Canyon Blaster
This is the country's largest indoor double-loop, double-corkscrew roller coaster. Carrying up to 28 passengers, the ride reaches speeds of 55 mph (88.5 km/h) as it makes several sudden, hair-raising vertical drops, twists, and turns.

Disk'O is an exhilarating ride that spins and rocks with upbeat disco music. Passengers face outwards on a pedestal seat with arms and legs free while moving at 22 mph (35 km/h).

Rim Runner
Passengers get thoroughly drenched after a leisurely boat ride turns into a wild plunge down a 60-ft (18-m) waterfall.

STAR FEATURES

★ Sling Shot
_____

★ Canyon Blaster

DOWNTOWN & FREMONT STREET

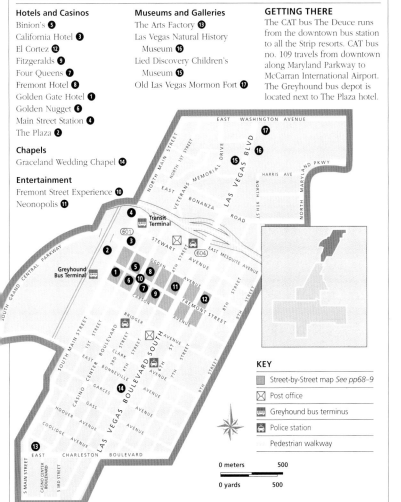

The city of Las Vegas and its now flourishing gambling industry grew up around Fremont Street in the early 1900s. This is where the first casinos and their colorful neon signs were originally located. Although the area has undergone a vast transformation since then, some vestiges of its heritage can still be seen.

Display, Fremont Street Experience

The Golden Gate hotel, for instance, has stood at the corner of Fremont and Main Street since 1906, and illuminated

landmarks, such as Vegas Vic, continue to light up the night sky. More recent attractions on this street, also known as Glitter Gulch, include the amazing light-and-sound shows of the Fremont Street Experience. In the near future, a new enhancement program will bring new and bigger resorts, and new restaurants to the area. For the present, however, downtown still offers unpretentious dining, lodging, and entertainment at affordable prices.

SIGHTS AT A GLANCE

Hotels and Casinos
Binion's **5**
California Hotel **3**
El Cortez **12**
Fitzgeralds **9**
Four Queens **7**
Fremont Hotel **8**
Golden Gate Hotel **1**
Golden Nugget **6**
Main Street Station **4**
The Plaza **2**

Chapels
Graceland Wedding Chapel **14**

Entertainment
Fremont Street Experience **10**
Neonopolis **11**

Museums and Galleries
The Arts Factory **13**
Las Vegas Natural History Museum **16**
Lied Discovery Children's Museum **15**
Old Las Vegas Mormon Fort **17**

GETTING THERE
The CAT bus The Deuce runs from the downtown bus station to all the Strip resorts. CAT bus no. 109 travels from downtown along Maryland Parkway to McCarran International Airport. The Greyhound bus depot is located next to The Plaza hotel.

KEY

▨	Street-by-Street map *See pp68–9*
⊠	Post office
🚌	Greyhound bus terminus
🚓	Police station
	Pedestrian walkway

0 meters 500

0 yards 500

◁ One of Las Vegas's most recognizable landmarks, Vegas Vic waves out to the crowd on Fremont Street *(see p73)*

Around Fremont Street

Originally known as Glitter Gulch, Fremont Street formed the heart of Las Vegas when the city was established in 1905. This is where the first casinos were founded, complete with stylish neon signs. Today, the area has outgrown its frontier heritage, but still boasts the best collection of neon lighting. The main attractions here are the shows at the Fremont Street Experience. The street also hosts dozens of shops and restaurants, as well as the new Fremont East Entertainment District between Las Vegas Boulevard North and Eighth Street.

The exterior of Main Street Station

Main Street Station
This classy hotel houses an enviable selection of antiques, artifacts, and collectibles ❹

California Hotel
Despite its name, the hotel has a Hawaiian ambience. Even the staff wears aloha shirts ❸

Binion's
A Las Vegas landmark, this hotel exemplifies, and once led, the Glitter Gulch casinos of bygone days ❺

Fremont Hotel
This is where the Midnight Idol and Vegas icon, Wayne Newton, made his singing debut ❽

Golden Gate Hotel
The city's oldest hotel, it is also known for introducing the shrimp cocktail to Las Vegas ❶

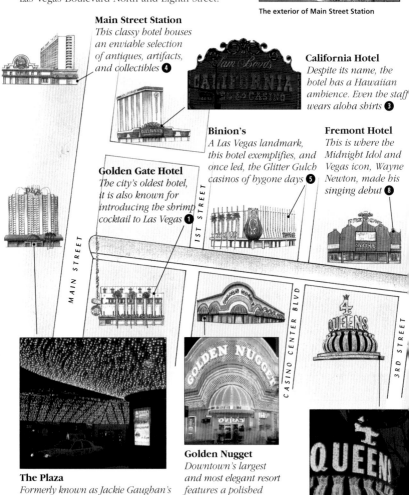

The Plaza
Formerly known as Jackie Gaughan's Plaza, this hotel was built in 1971 on the site of the original Union Pacific Railroad depot. It is also the only resort in town with a Greyhound bus station next door, and a rooftop swimming pool that overlooks Fremont Street ❷

Golden Nugget
Downtown's largest and most elegant resort features a polished white marble façade ❻

Four Queens
Built in 1966, this hotel was named after the original owner's four daughters ❼

Neonopolis
This multi-level mall is home to a range of shops and the Southern Nevada Museum of Fine Arts ⑪

LOCATOR MAP
See Street Finder maps 1 & 2

| 0 meters | 300 |
| 0 yards | 300 |

Fremont Street Experience
This open-air canopy generates a spectacular light-and-sound show nightly, and protects pedestrians from the harsh sun during the day ⑩

El Cortez
With a multi million dollar upgrade in 2008, El Cortez led the Downtown Vegas renaissance, however it still retains some of its 1950s architecture ⑫

4TH STREET

FREMONT STREET

LAS VEGAS BLVD

6TH STREET

Fremont East continues →

Fitzgeralds
Fitzgeralds Casino and Hotel claims to be the luckiest casino in Vegas. The casino offers great gaming action and several dining options ⑨

LAS VEGAS NEON

The neon sign remains the dominant icon of Las Vegas, despite the fact that many of the new themed mega resorts and shopping centers here have opted for a more understated look. Neon is a gas discovered by British chemist Sir William Ramsey in 1898. But it was a French inventor, Georges Claude, who, in 1910, found that when an electric current passed through a glass tube of neon, it emitted a powerful, shimmering light. In the 1940s and 50s, the craft of neon sign making was elevated to the status of an art in Vegas. The sidewalks near and around Neonopolis are home to an interesting collection of historic neon signs.

Glittering sign of Sassy Sally

Golden Gate Hotel ❶

1 Fremont St. **Map** 2 D3. **Tel** (702) 385-1906. ◯ 24 hours (see p118). ⓰ www.goldengatecasino.com

Located at the head of the Fremont Street Experience, Golden Gate, originally known as Hotel Nevada and later as Sal Sagev, was built in 1906 and is the city's oldest and smallest hotel. It also has the distinction of introducing Las Vegas to the shrimp cocktail, brought over from San Francisco by the hotel's owner in the 1950s. While the hotel has been expanded and modernized over the years, the casino and public areas retain a feeling of 19th-century San Francisco. Visitors can still get a great shrimp cocktail served in a tulip glass with a wedge of lemon. However, Golden Gate's 106 rooms have come a long way since the days of horse-drawn carriages, and are furnished with most modern amenities. The casino has about 500 slot and video poker machines, plus the usual table games.

The Plaza ❷

1 Main St. **Map** 2 D3. **Tel** (702) 386-2110. ◯ 24 hours (see p117). ⓰ www.plazahotelcasino.com

Established on land once owned by the railroad, The Plaza hotel has a Greyhound bus station next door. Located at the head of Fremont Street, the hotel was opened in 1971 by renowned hotelier Jackie Gaughan who sold it in 2004 to the Barrick Corporation.

The Plaza is mostly noted for its cascading neon waterfall along the façade of its tower. The hotel's 1,200 rooms include 136 suites and are spacious, comfortable, and airy. The decor is pleasant and features walnut veneer, and colorful patterns in the draperies and bedspreads.

Other amenities at The Plaza include a sports deck

The massive sign of California Hotel, as seen from the Strip at night

with a pool, jogging track, and the only tennis courts among the downtown casinos. The sports deck is often used as a venue for pool parties and other outdoor events during the summer months.

The hotel also hosts many eateries that offer a variety of cuisines from across the globe, as well as popular chains such as Subway and McDonalds.

California's staff in Hawaiian shirts

California Hotel ❸

12 Ogden Ave. **Map** 2 D3. **Tel** (702) 385-1222. ◯ 24 hours (see p117). ⓰ www.thecal.com

Despite its hip Hollywood implications, the California Hotel abounds with a tropical flavor and the aloha spirit. A part of the Boyd Gaming family of resorts, this 781-room hotel has been a Mecca for the Hawaiian tourist since it was built in 1975 – about 70 percent of the clientele are Hawaiians availing the resort's special tour packages. In keeping with the theme, the hotel staff wear colorful aloha shirts, the restaurants offer Polynesian and Oriental specialties, and the bars serve tropical drinks. Even California Hotel's casino, which is decorated with crystal chandeliers, etched glass, and Italian marble, has slot and video poker machines with Hawaiian names and themes. It also has a live keno lounge

and a sports book. The hotel's entertainment complex, Bridge Avenue, is home to several retail outlets and eateries such as the Cal Gift Shop, Aloha Specialities, and Vegas 808, as well as a video arcade.

As part of an expansion in 1996, a pedestrian walkway, which connects California Hotel with the Main Street Station resort, was constructed over Main Street.

Main Street Station ❹

200 N Main St. **Map** 2 D3. **Tel** (702) 387-1896. ◯ 24 hours (see p117). ⓰ www.mainstreetcasino.com

Although this hotel originally opened in 1991, it closed after a few months because of severe financial problems. Thereafter, Main Street Station was purchased by Boyd Gaming and, since

Slot machines lined up in the casino of Main Street Station

then, has emerged as one of downtown Las Vegas's classiest destinations.

The architecture suggests 1890s New Orleans with its brick promenade, magnolia trees, wrought-iron fences, and Victorian street lamps from pre-World War I Brussels. Inside, the hotel makes liberal use of hardwood and tile floors, gas lamps, brass fixtures, and enough antiques to fill a Southern mansion.

The hotel's lobby contains authentic hardwood railroad benches and bronze, dropped-dome chandeliers from the El Presidente Hotel in Buenos Aires. The stained-glass window greeting casino visitors is from singer Lillian Russell's Pennsylvania mansion, and the carved mahogany cabinetry behind the registration desk came from a Kentucky apothecary. The hotel also showcases President Theodore Roosevelt's Pullman railroad car, a fireplace from Scotland's Preswick Castle, US army scout and showman Buffalo Bill Cody's private rail car, and a section of the Berlin Wall.

Binion's ⑤

128 Fremont St. **Map** 2 D3. **Tel** (702) 382-1600. ◯ 24 hours (see p117). & www.binions.com

Formerly known as Binion's Horseshoe, this hotel was founded by Texan gambler and bootlegger Benny Binion in 1951 (see pp26–7), and was once the most popular gambling hall in downtown Las Vegas. During the 1960s and 1970s, the casino was packed day and night. However, after Binion's death in the 1990s, the casino went through a period of financial instability and was eventually sold to TLC Casino Enterprises in 2008.

Although much of the spark of the old Binion's has now gone, the casino still attracts many locals with its low-stake games and the opportunity to pose alongside its $1 million display.

The hotel's decor is true to its frontier heritage and reflects a Wild West theme with dark

Marble floors in the lobby at the Golden Nugget

wood panels, etched glass chandeliers, and antique furnishings. The ceilings are low, as is the lighting, reminiscent of the Binion's of the 1960s. Of the 366 guest rooms, 66 are part of the original hotel and feature Victorian wallpaper and brass or painted iron beds. The 300 tower rooms, annexed from the defunct Mint Hotel next door, are more modern in decor with plush carpeting, velvet headboards, and white-enameled furniture.

One of Binion's attractions was the World Series of Poker

Binion's, one of downtown's traditional casinos

competition (see p31), with its winner's pot of $5 million or more. The competition is no longer hosted here, but has moved to Rio (see p50).

Golden Nugget ⑥

129 Fremont St. **Map** 2 D3. **Tel** (702) 385-7111. ◯ 24 hours (see p118). & www.goldennugget.com

With its façade of polished white marble, gold trim, and white canopies, Golden Nugget stands out as a jewel among downtown hostelries. It is also the only casino in the area without a neon sign. Inside, the hotel hosts one of the world's largest gold nuggets, weighing an incredible 61 lb (27 kg). The hotel's elegant lobby has leaf-glass chandeliers, white marble floors and columns, etched glass panels, gold and brass accessories, and rich, red Oriental rugs. The white marble and gold trim-themed decor is evident throughout the restaurants and the common areas as well. The hotel's guest rooms are also among the most luxurious in town with plush cream-colored carpeting and wall coverings. Newer additions include a high-stakes salon, an expanded poker room and a pool complex.

Four Queens ❼

202 Fremont St. **Map** 2 D3.
Tel (702) 385-4011.
◯ 24 hours (see p117). ♿
www.fourqueens.com

Reflecting a New Orleans
motif, Four Queens is
the Grand Old Dame of
downtown Las Vegas. Built in
1966, the hotel was named in
honor of the original owner's
three daughters, and has one
of the best arrays of lights on
Fremont Street.

The Four Queen's decor
suggests the French Quarter
with its carved wood registration desk, brass trim, gilt
mirrors, and hurricane-lamp
chandeliers. The hotel has
690 rooms which were re-
modeled in 2008. They are
brightly furnished and feature
plush tan carpets, beautiful
brocade wallpaper, and dark
polished wood furniture.

The chandeliered casino
has plenty of action, with the
usual array of table games
and slot and video poker
machines that visitors to Las
Vegas would expect.

**Brightly illuminated sign of the
Four Queens hotel**

Fremont Hotel ❽

200 Fremont St. **Map** 2 D3. **Tel** (702)
385-3232. ◯ 24 hours (see p117).
♿ **www**.fremontcasino.com

This renowned casino was
built in 1956 and was
downtown's first high-rise
hotel. Fremont Hotel was
also the first to have a fully
carpeted casino at a time
when all other establishments
had sawdust-covered floors.

Slot machines in the Fremont Hotel casino

Moreover, it was here that
the famous Las Vegas headliner, Wayne Newton, made
his singing debut.

Today, the hotel's block-long
neon sign helps light up the
dazzling Fremont Street
Experience. The hotel is often
described as the heart of
Fremont Street and is
definitely close to all
the action in the area.
Across the street is its
sister resort, the
tropical-themed
California Hotel (see
p70). The Fremont's
447 guest rooms are
modern and comfort-
able, and have
attractive floral
patterns in hues of
emerald and burgundy.

The sprawling casino is
always busy as gamblers
flit from machine to machine
– there are more than
1,000 slot and video poker
machines to choose from.
And, during the football
season, Fremont Hotel's race
and sports book is one of
downtown's busiest.

Fitzgeralds ❾

301 Fremont St. **Map** 2 D3.
Tel (702) 388-2400.
◯ 24 hours (see p117). ♿
www.fitzgeraldslasvegas.com

Commonly referred to as
the "Fitz," this 638-room
resort is the tallest hotel in
downtown Las Vegas with
its 34-story tower. Located
next to the Fremont Street

**Sign of the Irish-
themed Fitzgeralds**

Experience, the hotel offers
an excellent vantage point to
see the light shows that take
place there each evening.

The hotel has an Irish
theme and hosts a piece of
the famous Blarney Stone
from Ireland's Blarney Castle.
The stone is
believed to
bestow the gift of
eloquence and
persuasiveness to
the one who kiss-
es it, and is a pop-
ular stop for visitors.

Fitzgeralds even
displays a gigantic neon
rainbow with a pot
of gold over the
hotel's entrance. On
St. Patrick's Day,
March 17, the place turns into
an Irish madhouse with parties, green-colored beer, and
much more.

In 1996, Fitzgeralds merged
with Holiday Inn and
underwent a $17-million
expansion that included new
restaurants, remodeled guest
rooms, and a larger casino
with a separate poker room.
The hotel was subsequently
sold to Detroit-based
businessman and casino
owner, Don Barden, in 2001.

Fitzgeralds has a universal
appeal and knows how to
attract a younger audience
with a McDonald's on site, as
well as a Krispy Kreme outlet.
For finer dining, there is also
Don B's Steakhouse, along
with the Courtyard Grill &
Buffet. The country tribute
band shows are a popular
and regular feature.

Fremont Street Experience ⑩

Map 2 D3. *Light shows: hourly 6pm–midnight daily.* 🚹
www.vegasexperience.com

Fremont Street has been at the heart of Las Vegas since it was established in 1905. When gambling was legalized in Nevada in 1931, this is where the first casinos were located. The street became known as "Glitter Gulch" when neon lighting became available, as stylish illuminated signs lit up the night sky.

In the 1980s and 1990s Fremont Street suffered in competition from more lavish attractions on the Strip and became a run-down city center, generally avoided by tourists. In 1994, an ambitious $70-million project to revitalize the area was initiated. A vast steel canopy now covers five blocks of the street, onto which is displayed the spectacular Fremont Street light-and-sound shows, which are collectively known as Viva Vision. The current shows on display include *KISS Over Vegas, Don McLean's*

The colorful, neon-lit façade of the Neonopolis entertainment center

American Pie and *A Tribute to Queen*. The canopy's ceiling showcases high-resolution images presented by more than 12 million synchronized LED modules with concert-quality sound controlled by 10 computers. The street is pedestrianized and visitors can stroll from casino to casino, stopping to snack and shop at kiosks on the way. Some of the famous 1950s and 60s neon signs gave way to the new show, but many of the dazzling façades belonging to some of the oldest and best-loved casinos remain.

Neonopolis ⑪

450 Fremont St. **Map** 2 E3.
🕐 *hours vary.* 🚹

This open-air, multi-level dining, shopping, and entertainment complex is located at the east end of the Fremont Street Experience. Unfortunately, Neonopolis has fallen onto fairly hard times during the past few years and a great deal of the complex is now vacant. However, this sad state of affairs is likely to change dramatically as there are plans to relocate the very popular Star Trek: The Experience here – previously at the Las Vegas Hilton *(see p62)* – in 2010. The Experience will be significantly different from the one at the Hilton and will include more elements from *Star Trek: The Original Series* and the 2009 *Star Trek* movie.

Although this massive mall has experienced a decline in popularity, retail shops and eateries such as Del Prado Jewelers, El Nopal, and a delicatessen, Taste of California make it worth a visit. Hennessey's Irish Tavern and the Mickie Finnz Fish House & Bar are located just across the street from the complex.

Neonopolis is situated at the gateway to the Fremont East District, which features wide sidewalks, lighted gateways, and tall, retro-looking neon signs that revive the glitz of vintage Las Vegas. Popular nightclubs in the area include Beauty Bar, Downtown Cocktail Room *(see p150)*, The Griffin, and Take 1.

The spectacular light-and-sound show at the Fremont Street Experience

El Cortez, one of the few hotels to retain parts of its original architecture

El Cortez ⑫

600 E Fremont St. **Map** 2 E3. **Tel** (702) 385-5200. ⬭ 24 hours (see p117). ♿ www.elcortezhotelcasino.com

One of Las Vegas's most recognized landmarks, the El Cortez hotel was built in 1941 and holds the distinction of being the oldest casino in town. Leading the Fremont East rejuvenation, El Cortez upgraded the exterior in 2008 adding a modern entrance and a new tower, at a cost of $6 million. However, it still retains some of its original architecture.

The hotel's original guest rooms with their hardwood floors and tile baths are still intact and are reached via a creaky staircase just off the casino floor. For those looking for more modern accommodation, there is a 14-story, 200-room tower with pleasant and comfortable rooms.

The hotel was once owned by Benjamin "Bugsy" Siegel (see p26) who sold it when he needed to raise cash to build his famous Flamingo hotel on the Strip. It is currently owned by Jackie Gaughan, one of Las Vegas's true pioneers. Gaughan owned several other hotels and casinos in downtown Las Vegas, including The Plaza, Vegas Club, Western Hotel, and Gold Spike, all of which he sold in 2004. However, he retained El Cortez, where he still lives

in a penthouse apartment.

Today, El Cortez caters mostly to budget travelers, senior citizens, and slot machine players who enjoy playing in the ambience of an "old Las Vegas" style casino. Video poker and video keno are two of the most popular games in the sprawling casino, which is crammed with rows of machines of every type and coinage. Because there are so many nickel poker and keno machines, the action here is often intense, noisy, and packed. The El Cortez casino also has a race and sports book.

The Arts Factory ⑬

101–109 E Charleston Blvd. **Map** 1 C4. **Tel** (702) 676-1111. ⬭ daily, varies for each gallery. ♿ www.theartsfactory.com

Located just about a mile (1.6 km) south of Fremont Street, in the Gateway Arts District, The Arts Factory is an eclectic collection of local artists who have set up shop in a long strip of storefront

The charming and quaint exterior of Graceland Wedding Chapel

buildings. Included in the mix are artists, graphic designers, architects, photographers, interior designers, and other craftspeople who enjoy the creative energy of working under one roof.

The Factory also houses several galleries and studios, such as Jawa Studio, Rever Gallery, Trifecta Gallery, Joseph Watson Collection, Studio West Photography, and Cricket Studio, where the artists can showcase their works. The building, like the others in the neighborhood, is old and somewhat neglected, but the artists have plied their talents to create a pleasing venue for their work. On the first Friday of each month, the center organizes an event that features works by local artists, along with live music and other forms of entertainment.

A bridal bouquet

Graceland Wedding Chapel ⑭

619 Las Vegas Blvd S. **Map** 2 D4. **Tel** (702) 382-0091. ⬭ hours vary. ♿ www.gracelandchapel.com

Established more than half a century ago, the Graceland Wedding Chapel is quintessential Las Vegas. Located about a mile south of downtown, it is the birthplace of the original Elvis-themed wedding that has since become a Vegas tradition. The spire-like bell tower and sloped roof of this quaint chapel exude a Victorian flavor. Over the years, the chapel has seen many celebrities walk down its aisle. Among the more recent are Billy Ray and Tish Cyrus, Jon Bon Jovi, TV personality Jay Leno, and singers such as Aaron Neville and Roger Glover of the hard rock music group, Deep Purple. The chapel offers several wedding packages and a choice of floral arrangements, photographers, and even a limousine service (see p167).

◁ Hundreds of visitors take in the light-and-sound shows at the Fremont Street Experience (see p73)

Exterior of Lied Discovery Children's Museum

Lied Discovery Children's Museum ⓯

833 Las Vegas Blvd. **Map** 2 E2. **Tel** (702) 382-3445. ◯ Jun–early Sep: 10am–5pm Mon–Sat, noon–5pm Sun; early Sep–May: 9am–4pm Tue–Fri, 10am–5pm Sat, noon–5pm Sun, & most school holidays. ◉ major hols. ⌕ ♿ www.ldcm.org

A conical, concrete teepee forms part of this striking building, which also houses a branch of the Las Vegas City Library. Opened in 1990, this excellent museum is devoted to interactive exhibits that are fun for both adults and kids. The first floor focuses on the arts, providing opportunities for imaginary and dramatic play. It is dedicated to children who are not yet able to read. Children can stand inside a gigantic bubble, freeze their shadows on a wall, and hear simple phrases translated into different languages, including Navajo. The second floor features the in-house radio station. In total there are approximately 100 exhibits covering the arts, sciences, and humanities.

The Las Vegas Natural History Museum ⓰

900 Las Vegas Blvd N. **Map** 2 E2. **Tel** (702) 384-3466. ◯ 9am–4pm daily. ◉ major hols. ⌕ ♿ www.lvnhm.org

This museum attracts families with its appealing range of exhibits. Dioramas re-create the African savanna and display a variety of wildlife from leopards to several African antelope species such as bush boks and duikers. The Wild Nevada Room displays the flora and fauna of the Mojave Desert. Animatronic dinosaurs include a 35-ft- (10.5-m-) long Tyrannosaurus rex, while the marine exhibit has live sharks and eels. In the hands-on discovery room visitors can dig for fossils and explore the five senses. An exhibition on Egypt opened in 2009, following the generous donation of Tutankhamen artifacts by Luxor *(see p42)*.

Old Las Vegas Mormon Fort ⓱

500 E Washington Blvd. **Map** 2 E2. **Tel** (702) 486-3511. ◯ 8am–4:30pm Tue–Sat. ◉ public hols. ⌕ ♿ www.parks.nv.gov/olvmf.htm

Located just a short distance from the Lied Discovery Children's Museum, the small soft-pink adobe building that is the only remains of the Mormon Fort is a tranquil spot. The oldest building in Las Vegas, the fort dates back to 1855, when the first group of Mormon settlers arrived in the area *(see p18)*. They constructed an adobe fort arranged around a 150-ft (45-m) long *placita* – a small rectangular plaza – with 14-ft (4-m) high walls, but abandoned it three years later. The fort became part of a ranch in the 1880s and was run by Las Vegas pioneer Helen Stewart. The City of Las Vegas bought the site in 1971, and restoration work has been ongoing since.

Today, visitors enter a reconstruction of the original adobe house with its simply furnished interior much as it would have been under Mormon occupation. The building also contains an exhibition that describes the Mormon missions and their impact on Las Vegas.

An animatronic Tyrannosaurus rex in roaring form at the Las Vegas Natural History Museum

FARTHER AFIELD

Beyond the neon glow of the downtown district and the monetary lure of the Strip casinos, lies a land of diversity filled with scenic and historical treasures. Canyons, mountains, deserts, and some of the most magnificent wilderness that the US has to offer can be seen in almost every direction just beyond Vegas's bright lights, and present a sharp contrast to the artificial wonders of the city. A short drive away are the lush, alpine forests and snow-laden peaks of Mount Charleston, the steep gullies, bristlecone canyons, and red sandstone escarpments of Red Rock Canyon and Valley of Fire State Park, and the expansive shoreline and scenic blue splendor of Lake Mead. For admirers of contemporary architecture, the modern day marvel of Hoover Dam is a must-see. Hailed as an engineering victory, the dam offers splendid views of the surrounding badlands from the top of its visitor center, and is a highly popular tourist destination. Situated a comfortable distance southeast of Las Vegas are two inviting and well-planned cities – Henderson and Boulder City – each with its own distinct character. Most of these side trips can be enjoyed in just a few hours or as a day excursion, and all offer a chance to renew body and spirit.

Sign of Lake Mead Cruises

SIGHTS AT A GLANCE

Areas of Natural Beauty
Lake Mead National Recreation Area **5**
Mount Charleston **3**
Red Rock Canyon Tour p80 **1**
Valley of Fire State Park **4**

Historic Cities
Boulder City **6**
Henderson **7**

Landmarks
Hoover Dam p83 **8**

Entertainment
Bonnie Springs Ranch/Old Nevada **2**

KEY
▨	Major sight
☐	Urban area
✈	International airport
═	National highway
▬	Major road
═	Minor road
—	Railroad
·—	State line

0 kilometers 20

0 miles 20

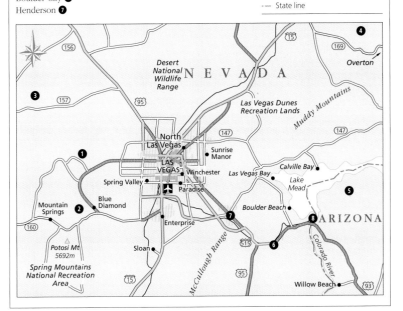

◁ **Crowded marina in the picturesque Lake Mead Recreational Area *(see p82)***

Red Rock Canyon Tour ❶

Pictographs on prehistoric rocks

The centerpiece of Red Rock Canyon is a yellow and red sandstone escarpment incised with numerous deep canyons formed by years of erosion. These spectacular rock formations are the geological result of the Keystone Thrust fault where the earth's tectonic plates collided with such force so as to thrust one rock plate over another. Perennial and seasonal springs encourage lush vegetation in relatively shaded places in contrast with the arid desert floor.

TIPS FOR DRIVERS

Tour Length: 13 miles (21 km). *Getting there:* 17 miles (27 km) west on Charleston Blvd (Hwy 159) from Las Vegas. *When to go:* The Scenic Loop Drive opens daily at 6am. Closing hours: 7pm Mar & Oct; 8pm Apr–Sep; 5pm Nov–Feb. The weather is good all year, except for flash floods.

Keystone Thrust ③
This fracture in the earth's crust details the sharp contrast between the older gray limestone and the younger red sandstone rock formations where the "thrust" of the tectonic plates took place.

Calico Hills ②
The two Calico Vista points here offer great panoramic views of the striking and flame-colored sandstone bluffs.

Willow Springs ④
Located just past the halfway point on the drive, this is an idyllic picnic spot. It is also a good place to see ancient rock carvings.

Ice Box Canyon ⑤
This popular trail features huge vertical cliffs and three water-falls that keep this area cool all year.

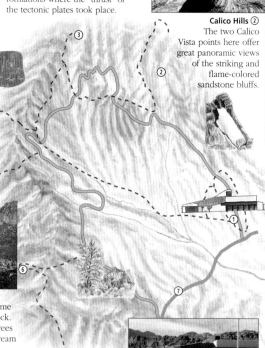

Pine Creek Canyon ⑥
This canyon is home to some of the best trails in Red Rock. Rows of ponderosa pine trees and a meandering clear stream add to the tranquil beauty of the area.

Red Rock Overlook ⑦
Although not part of the Scenic Loop, this vantage point offers excellent views over the canyon.

Visitor Center ①
Set against a backdrop of sandstone cliffs, the center provides maps and information on the geology, wildlife, and history of the region.

KEY

— Tour route

-- Hiking trail

— Highway

0 kilometers   2

0 miles   2

Bonnie Springs Ranch/Old Nevada ②

1 Gunfighter Lane, Blue Mountain, Nevada. *Tel* (702) 875-4191.
⬤ *summer: 10:30am–6pm Wed–Sun; winter: 10:30am–5pm Wed–Sun.* 🖼 🔥 **www.** bonniesprings.com

Located a short distance from Red Rock Canyon, Bonnie Springs Ranch and Old Nevada provide wholesome family entertainment. Built in 1843 as a cattle ranch and watering hole for wagon trains on their way to California, Bonnie Springs, today, has a petting zoo, duck pond, bird aviary, and riding stables.

Next door, Old Nevada is a full-scale restoration of an old Western mining town. Although it looks like a movie set, there are no false fronts here. The weathered buildings include country stores, an ice cream parlor, a shooting gallery, and a chapel. Throughout the day, fake gunfights are held in the street. Visitors can also ride a miniature train along the outskirts of the town.

Mount Charleston ③

Tel (702) 515-5400 (Forest Service).
🚌 *Las Vegas.* Ⓐ
www.fs.fed.us/r4/htnf

Rising out of the **Toiyabe National Forest** at a considerable height of 11,918 ft (3,632 m), Mount Charleston

Pine-, aspen-, and fir-covered peaks of Mount Charleston

is covered with pine, aspen, mountain mahogany, and fir. Located just about 45 miles (72 km) northwest of Las Vegas, the region is also known as the Spring Mountain Recreation Area, and offers refuge from the city's summer heat with a variety of hiking trails and picnic areas. In winter, snowboarding and skiing are popular (see p155).

Among the many hikes available, two of the most demanding trails that snake up to the summit are the 11-mile (18-km) North Loop Trail and the 9-mile (14-km) South Loop Trail. Easier walks on the slopes are also marked, such as a one-hour hike up Cathedral Rock. This walk starts from a picnic area at the end of Nevada State Highway 157. This is the more southerly of the two byroads leading to Mount Charleston off Highway 95; the other is Highway 156 that runs to the Lee Canyon Ski Area, catering to both skiers and snowboarders.

Valley of Fire State Park ④

Tel (702) 397-2088. 🚌 *Las Vegas.* 🖼 🔥 *partial.* Ⓐ **http://** parks.nv.gov/vf.htm

This spectacularly scenic state park has a remote, desert location some 60 miles (97 km) northeast of Las Vegas. Its name derives from the red sandstone formations that began as huge, shifting sand dunes about 150 million years ago. There are four well-maintained trails across this wilderness, including the Petroglyph Canyon Trail, an easy half-mile (0.8-km) loop, which takes in several fine prehistoric Ancestral Puebloan rock carvings. Here, summer temperatures often reach 44°C (112°F). The best time to visit is in spring or fall.

The nearby town of Overton lies along the Muddy River. Ancestral Puebloan people settled here in around 300 BC but left some 1,500 years later, perhaps because of a long drought. Archaeologists have unearthed hundreds of prehistoric artifacts in the area since the first digs began in the 1920s. Overton's **Lost City Museum of Archaeology**, which is located just outside the town, has a large collection, including pottery, beads, woven baskets, and delicate turquoise jewelry.

🏛 Lost City Museum of Archaeology
721 S Moapa Valley Blvd, Overton.
Tel (702) 397-2193. ⬤ *8:30am– 4:30pm Thu–Sun.* ⬤ *Thanksgiving, Dec 25, Jan 1* 🖼 🔥

Lake Mead National Recreation Area ❺

US 93 W of Las Vegas. **Tel** (702) 293-8906; Alan Bible Visitor Center (702) 293-8990. 🚌 Las Vegas. ⏰ 8:30am–4:30pm daily. ◔ Thanksgiving, Dec 25, Jan 1. 📷 ♿ limited. ⚠
www.nps.gov/lame

After the completion of the Hoover Dam, the waters of the Colorado River filled the deep canyons that once towered above the river to create a huge reservoir. This lake, with its 700 miles (1,130 km) of shoreline, boasts forests and flower-rich meadows, and is the centerpiece of Lake Mead National Recreation Area, a remarkably expansive tract of land. The focus is on water sports, especially sailing, waterskiing, boating, and fishing. Striped bass and rainbow trout are popular catches. There are also several campgrounds and marinas.

The lake and its main marina are easily accessed through Boulder City. However, a more scenic route is available via the Lakeshore and Northshore Drives along the lake's northern finger. These vistas offer panoramic views of Lake Mead with the desert and mountains for a backdrop.

Power boating on Lake Mead

Speedboats moored on either side of a jetty on Lake Mead

The serene setting of Green Valley Ranch Resort, Henderson

Boulder City ❻

US 93 SE of Las Vegas. 👥 102,000. ✈ 🚌

Just eight miles (13 km) west of the colossal Hoover Dam, Boulder City was built as a model community to house the dam's construction workers. With its neat yards and suburban streets, it is one of Nevada's most attractive and well-ordered towns. Its Christian founders banned casinos, and there are none here even today. Several of its original 1930s buildings remain, including the restored 1933 Boulder Dam Hotel, which houses the **Hoover Dam Museum**. Posters, memorabilia, photographs, films, and other exhibits that provide an insight into the dam and the people who built it are on display here.

🏛 **Hoover Dam Museum**
1305 Arizona St, Boulder City.
Tel (702) 294-1988. ⏰ 11am–5pm Mon–Sat; 12–5pm Sun. ◔ Jan 1, Easter Sun, Mother's Day, Thanksgiving, Dec 25. 📷 ♿
www.bcmha.org

Henderson ❼

US 93 SE of Las Vegas. 👥 256,000. ✈ 🚌 ℹ Henderson Convention Center and Visitors Bureau (702) 267-2171. www.cityofhenderson.com

Often mistaken as a suburb of Las Vegas, Henderson is an incorporated city that is now the state's second largest.

The city has something of a split personality – its oldest sections have changed little since the town was incorporated in 1944. With street names such as Titanium and Magnesium, these working class neighborhoods are lined with humble, concrete block bungalows that have stood the test of time. Conversely, Henderson is home to one of southern Nevada's most upscale planned communities, Green Valley, where championship golf courses intermingle with million-dollar estates and villas. The city also developed a gaming industry of its own, once again split between the blue-collar casinos of its downtown, and the more fashionable resorts such as the **Green Valley Ranch Resort** (see p119), which features Mediterranean architecture and some great dining options.

One of the main attractions in Henderson is the **Ethel M Chocolates** factory. The "M" stands for Mars, as in Mars Bars, who are the makers of candies such as Milky Way, Snickers, Twix, and M&Ms, as well as Ethel M Chocolates, which are now produced exclusively in Las Vegas. Free tours are available to view the gourmet chocolates being created.

Green Valley Ranch Resort
2300 Paseo Verde Pkwy, Henderson. **Tel** (702) 617-7777. ⏰ 24 hours. ♿ www.greenvalley ranchresort.com

Ethel M Chocolates
2 Cactus Garden Dr, Henderson. **Tel** (702) 433-2500. ⏰ 8:30am–6pm. ♿ 📷
www.ethelm.com

Hoover Dam ❽

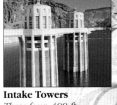

Originally known as the Boulder Dam, the Hoover Dam project began in 1931 and was completed in 1935, ahead of schedule and under budget. Hailed as an engineering victory, this massive concrete structure stands 54-stories tall, has a 600-ft (183-m) thick base, and controls the flow of the Colorado River. Today, the dam provides this desert region with a reliable supply of water and electricity and is a major tourist attraction. Due to security restrictions, the only way to tour the dam is through the visitor center. Certain vehicles are restricted from driving over the dam.

Hoover Dam workers memorial

VISITORS' CHECKLIST

US Hwy 95 S past Boulder City. 🛈 *Hoover Dam Visitor Center (702) 494-2517; (866) 730-9097.* ⭕ *9am–5:15pm (4:15pm winter).* ⬤ *Thanksgiving, Dec 25.* 🎦 *gallery, exhibitions.* ♿ 🎟 **www**.ubr.gov/lc/hooverdam

The Colorado River, flowing along its 1,400-mile (2,253-km) journey from the Rocky Mountains to the Gulf of Mexico, is the source of all power generated by the dam.

Intake Towers
These four, 400-ft (122-m) tall towers, two on either side of the dam, control water flow through the electric turbines.

★ Visitor Center
This three-level center features audiovisual and theater presentations as well as multimedia exhibits that explain the processes involved in building the dam.

Art Deco Details
Large cast-concrete panels on the entrance towers, as well as the dam's design and craftsmanship, reflect Art Deco elements in the architecture.

★ Hydroelectric Power Generators
The dam's 17 turbine-driven generators supply electricity to the states of California, Nevada, and Arizona.

STAR FEATURES

★ Visitor Center

★ Hydroelectric Power Generators

TWO GUIDED WALKS AND A DRIVE

Las Vegas is a fascinating and diverse city with multifold layers that can both charm and intrigue those who venture to explore it. The following walks and drive have been chosen to capture a distinct view of a neo-Southwestern city, where brightly lit, ultra-modern casinos exist alongside unexpected, yet vivid vestiges reminiscent of the town's frontier heritage.

Breaking from the flamboyance of the Strip, the first walk offers a contrasting perspective to the main area of the city. The university campus is a sanctuary for the arts, culture, literature, and history of Southern Nevada, and teems with youthful and intellectual vibrancy. The second walk intro-

Marble statue, Monte Carlo

duces Las Vegas's famous "themed" resorts that meticulously re-create the architectural beauty of man-made sights and landmarks from all around the world. En route you can gaze at the Eiffel Tower, walk across the Brooklyn Bridge, and admire the opulent grandeur of the Roman Colosseum.

Finally, a scenic drive takes visitors beyond the neon and through several generations of the city's neighborhoods. It covers the downtown residential district where the city was born and the midtown estates where the community's founding fathers used to live.

Remember that Las Vegas is situated in a desert, so wear appropriate clothing, sensible shoes, and sunscreen, and carry drinking water.

CHOOSING A WALK OR A DRIVE

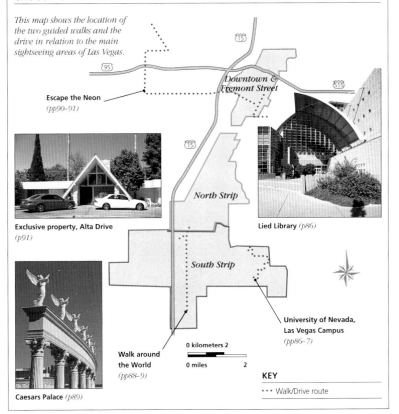

This map shows the location of the two guided walks and the drive in relation to the main sightseeing areas of Las Vegas.

Escape the Neon
(pp90–91)

Downtown & Fremont Street

North Strip

Exclusive property, Alta Drive
(p91)

Lied Library *(p86)*

South Strip

Caesars Palace *(p89)*

Walk around the World
(pp88–9)

0 kilometers 2

0 miles 2

University of Nevada, Las Vegas Campus
(pp86–7)

KEY

••• Walk/Drive route

◁ Fall leaves at the University of Nevada, Las Vegas campus **(see pp86–7)**

A 90-Minute Walk around the University of Nevada, Las Vegas Campus (UNLV)

This walk offers a stimulating glimpse into the University of Nevada, Las Vegas, which serves as the intellectual and cultural center of the city. Each year, UNLV's performing arts venues showcase ballets, operas, theatrical productions, and classical musical concerts by world-renowned artists. In addition, the university features fine arts galleries, museums, and an extensive library – its collection of casino memorabilia is the most comprehensive in the state of Nevada. The surrounding area offers various off-campus diversions that provide a respite from university life.

Front façade of the Lied Library ②

Thomas & Mack Center to the Lied Library

At the southwest end of the UNLV campus, located just off Swenson Street is the Thomas & Mack Center ①. This 18,000-seat sports and entertainment arena is home to the school's Runnin' Rebels basketball team. It is also the site of various community events, such as the annual National Finals Rodeo *(see p32)*, the Mountain West Conference basketball tournaments, rock shows, Disney musicals on ice, and more. The adjoining 3,000-seat Cox Pavilion, added to the center in 2001, is the venue for UNLV's volleyball and women's basketball games.

From Thomas & Mack, walk about two blocks north along Gym Road to Lied Library ② for a must-see visit to its Special Collections section. Thousands of maps, manuscripts, periodicals, drawings, and pictures document the history, art, and culture of Las Vegas. A good place to start is the

Marjorie Barrick Museum ③

public reading room, stocked with volumes dating back to the 18th century and earlier. You can also head for the oral history room that has audio- and videotapes of interviews and documentaries on famous Las Vegans. The library has a wide selection of gaming memorabilia as well.

UNLV Marjorie Barrick Museum to Donna Beam Gallery

From the library, walk across Gym Road to the UNLV Marjorie Barrick Museum of Natural History ③ *(see p45)*. Exhibits here focus on the area's flora and fauna. There is also a fine collection of Native American and Meso-American cultural artifacts, such as textiles and dance masks. The museum also chronicles the history of ancient peoples such as the Anasazi and the Hopi Indians. Situated at the entrance to the museum is the Xeric Garden ④, which features an attractive landscape of indigenous plant life, paved pathways, and striated sandstone boulders. Continue east till Brussels Street and then head north to the Donna Beam Fine Arts Gallery ⑤. Located in the Alta Ham Fine Arts Building, the

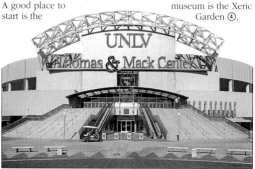

Entrance to the massive sports arena, Thomas & Mark Center ①

gallery showcases an eclectic collection of works by acclaimed contemporary artists, as well as by students and faculty of the university's Department of Art. The ever-changing exhibitions include those organized by renowned art companies, such as Crayola Crayon Inc., National Council on Education for the Ceramic Arts, and American College Theater Festival.

Nuclear bomb, Atomic Testing Museum ⑦

Flashlight Sculpture to the Atomic Testing Museum

The Fine Arts building and Donna Beam Gallery are just a few steps from the performing Arts Center, which houses the Artemus Ham Concert Hall and the Judy Bayley Theater – two of UNLV's most prominent entertainment venues for various cultural shows. On the plaza between these two venues, stands a massive sculpture, the 38-ft (11.5-m) tall *Flashlight* ⑥, created by Swedish-born artist Claes Oldenburg. Installed in 1981, the pop art sculpture has become a favorite on campus. Head east from here till you reach Maryland Parkway, one the city's oldest boulevards, connecting the area east of downtown with McCarran Airport. The section near UNLV is home to a wide selection of shops, bookstores, coffee houses, restaurants, and bars, and is always crowded with students. Walk north on Maryland and turn east on Cottage Grove Avenue.

FlashLight sculpture ⑥

TIPS FOR WALKERS

Starting point: *Thomas & Mack Center.*
Length: *2 miles (3.2 km).*
Getting there: *Take the CAT bus no. 201 on Tropicana Avenue heading east from the Strip and get off at Swenson Street. From downtown you can take CAT bus no. 108 south on Paradise Road all the way to the airport, at which point the bus loops and returns via Swenson Street.*
Stopping-off points: *Maryland Parkway has an array of good eateries to choose from, including Paymon's Mediterranean Café, which serves excellent Middle Eastern cuisine, or Einstein Bagels for a quick and tasty snack.*

At the north end of the UNLV campus is the Desert Research Institute (DRI), home to the Atomic Testing Museum ⑦. Some of the most notable displays here are the Nevada Test Site's *(see p22)* vast collection of photographs and memorabilia, a one-fifth-scale model of a test canister used in underground nuclear experiments, and a letter written by eminent scientist Albert Einstein to President Franklin D. Roosevelt. The museum also features interactive multimedia exhibits, the Ground Zero Theater that shows films of actual atomic tests, and works from the Smithsonian Institution.

A painting by actor Tony Curtis at the Donna Beam Fine Arts Gallery ⑤

NGO ROAD

MARYLAND CIR

COTTAGE CIR
GROVE CIR
FAIRFAX CIR

GE GROVE AVE

⑥

⑤

P

MARYLAND PARKWAY

BRUSSELS ST

④

P

UNIVERSITY ROAD

BRUSSELS ST

DOROTHY AVE

CANA AVENUE

| 0 meters | 200 |
| 0 yards | 200 |

KEY

••• Tour route

P Parking

A Two-Hour Walk around the World

Nothing characterizes Las Vegas like its imaginatively conceived and exquisitely designed, themed mega resorts. Lined along the Strip, these opulent hotels pay tribute to some of the most renowned cities and countries in the world through remarkable re-creations of their architectural landscape. This walk allows you to stroll along the streets of Venice, marvel at international landmarks such as the Eiffel Tower, Brooklyn Bridge, and the Egyptian sphinx, and see beautiful Roman sculptures and fountains – all within a short period of time.

A replica of the Brooklyn Bridge at New York-New York ②

Egypt to New York

Begin the walk at the corner of Las Vegas Boulevard and Hacienda Avenue to see one of the city's most spectacular resorts – Luxor ① *(see p42)*. The main building consists of a 30-story high pyramid, encased in dark reflective glass with its entrance guarded by a ten-story high sphinx, flanked by a sandstone obelisk, lagoon, palm trees, and statues of pharaohs. Two permanent and fascinating exhibitions are housed here: Titanic and Bodies. Real full-bodies and organs are displayed, giving a detailed, 3D vision of the human form rarely seen outside of an anatomy lab or morgue.

From Luxor, take a free monorail to Excalibur *(see p42)*, where it's just a short walk across the street to New York-New York ② *(see p43)*. A replica of the Statue of Liberty marks the entrance to this hotel. In front of the statue is a memorial for the victims of the September 11,

2001 attack on New York's World Trade Center. The hotel's towers contain replicas of other famous landmarks, including the Empire State Building and the Chrysler Building. The casino also duplicates New York icons such as Times Square, which hosts nightly New Year's Eve parties, and a replica of Coney Island,

A majestic reproduction of the Great Sphinx, Luxor ①

(see p42), *(see p42)*, *(see p43)*

KEY

••• Tour route

🅿 Las Vegas Monorail

🅿 Free monorail

— Monorail route

featuring an arcade with video games and bumper cars. When it's time to leave, walk across the Brooklyn Bridge, and head north towards Monte Carlo ③ *(see p43)*.

Monte Carlo to Paris

From the sidewalk, admire the European-style architecture at Monte Carlo, an impressive array of elegant alabaster columns, Renaissance statues, and a gleaming marble lobby. From here you can view the pool area with its lush landscaping, wave pool, and a lazy river. Bring some quarters as the Street of Dreams has a games arcade where visitors can enjoy motion simulated rides or tee off on a virtual reality golf game.

From here, continue walking north along the Strip, or head across the road to MGM Grand where you can take the monorail to Bally's, which is just a short stroll away from Paris Las Vegas ④ *(see p46)*. Designed to resemble a mini version of the French capital, this resort has an impressive half-size replica of the iconic Eiffel Tower, as well as copies of buildings such as l'Opera, Louvre, and Arc de Triomphe. Cobblestone pathways, French wrought-iron street lamps, and a faithful replica of the Pont Alexandre bridge complete the Parisian scene.

Tuscany to Venice Via Rome

Take the overpass crosswalk across Las Vegas Boulevard to Bellagio ⑤ *(see pp48–9)*. One of the main attractions at this chic Tuscan-themed hotel is the 8.5-acre (3.4-ha) lake in front. Each night, the lake comes alive with dancing fountains set to the music of artists ranging from Sinatra to Pavarotti. The hotel's lobby is adorned with a breathtaking glass flowers sculpture. A short walk from the lobby is the Conservatory, a massive atrium filled with beautiful plants and flowers that change with the seasons. If you have

Tuscan-style architecture comes to life at Bellagio ⑤

the time, visit the Bellagio Gallery of Fine Art, which showcases original works by artists such as Monet, Renoir, Picasso, and van Gogh, and also holds temporary exhibitions throughout the year. On the way out, stroll along Via Bellagio *(see p137)*, a promenade of upscale shops. Use the overhead sidewalk to make your way across Flamingo Road to Caesars Palace ⑥ *(see p50)*. Marble statues, Roman fountains, imported cypress trees, and toga-clad cocktail waitresses contribute to the resort's opulent and lavish Roman theme. On your way into the casino, note the imposing Colosseum and the Roman aqueducts. From Caesars Palace, it is a comfortable stroll north to the Venetian ⑦ *(see pp58–9)*.

Artistic fountains, Monte Carlo ③

Graceful bridges, bustling piazzas, and stone walkways meander among replicas of landmarks, including the Doge's Palace, Rialto Bridge, St. Mark's Square, and the 315-ft (96-m) high Campanile Tower – all successfully re-creating the charm of Venice. The casino is tastefully decorated with Italian-style frescoes, gilded ceilings, marble floors, and plush furnishings. Just off the casino floor is the Grand Canal Shoppes *(see p137)*, a shopping arcade built along winding canals, with authentic gondolas and singing gondoliers adding to the flavor.

The grandeur of the Colosseum as seen at night, Caesars Palace ⑥

Escape the Neon Drive

Most visitors are unaware of the many attractions Las Vegas has to offer beyond the bright lights of the Strip. But hidden in the jumbled cityscape, not far from the pulsating excitement of gambling resorts, are various unique, yet generally unknown, sights and symbols that represent the history and culture of Las Vegas. Because the city is spread across a large area, the best way to experience the municipal kaleidoscope is by car. This drive not only takes a trip into Las Vegas's past, but also affords a closer glimpse at the path it took in becoming one of the most modern and fastest growing cities in the world today.

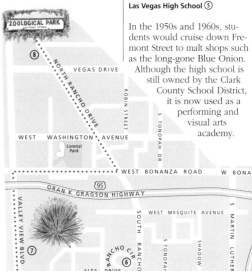

Carvings above the entrance of Las Vegas High School ⑤

In the 1950s and 1960s, students would cruise down Fremont Street to malt shops such as the long-gone Blue Onion. Although the high school is still owned by the Clark County School District, it is now used as a performing and visual arts academy.

Guest enjoying a meal at the lunch counter, Huntridge Drug Store ②

Huntridge Theater to Las Vegas High School

Start a few blocks south of Fremont Street at the junction of Charleston Boulevard and Maryland Parkway. You can't miss the tall, Art Deco façade of the Huntridge Theater ①. Built in the 1940s, Huntridge was once the most popular movie theater in the city. It was also a well-known launch pad for several musical groups, including Foo Fighters, Red Hot Chili Peppers, Smashing Pumpkins, and many more. Unfortunately this interesting building is no longer open to visits from the public.

Directly across Maryland Parkway is the Huntridge Drug Store ②, one of the few independent drug stores that hasn't been driven out by pharmaceutical giants such as Walgreens or Sav-on. The old-fashioned lunch counter still serves its specialty of tuna and grilled cheese sandwiches, along with plenty of pleasant conversation. Drive west on Charleston and turn left on Eighth Street, then immediately turn right and continue

west to Park Avenue. The large white building is Hartland Mansion ③, which was once visited by Elvis Presley.

Drive back on to Charleston, and turn into Seventh Street, heading toward Fremont. You'll pass through a pleasant neighborhood of modest Tudor-style homes ④, many of which have been converted to offices by local attorneys and accountants.

The building near the intersection of Seventh Street and Bridger Avenue is the old Las Vegas High School ⑤, and a great example of the Gothic architecture of the 1930s.

Tudor-style house, today a law office ④

Rancho Circle to Springs Preserve

Leaving the Fremont Street neighborhood, drive south to Bonneville Avenue and turn right. Continue about 2 miles (3.2 km) along this route to Rancho Drive, home to two of the most exclusive neighborhoods in the city – Rancho Circle ⑥ and Rancho Bel Air. Since both are gated neighborhoods, one can only peek at the homes from the perimeter. For the best view drive west along Alta Drive. The first home on your right, at the corner, once belonged to Frank Hawkins, a former city councilman and football player for the Oakland Raiders. Continue along Alta past old money estates that are home to Vegas icons such as hotelier Bob Stupak, Blues singer B. B. King, Phyllis McGuire of the McGuire Sisters singing trio, and the Herbsts, one of the city's richest business families. Take Alta as far as Valley View, turn right and drive back to

Samples of the desert's plant life at Springs Preserve ⑦

Charleston. For an insight into the desert's plant life, stop at Springs Preserve ⑦. Here you can explore the history of the Las Vegas Valley from early American cultures to Anglo-European settlers. Other features include botanical gardens and the Desert Living Center.

Nevada State Museum to Zoological Park

From Las Vegas Springs Preserve, drive north and turn right on Bonanza Road until Lorenzi Park. This is home to the Nevada State Museum and Historical Society that has displays, artifacts, newspaper clippings, and photographs illustrating southern Nevada's history.

KEY

••• Tour route

Greyhound bus terminal

TIPS FOR DRIVERS

Starting point: *Huntridge Theater at the corner of Charleston Boulevard and Maryland Parkway.*
Length: *15 miles (24 km).*
Getting there: *From Fremont Street, drive east to Maryland Parkway and then south to Charleston. You can also drive along Las Vegas Boulevard to Charleston, turn east and drive to Maryland Parkway.*
Stopping-off points: *The 1930s old Gothic architecture at Las Vegas High School provides an interesting snapshot. The pastoral setting of Lorenzi Park is a nice spot for relaxing or a picnic. The Omelet House, between Rancho and Valley View, serves great burgers.*

An enormous Columbian mammoth dominates the complex, as does a full-sized model of a 48-ft (14.6-m) long ichthyosaur, along with many other archaeological exhibits. Head north on Rancho Drive to the Southern Nevada Zoological Park ⑧, Las Vegas's only zoo. Though smaller than those in most large cities, it presents an impressive exhibit of native wildlife and plants, and a petting zoo that children love. The zoo is also home to more than 40 endangered species, including a family of Barbary apes, the last such group in existence in the US. The zoo provides refuge to animals rescued from the wild as well.

Skeleton of a massive Columbian mammoth at Nevada State Museum

BEYOND LAS VEGAS

Exploring Beyond Las Vegas

The wilderness areas beyond Nevada's borders are home to some of the country's most dramatic and fascinating natural wonders and treasures. Heading west and just two hours away from Las Vegas is the austere but quietly breathtaking Death Valley, a giant geological lab containing salt beds, sand dunes, and multi-tiered hills whose layers are windows to the history of the Earth. Within a few hours' drive northeast of Vegas are the soaring peaks, sandstone crags, and lush rolling meadows of the Zion and Bryce Canyon National Parks in Southern Utah. And located east of Las Vegas is the most spectacular marvel of them all, the Grand Canyon with its awe-inspiring dimensions. Each of these regions has its own distinct flora and fauna, with some species found nowhere else on Earth.

Flowers of a Mojave yucca plant, Mojave Desert

SIGHTS AT A GLANCE

Bryce Canyon National Park ②
Cedar City ③
A Tour of Death Valley
   pp106–107 ⑧
Grand Canyon pp96–101 ①
Mojave Desert ⑦
Rhyolite ⑥
St. George ⑤
Zion National Park ④

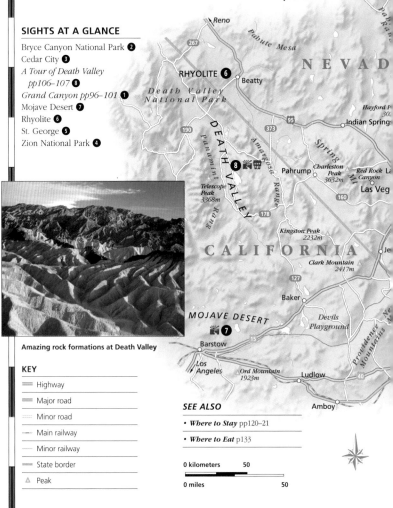

Amazing rock formations at Death Valley

KEY

═══	Highway
▬▬	Major road
┄┄	Minor road
┈╾┈	Main railway
───	Minor railway
═══	State border
△	Peak

SEE ALSO

- *Where to Stay* pp120–21
- *Where to Eat* p133

0 kilometers   50

0 miles   50

◁ **Striking landscape and sun-soaked cliffs of Grand Canyon** *(see pp96–101)*

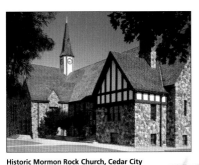

Historic Mormon Rock Church, Cedar City

GETTING AROUND

There are several Las Vegas tour operators that fly regularly to the Grand Canyon. In addition, some commercial airlines fly from McCarran Airport to a few of these areas. The I-15 north from Las Vegas leads to St. George, Cedar City, and Zion and Bryce Canyon National Parks. For Death Valley, drive northwest on US 95, which also accesses the historic towns of Beatty and Rhyolite. To reach the Grand Canyon's South Rim, drive southeast on US 95, then head east on Route 40, and drive north on Route 64 to Grand Canyon Village.

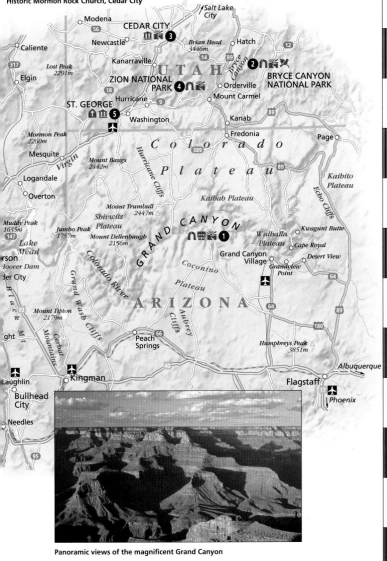

Panoramic views of the magnificent Grand Canyon

For additional map symbols *see back flap*

Grand Canyon ❶

Grand Canyon is one of the world's great natural wonders and an instantly recognizable symbol of the Southwest. The canyon runs through Grand Canyon National Park *(see pp98–101)*, and is 277 miles (446 km) long, an average of 10 miles (16 km) wide, and around 5,000 ft (1,500 m) deep. It was formed over a period of six million years by the Colorado River, whose waters sliced their way through the Colorado Plateau, which includes the gorge and most of Northern Arizona and the Four Corners region. The plateau's geological vagaries have defined the river's twisted course, and exposed vast cliffs and pinnacles that are ringed by rocks of different colors, variegated hues of limestone, sandstone, and shale. The canyon is spectacular by any standard, but its beauty is in the colors that the rocks take on – bleached white at midday, but red and ocher at sunset. The South Rim, which is easier to access than the North Rim, is a five-hour drive from Las Vegas.

Mule Trip Convoy
A mule ride is a popular method of exploring the canyon's narrow trails.

Havasu Canyon
The 10-mile (16-km) trail to the beautiful Havasu Falls is a popular hike. The land is owned by the Havasupai tribe, who offer horseback rides and guided tours into the canyon.

Grandview Point
At 7,400 ft (2,250 m), Grandview Point is one of the highest places on the South Rim, the canyon's southern edge. It is one of the stops along Desert View Drive (see p99). The point is thought to be the spot from where the Spanish had their first glimpse of the canyon in 1540.

North Rim

The North Rim receives roughly one-tenth the number of visitors of the South Rim. While less accessible, it is a more peaceful destination offering a sense of unexplored wilderness. It has a range of hikes, such as the North Kaibah Trail, a steep descent down to Phantom Ranch on the canyon floor.

Grand Canyon Skywalk

This horseshoe-shaped glass walkway is suspended 4,000 ft (1,200 m) above the Colorado River. Some 450 tons of steel were used in the construction of this spectacular structure.

YAVAPAI POINT AT THE SOUTH RIM

Situated 5 miles (8 km) north of the canyon's South Entrance, along a stretch of the Rim Trail, is Yavapai Point. Its observation station offers spectacular views of the canyon, and a viewing panel identifies several of the central canyon's landmarks.

Bright Angel Trail

Used by both Native Americans and early settlers, the Bright Angel Trail follows a natural route along one of the canyon's enormous fault lines. It is an appealing option for day hikers because, unlike some other trails in the area, it offers shade and several seasonal water sources.

Grand Canyon National Park

A World Heritage Site, Grand Canyon National Park is located entirely within the state of Arizona. The park covers 1,904 sq miles (4,930 sq km), and is made up of the canyon itself, which starts where the Paria River empties into the Colorado, and stretches from Lees Ferry to Lake Mead *(see p82)*. The area won protective status as a National Monument in 1908 after Theodore Roosevelt visited it in 1903, observing that it should be kept intact for future generations as "… the one great sight which every American … should see." The National Park was created in 1919 and has two main entrances, on the North and South Rims of the canyon. The southern section of the park receives the most visitors and is often congested during the summer season *(see pp100–1).*

North Kaibab Trail follows the Bright Angel Creek bed, past Roaring Springs, and descends to Phantom Ranch.

North Rim Entrance Station

Point Sublime

Crystal Creek

Bright Angel Poi

Shiva Temple

Colorado River

Isis Temple

HAVASU CANYON

Diana Temple

Hopi Point

BRIGHT CA

Yavapai Point

Grand Canyo Village

Yaki P

Hermits Rest

64

FLAGSTAFF WILLIAM

Tusayan

Grand Canyon Lodge
Perched above the canyon at Bright Angel Point, the Grand Canyon Lodge has rooms and a number of dining options (see p101).

Bright Angel Trail starts from the South Rim. It is well maintained but demanding. It descends into the canyon and connects with the North Kaibab Trail up on the North Rim.

Phantom Ranch *(see p121)* is the only lodge on the canyon floor, and is accessible by mule, raft, or on foot.

Hermit Road
A free shuttle bus runs along this route to the Hermits Rest viewpoint during the summer. It is closed to private vehicles from March to November.

Kolb Studio
Built in 1904 by brothers Emery and Ellsworth Kolb, who photographed the canyon extensively, the Kolb Studio is now a National Historic Site and bookstore.

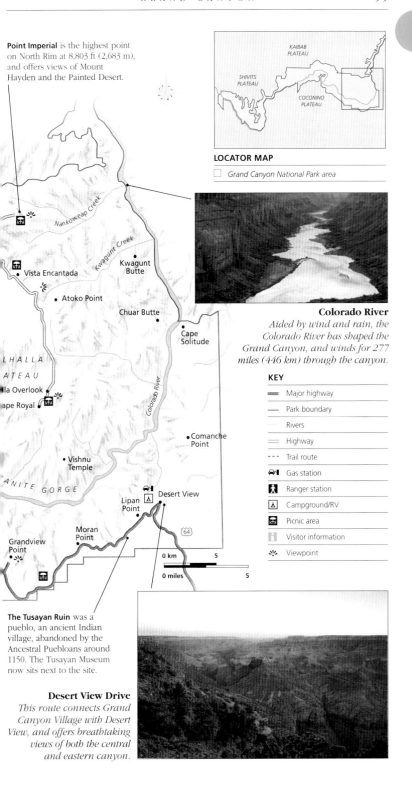

Point Imperial is the highest point on North Rim at 8,803 ft (2,683 m), and offers views of Mount Hayden and the Painted Desert.

LOCATOR MAP

☐ *Grand Canyon National Park area*

Colorado River
Aided by wind and rain, the Colorado River has shaped the Grand Canyon, and winds for 277 miles (446 km) through the canyon.

KEY

▬▬▬	Major highway
—	Park boundary
══	Rivers
═══	Highway
---	Trail route
🚗	Gas station
🚶	Ranger station
Δ	Campground/RV
🏠	Picnic area
ℹ	Visitor information
☀	Viewpoint

The Tusayan Ruin was a pueblo, an ancient Indian village, abandoned by the Ancestral Puebloans around 1150. The Tusayan Museum now sits next to the site.

Desert View Drive
This route connects Grand Canyon Village with Desert View, and offers breathtaking views of both the central and eastern canyon.

Exploring Grand Canyon National Park

Grand Canyon offers awe-inspiring beauty on a vast scale. The magnificent rock formations with towers, cliffs, steep walls, and buttes recede as far as the eye can see, their bands of colored rock varying in shade as light changes through the day. The park's main roads, Hermit Road and Desert View Drive, both accessible from the South Entrance, overlook the canyon. Grand Canyon Village is located on the South Rim and offers many facilities. Visitors can also enter the park from the north, although this route (Highway 67) is closed during winter. Walking trails along the North and South Rims offer staggering views but, to experience the canyon at its most fascinating, the trails that go down toward the canyon floor should be explored.

Bell near Hermits Rest

The Bright Angel Trail on the South Rim, and the North Kaibab Trail on the North Rim, descend to the canyon floor, and are tough hikes involving an overnight stop.

is not only the starting point for most of the mule trips through the canyon, but also the terminus for the Grand Canyon Railway.

South Rim

Most of the Grand Canyon's 4.3 million annual visitors come to the South Rim, since, unlike the North Rim, it is open year-round and is easily accessible along Highway 180/64 from both Flagstaff and Williams. **Hermit Road** and **Desert View Drive** (Highway 64) start at Grand Canyon Village and encompass a selection of the choicest views of the gorge. Hermit Road is closed to private vehicles from March to November each year; free shuttle buses are available. Desert View Drive is open all year.

From the village, Hermit Road meanders along the South Rim, extending for 8 miles (13 km). Its first viewpoint is **Trailview Overlook**, which provides an overview of the canyon and the winding course of the Bright Angel Trail. Moving on, **Maricopa Point** offers especially panoramic views of the canyon but not of Colorado River, which is more apparent from nearby **Hopi Point**. At the end of Hermit Road lies Hermits Rest, where a gift shop, decorated in rustic style, is located in yet another Mary Colter-designed building. The longer Desert View Drive runs in the opposite direction, and covers 26 miles (42 km). It winds for 12 miles (20 km) before reaching **Grandview Point**, where the Spaniards are believed to have had their first glimpse of the

Adobe pueblo-style architecture of Hopi House, Grand Canyon Village

🏛 Grand Canyon Village

Grand Canyon National Park.
Tel (928) 638-7888. 🔥 *partial.*
Grand Canyon Village has its roots in the late 19th century. The extensive building of visitor accommodations started after the Santa Fe Railroad opened a branch line here from Williams in 1901, though some hotels had been built in the late 1890s. The Fred Harvey Company constructed a clutch of well-designed, attractive buildings. The most prominent is **El Tovar Hotel** *(see p121)*. Opened in 1905, it is named after the Spanish explorers who reached the gorge in 1540. The **Hopi House**, a rendition of a traditional Hopi Indian dwelling, where locals could sell their craftwork as souvenirs, also opened in 1905. It was built by Hopi craftsmen and

designed by Mary E. J. Colter. An ex-schoolteacher and trained architect, Colter drew on Southwestern influences, mixing both Native American and Hispanic styles. She is responsible for many of the historic structures that now grace the South Rim, including the 1914 **Lookout Studio** and **Hermits Rest**, and the rustic 1922 **Phantom Ranch** on the canyon floor.

Today, Grand Canyon Village has a wide range of hotels, restaurants, and stores. It is surprisingly easy to get lost here since the buildings are spread out and discreetly placed among wooded areas. The village

The interior of the Hermits Rest gift store with crafts for sale lining the walls

Desert View's stone watchtower, on Desert View Drive

CALIFORNIA CONDORS

America's largest bird, the California condor, has a wingspan of over 9 ft (2.7 m). Nearly extinct in the 1980s, the last 22 condors were captured for breeding in captivity. In 1996, the first captive-bred birds were released in Northern Arizona. Today, 67 condors fly over the skies of Arizona. They are frequent visitors to the South Rim, though visitors should not approach or attempt to feed them.

A pair of California condors

canyon in 1540. About 10 miles (16 km) farther on lie the pueblo remains of Tusayan Ruin, where there is a small museum with exhibits on Ancestral Puebloan life. The road continues on to the stunning overlook of Desert View. The watchtower here was Colter's most fanciful creation, its upper floor decorated with early 20th-century Hopi murals.

Just east of Grand Canyon Village is **Yavapai Point** from where it is possible to see Phantom Ranch *(see p121)*. This is the only roofed accommodation available on the canyon floor, across the Colorado River.

North Rim

Standing at about 8,000 ft (2,400 m), the North Rim is higher, cooler, and greener than the South Rim, with dense forests of ponderosa pine, aspen, and Douglas fir. Visitors are most likely to spot wildlife such as the mule deer, Kaibab squirrel, and wild turkey on the North Rim.

The Rim can be reached via Highway 67, off Highway 89A, ending at **Grand Canyon Lodge**, where there are visitor services, a campground, restaurant, a gas station, and a general store. Nearby, there is a National Park Service information center, which offers maps of the area. The North Rim and all its facilities are closed from mid-October to mid-May, when it is often snowed in.

The North Rim is twice as far from the river as the South Rim, and the canyon really stretches out from the overlooks giving a sense of its 10-mile (16-km) width. There are about 30 miles (45 km) of scenic roads along the North Rim, as well as hiking trails to high viewpoints or down to the canyon floor, particularly the **North Kaibab Trail** that links to the South Rim's Bright Angel Trail. The picturesque **Cape Royal Drive** starts north of Grand Canyon Lodge and travels 23 miles (37 km) to Cape Royal on the Walhalla Plateau. From here, several famous buttes and peaks can be seen, including Wotans Throne and Vishnu Temple. There are also several short walking trails around Cape Royal. A 3-mile (5-km) detour leads to **Point Imperial**, the highest point on the canyon rim, while along the way the **Vista Encantada** has delightful views and picnic tables overlooking the gorge.

Mule deer on the canyon's North Rim

Bright Angel Trail

This is the most popular of all Grand Canyon hiking trails. The Bright Angel trailhead is at Grand Canyon Village on the South Rim. The trail begins near the **Kolb Studio** at the western end of the village. It then switches dramatically down the side of the canyon for 9 miles (14 km). The trail crosses the river over a suspension bridge, ending a little farther on at Phantom Ranch. There are two resthouses and a fully-equipped campground along the way. It is not advisable to attempt the whole trip in one day. Many walk from the South Rim to one of the rest stops and then return up to the Rim. Temperatures at the bottom of the canyon can reach 43°C (110°F) or higher during the summer. Day hikers should, therefore, carry a quart (just over a liter) of water per person per hour for summer hiking. Carrying a first-aid kit is also recommended.

Hikers taking a break on the South Rim's Bright Angel Trail

The naturally created Thor's Hammer hoodoo, Bryce Canyon

Bryce Canyon National Park ➋

Hwy 63 off Hwy 12. *Tel* (435) 834-5322. ✈ Bryce Canyon Airport. 🚌 shuttle service in summer from Bryce Point. ◯ daily. ● Thanksgiving, Dec 25, Jan 1. 🎫 ♿ 🗂 🚻 🏔 www.nps.gov/brca

A series of deep, cavernous amphitheaters filled with striking, flame-colored rock formations called hoodoos are the hallmark of Bryce Canyon National Park. High in altitude, Bryce reaches elevations of 8,000–9,000 ft (2,400–2,700 m), with a scenic road traveling for 18 miles (30 km) along the rim of Paunsaugunt Plateau. The highlights here are the fields of pink, orange, and red spires. The Paiute Indians, once hunters here, described them as "red rocks standing like men in a bowl-shaped recess."

During winter, the panoramic vista of snow-covered rock spires from the Bryce amphitheater is a popular vantage point. The Agua Canyon overlook has views of the layered pink sandstone cliffs of the Paunsaugunt Plateau. One of the park's most famous hoodoos – Thor's Hammer – was formed by wind, ice, and rain. The natural bridge, near the park's highway was formed by the same forces.

Cedar City ➌

🏙 27,000. 🛈 581 N Main St, (435) 586-5124. ✈ 🚌 www.scenicsouthernutah.com

Founded by Mormons in 1851, this town developed as a center for mining and smelting iron in the latter part of the 19th century. Today, it offers hotels and restaurants within an hour's drive of the lovely Zion National Park.

The **Iron Mission State Park and Museum** pays tribute to the early Mormons, and displays a collection of more than 300 wagons and vehicles, including an original Wells Fargo overland stagecoach. The city's Shakespeare Festival runs annually from June to October and is staged in a replica of London's neo-Elizabethan Globe Theatre.

Around 15 miles (24 km) east of the town, along Highway 14, **Cedar Breaks National Monument** features an array of pink and orange limestone cliffs, topped by deep green forest. The monument closes in winter, but remains a popular destination for cross-country skiers.

🏛 Iron Mission State Park and Museum
635 N Main. *Tel* (435) 586-9290. ◯ 9am–5pm Mon–Sat. 🖥 www.stateparks.utah.gov/park_pages/iron.htm

🏛 Cedar Breaks National Monument
Tel (435) 586-0787 ext. 31. ◯ daily. Visitor Center ◯ Jun–mid-Oct: 8am–6pm daily. 🎫 www.nps.gov/cebr

Zion National Park ➍

Hwy 9, near Springdale. 🛈 Zion Canyon Visitor Center (435) 772-3256. ◯ 8am–6pm daily (to 5pm in winter, to 8pm in summer). ● Dec 25. 🎫 ♿ partial. 🗂 🚻 🏔 www.nps.gov/zion

Zion Canyon lies at the heart of this beautiful national park and is arguably Utah's most famous natural wonder. The canyon was carved by the powerful waters of the Virgin River and then sculpted, widened, and reshaped by wind, rain, and ice. The canyon walls rise up to 2,000 ft (600 m), and form jagged peaks and formations in shades of red and white. One of the best routes in Zion is the Zion–Mt. Carmel highway with splendid views of the canyon and the pastel-colored sandstone of the peaks.

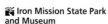

Wild flowers in Zion National Park

The park shuttle is the only way into the canyon from April to November. The shuttle's stops along the way lead to marked trails for a 16-mile (26-km) hike through the park.

The Virgin River weaves a scenic trail through Zion National Park

◁ Breathtaking flame-colored rock formations at Bryce Canyon National Park

Façade of Brigham Young's winter home in St. George

St. George ❺

🏠 76,000. 🛈 97 E St, George Blvd. (435) 628-1658. ✖ 🚌 🛈 Visitor Center. ◯ 9am–5pm Mon–Fri.

Established by Mormons in 1861, St. George recently experienced a population boom as retirees from all over the US discovered its mild climate and tranquil atmosphere. The towering gold spire that can be seen over the city belongs to Utah's first Mormon Temple, finished in 1877. A beloved project of Mormon leader and visionary Brigham Young (1801–77), it remains a key site. Only Mormons are allowed inside the temple, but the Visitor Center, which relates its history, is open to all.

Brigham Young's association with St. George began when he decided to construct a winter home here in 1871. The elegant and spacious **Brigham Young Winter Home Historic Site** is now a museum and has preserved much of its first owner's original furnishings.

Five miles (8 km) northwest of town on Highway 18 lies Snow Canyon State Park. It features hiking trails that lead to volcanic caves and million-year-old lava flows. A paved bike path winds its way through the park and back to St. George.

🏛 **Brigham Young Winter Home Historic Site**
89 W St N. **Tel** (435) 673-5181.
◯ 9am–5pm daily (to 7pm in spring, to 8pm in summer). 🎟

Rhyolite ❻

Off Hwy 374, 4 miles W from Beatty.
🏠 45,000. 🛈 Beatty Chamber of Commerce, 119 E Main St, (775) 553-2424.

This once prosperous community is located about 120 miles (193 km) northwest of Las Vegas and was founded in 1905. The presence of rich gold mines fueled a growth that made Rhyolite one of Nevada's top cities within just a couple of years. At its peak in 1908, the city had 6,000 people, three railroads, four local newspapers, four banks, an opera house, board of trade, and a telephone exchange. However, when the ore ran out, the mills began to shut down and people started to leave. By 1920 the city was nearly empty. Today, Rhyolite is

Ruins of a building in the ghost town of Rhyolite, Nevada

primarily known for its historic ruins. One of its most famous and unique attractions is the bottle house, which was built in 1906 and is made of about 20,000–50,000 discarded liquor and medicine bottles held together with adobe mud.

Every March, the town comes alive as nearby residents and visitors celebrate its annual Resurrection Festival.

Mojave Desert ❼

Barstow. 🚌 🛈 681 N First Ave, (760) 256-8617.
www.barstowchamber.com

Lying at an altitude of 2,000 ft (600 m), the Mojave or High Desert was the gateway to California for traders in the 19th century. Barstow, the largest town, is a stopover between Los Angeles and Las Vegas. In the 1870s, gold and silver were discovered in this area, and towns such as Calico sprang up. However, when the mines became exhausted, they were soon abandoned and turned into ghost towns. Many of Calico's buildings are still intact, and visitors can ride in an actual mine train.

To the west, Edwards Air Force Base is famous for its space shuttle landings. The Kelso Dunes, in the Mojave National Preserve, can reach up to 650 ft (200 m), while the Mitchell Caverns have limestone formations. Northern Mojave is dominated by the Death Valley National Park (see pp106–107).

A Tour of Death Valley ❽

The native Americans called the valley Tomesha, "the land where the ground is on fire" – an apt name for the site of the highest recorded temperature in the United States: 57°C (134°F) in the shade, in July 1913. Death Valley stretches for some 140 miles (225 km) north to south and was once an insurmountable barrier to miners and emigrants. The valley and surrounding area were declared a National Park in 1994. Death Valley is now accessible to visitors, who can discover this stark and unique landscape by car and by taking short walks from the main roads to spectacular viewpoints. However, this remains the California desert at its harshest and most awe-inspiring.

Scotty's Castle ⑧

This incongruous Moorish-style castle was commissioned by Albert Johnson at a cost of $2.4 million. However, the public believed it belonged to Walter Scott, an eccentric prospector. The house remained unfinished after Johnson lost his money in the Wall Street Crash of 1929. In 1970 the building was bought by the National Park Service, which now holds hourly guided tours of the interior.

Ubehebe Crater ⑦

This is one of a dozen volcanic craters in the Mojave area. The Ubehebe Crater is 3,000 years old. It is more than 900 yds (800 m) wide and 500 ft (150 m) deep.

DEATH VALLEY SCOTTY

Walter Scott, would-be miner, beloved charlatan, and sometime performer in Buffalo Bill's Wild West Show, liked to tell visitors to his home that his wealth lay in a secret gold mine. That "mine" was his friend Albert Johnson, a Chicago insurance executive, who not only paid for the castle where Scott lived but all his bills as well. "He repays me in laughs," said Johnson. Built in the 1920s by European craftsmen and local Native American labor, the castle represents a mixture of architectural styles and has a Moorish feel. Although Scott died in 1954, the edifice is still known as Scotty's Castle.

Grandiose Scotty's Castle

Stovepipe Wells ⑥

Founded in 1926, Stovepipe Wells Village was the valley's first tourist resort. According to legend, a lumberjack traveling west struck water here and stayed. An old stovepipe, similar to the ones that were then used to form the walls of wells, marks the site.

KEY

▨▨▨	Tour route
═══	Other roads
ℍ	Tourist information
⤲	Ranger station
⛽	Gas station

Zabriskie Point ②
Made famous by Antonioni's 1970 film of the same name, Zabriskie Point offers views of the multicolored mud hills of Golden Canyon. The spot was named after a former general manager of the borax operations in Death Valley.

Furnace Creek ①
The springs here are one of the few freshwater sources in the desert. They are thought to have saved the lives of hundreds of gold prospectors crossing the desert on their way to the Sierra foothills. The Death Valley Museum and Visitor Center features exhibits detailing the area's history.

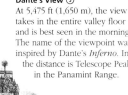

Dante's View ③
At 5,475 ft (1,650 m), the view takes in the entire valley floor and is best seen in the morning. The name of the viewpoint was inspired by Dante's *Inferno*. In the distance is Telescope Peak in the Panamint Range.

TIPS FOR DRIVERS
Tour length: 236 miles (380 km).

When to go: The best time to visit is October to April, when temperatures average 18°C (65°F). May to September, when the ground temperature can be extremely hot, should be avoided. Try for an early start, especially if you are planning to take any hikes. Always wear a hat and use plenty of sunblock.

Precautions: Check the weather forecast before you leave and always carry water, a map, a first aid and snake-bite kit, a cell phone, a jack, and a spare tire. Remain near your vehicle if you break down. If you plan to travel in remote areas, inform someone of where you are going and when you plan to return. The area is not suitable for rock climbing. Do not feed wild animals or reach into burrows or holes.

Stopping-off points: Furnace Creek Ranch, Furnace Creek Inn, Stovepipe Wells Village, and Panamint Springs are the only lodging and eating places in the park. Shoshone, Amargosa, and Tecopa, outside the park, also have motels.

Emergency: Phone park rangers on 911 or (760) 786-2331. **www**.nps.gov/deva

(Map: Death Valley)

x Museum

ek (190)

Death Valley Museum and Visitor Center

Golden Canyon

① ②

DEATH VALLEY JUNCTION

(190)

Furnace Creek Wash

⑤

Devil's Golf Course

④ ③

(178)

TECOPA HOT SPRINGS

Badwater ④
Badwater is the lowest point in the western hemisphere. It lies 282 ft (85 m) below sea level and is one of the world's hottest places. The water is not poisonous, but it is unpalatable, filled with sodium chloride and sulfates.

Artist's Palette ⑤
These multicolored hills were created by mineral deposits and volcanic ash. The colors are at their most intense in the late afternoon sun.

0 kilometers 10

0 miles 10

TRAVELERS'
NEEDS

WHERE TO STAY

Sphinx outside Luxor hotel

Recognized as one of the most-popular tourist destinations in the US, Las Vegas has over 130,000 hotel rooms – more than any other American city. This number is expected to continue increasing. Visitors to the city can choose from an extensive range of accommodations that caters to every budget and taste. From fantasy-inspired mega resorts to convenient motels, and from fully-equiped apartments to cozy inns, Las Vegas has it all.

The larger resorts in the city feature attractions such as casinos, restaurants, nightclubs, and shopping promenades. There are also many non-gaming hotels, mostly clustered around the Convention Center, designed with the family or business traveler in mind. Outdoor enthusiasts can access any of the many campgrounds and RV parks. The listings on pages 112–121 recommend a variety of places to stay, within a selection of price ranges.

An elegant room at the Venetian (see p117)

HOTEL CLASSIFICATIONS

Las Vegas hotels are known for their quality accommodations and range of amenities, which can be extensive. Travelers can use the diamond rating system of the American Automobile Association (AAA) *(see p188)* as a guideline. Every accommodation, from the one-diamond motel to the five-diamond resort hotel, is rated for service, cleanliness, and facilities offered.

HOTELS

Most of the opulent resorts in Las Vegas are located along the Strip or downtown, and showcase theme-based attractions, such as Egyptian pyramids at Luxor *(see p42)* and circus acts at Circus Circus *(see pp64–5)*. The newer hotels such as Wynn Las Vegas *(see pp60–61)*, however, rely less on gimmicks and more on amenities, tempting guests with full-scale health spas, upscale shops, fine restaurants, and star-quality entertainment.

Bellagio *(see pp48–9)*, for instance, is a European-style confection of polished marble and beautiful flowers, which has an unparalleled selection of prestigious restaurants and high-end retailers. Many of the "older" Strip hotels, such as Flamingo *(see p51)* and Caesars Palace *(see p50)*, have also undergone expansions in an attempt to modernize, while successfully retaining a pre-corporate charm that hints of old Las Vegas.

The downtown casino-hotels also provide lavish accommodations, although their dining and entertainment options are more limited than those on the Strip. Since a large number of hotels offer various amusements as means of attracting guests, their amenities often supercede their guest services. As a result, with a few lively exceptions that include the mega resorts, most Las Vegas hotel rooms tend to offer clean and modern accommodations, but nothing that would rival a Bellagio.

CHAIN HOTELS AND MOTELS

In addition to the unique gaming resorts, Las Vegas is home to a range of national chain hotels and motels, any one of which provide efficient service in comfortable surroundings at moderate prices. The most popular chains include **Holiday Inn**, **Best Western**, **Ramada**, and the **Marriott**. Visitors will also find good value at suite hotels such as **Residence Inns**, **Courtyard**, **Hyatt Place**, **Budget Suites**, and **Embassy Suites**, which offer separate living rooms and attached kitchenettes for a little more than the cost of a basic hotel

Guests enjoying the pool at Flamingo Las Vegas (see p114)

◁ **Ornate chandeliers and bright lights of the Main Street Station casino (see pp70–71)**

Fresh flowers and muted lighting in a room at Golden Nugget *(see p118)*

room. Moreover, chain hotels have a central reservation system that can help you find a room at peak times. Motels usually provide rooms that are accessible from the parking lot and are often the only option in outlying getaways such as Red Rock Canyon, Valley of Fire Park, and Boulder City.

HOTEL RATES

No matter where you stay in Vegas hotel prices are among the country's best, generally 10–20 percent below those of other resort and convention cities. Rates are usually substantially lower on weekdays, so check the prices for a Monday through Thursday arrival. Weekend rates begin with a Friday arrival, and many hotels will not even book a room for a Saturday arrival. Rooms at downtown hotels are typically 25–50 percent lower than their Strip counterparts.

Rates are often higher on holiday weekends and during major conventions. But you can find bargain room prices during the period from Thanksgiving to Christmas (except for 10 days in early December when the National Finals Rodeo is in town), and the days preceeding and following New Year. The city is busiest during March, when rates increase considerably. It is a good idea to make reservations as far in advance as possible. Ask for a special rate if you are staying for a few days.

HIDDEN EXTRAS

Room rates in Las Vegas hotels are usually quoted exclusive of sales and a county-wide tax, which adds about 11 percent to the price

of the room. The rates are usually for double occupancy, exclusive of children or additional persons. Most hotels charge about $25–50 for extra persons in the room, though children under the age of 12 can usually stay free. Some hotels charge a fixed amount for local phone calls, and long distance calls are often quite expensive – up to $10 a minute and more. Thus it might be prudent to bring your cell phone with you.

A secluded and shaded campsite at Lake Mead Recreational Area

CAMPGROUNDS AND RV PARKS

Camping in state and national parks is allowed in spaces designated for that use. While most of these parks follow a first come, first served policy, other campgrounds require reservations, so be sure to book in advance. Check with the **National Forest Service** for camping information at Mount Charleston, Lake Mead, and Red Rock Canyon. Facilities at campgrounds can range from extremely basic to those with running water and limited RV hook-ups.

Recreational vehicles have many ports of call in the city. These include hotels, such as

DIRECTORY

CHAIN HOTELS AND MOTELS

Best Western
Tel (800) 780-7234.
www.bestwestern.com

Budget Suites
Tel (866) 877-2000.
www.budgetsuites.com

Courtyard
Tel (800) 321-2211.
www.courtyard.com

Embassy Suites
Tel (800) 362-2779.
www.embassysuites.com

Holiday Inn
Tel (866) 655-4669.
www.holiday-inn.com

Hyatt Place
Tel (702) 369-3366.
www.hyattplace.com

Marriott
Tel (800) 228-9290.
www.marriott.com

Ramada
Tel (800) 272 6232.
www.ramada.com

Residence Inns
Tel (800) 331-3131.
www.residenceinn.com

CAMPGROUNDS AND RV PARKS

KOA at Circus Circus
500 Circus Circus Dr. **Map** 3 C2.
Tel (702) 733-9707.

National Forest Service
4701 N Torrey Pines Dr.
Tel (877) 444-6777.

Sam's Town RV Park
4040 S Nellis Blvd.
Tel (702) 454-8055.

Main Street Station RV Park
200 North Main St. **Map** 2 D3.
Tel (702) 387-1896; (800) 465 0711.

Sam's Town RV Park, KOA at Circus Circus, and **Main Street Station RV Park**. Most of the parks offer competitive rates – many cost less than $20 a day – full hook-ups, laundry facilities, flush toilets, showers, convenience store, and even a pool. They also accept pets. Advance reservations are recommended.

Choosing a Hotel

These hotels have been selected for their good value, facilities, and location. Rooms have air conditioning, TV, and are wheelchair accessible unless otherwise noted. Hotels are listed by area, and alphabetically within each price category. This chart highlights factors that may influence your choice. For map references, see pages 192–5.

PRICE CATEGORIES
For a standard double room per night, exclusive of breakfast and inclusive of any additional taxes:

$ under $50
$$ $50–$100
$$$ $100–$150
$$$$ $150–$200
$$$$$ over $200

SOUTH STRIP

Motel 6 $

195 E Tropicana Ave, 89109 **Tel** *(702) 798-0728* **Fax** *(702) 798-5657* **Rooms** *608*   **Map** *4 D4*

The largest property of the Motel 6 chain of hotels in the country. A favorite with families, the two-story U-shaped building wraps around the popular pool and play area for youngsters. Children below the age of 17 are allowed to stay for free if they are sharing a room with an adult family member. **www.motel6.com**

Wild Wild West Gambling Hall and Hotel $

3330 W Tropicana Ave, 89103 **Tel** *(702) 740-0000* **Fax** *(702) 736-7106* **Rooms** *262*   **Map** *3 B4*

Many of the motel-style rooms here offer great views of the Strip, located at a distance of about half a mile. It is also at a comfortable distance from McCarran International Airport. The hyperactive casino has a large collection of slot and video poker machines. Also features a heated pool and spa area. **www.wwwesthotelcasino.com**

Airport Inn and Suites $$

5100 Paradise Rd, 89119 **Tel** *(702) 798-2777* **Fax** *(702) 736-8295* **Rooms** *325*   **Map** *4 D4*

Roll out of a long flight and find comfort close at hand. Located less than a mile (1.6 km) from McCarran International Airport, this hotel is also within walking distance from the University of Nevada, Las Vegas. All rooms come with cable television with free HBO channels. **www.airportinnlasvegas.com**

Ambassador Strip Inn Travelodge $$

5075 Koval Lane, 89109 **Tel** *(702) 736-3600* **Fax** *(702) 736-0726* **Rooms** *106*   **Map** *3 C4*

Conveniently located near the MGM Grand and New York-New York hotels, the inn is also within half a mile of McCarran International Airport. The Southwestern-style rooms feature modern conveniences such as coffeemakers, hair dryers, and refrigerators. Also offers a daily complimentary Continental breakfast. **www.lvtravelodge.com**

Best Western Mardi Gras Hotel & Casino $$

3500 Paradise Rd, 89109 **Tel** *(702) 731-2020* **Fax** *(702) 731-4005* **Rooms** *314*   **Map** *4 D3*

Within walking distance from the Sands and Las Vegas Convention Centers. Each of the guest rooms is a mini-suite with separate sitting areas and conveniences that include a coffeemaker, high-speed Internet access, refrigerator, on-demand movies, and a wet bar. Also has a whirlpool spa and gift shop. **www.mardigrasinn.com**

Budget Suites – Tropicana $$

3655 W Tropicana Ave, 89103 **Tel** *(702) 739-1000* **Fax** *(702) 262-6713* **Rooms** *480*   **Map** *3 B4*

One of the Budget Suites of America chain hotels. Located at a convenient distance from both the Strip and McCarran International Airport, the hotel has several suites with adjoining kitchenettes and other conveniences. Ideal for extended stopovers, the resort also offers hot tubs for relaxation. **www.budgetsuites.com**

Casino Royale & Hotel $$

3411 Las Vegas Blvd S, 89109 **Tel** *(702) 737-3500* **Fax** *(702) 650-4743* **Rooms** *152*   **Map** *3 C3*

The hotel's whimsical New England fishing village façade is sandwiched between Harrah's and the Venetian. Guest rooms offer an uninterrupted view of the Mirage's erupting volcano. The rooms are also among the better bargains on the Strip and feature amenities such as coffeemakers and safes. **www.casinoroyalehotel.com**

Gold Coast $$

4000 W Flamingo Rd, 89103 **Tel** *(702) 367-7111* **Fax** *(702) 367-8575* **Rooms** *711*   **Map** *3 B3*

One of the most popular casinos among the local population. A massive bowling alley, large bingo hall, video games arcade, beauty salon, and a sprawling casino with an extensive selection of video poker machines, are just some of the attractions here. The hotel presents a range of dining options as well. **www.goldcoastcasino.com**

New York-New York $$

3790 Las Vegas Blvd S, 89109 **Tel** *(702) 740-6969* **Fax** *(702) 740-6700* **Rooms** *2,023*   **Map** *3 C4*

An impressive replica of one of the world's most exciting cities, with towers that imitate famous New York landmarks. Rooms are decorated in authentic Art Deco style, with lots of inlaid wood. Adults and kids alike enjoy taking a ride on the roller coaster located in front of the casino. **www.nynyhotelcasino.com**

Key to Symbols *see back cover flap*

St. Tropez All Suite Hotel

$$

455 E Harmon Ave, 89109 **Tel** *(702) 369-5400* **Fax** *(702) 369-8901* **Rooms** *149*   **Map** *4 D4*

This European-style resort has pink stucco walls, a red-tile roof, and palm trees. Inside, the spacious suites feature virtually every amenity from refrigerators and ironing boards to blow dryers and bathrobes. This non-gaming resort is a short distance from the Strip and McCarran International Airport. **www.sttropezlasvegas.com**

The Orleans

$$

4500 W Tropicana Ave, 89103 **Tel** *(702) 365-7111* **Fax** *(702) 365-7500* **Rooms** *1886*   **Map** *3 A4*

A playful Mardi Gras theme runs throughout the property. The massive gambling hall has thousands of video poker and keno machines. Features an excellent bowling center and a huge movie theater complex. Rooms are spacious and well equipped with modern conveniences. Also hosts several popular restaurants. **www.orleanscasino.com**

Tuscany Suites & Casino

$$

255 E Flamingo Rd, 89109 **Tel** *(702) 893-8933* **Fax** *(702) 947-5994* **Rooms** *716*   **Map** *4 D3*

The best kept secret in Vegas, Tuscany offers extremely large rooms in a villa-like setting. These are equipped with all modern amenities, including coffeemakers, refrigerators, hair dryers, large bathrooms, and writing desks, as well as dry cleaning and same-day laundry services. **www.tuscanylasvegas.com**

Bally's

$$$

3645 Las Vegas Blvd S, 89109 **Tel** *(702) 739-4111* **Fax** *(702) 967-3890* **Rooms** *2,814*   **Map** *3 C3*

A row of neon columns marks the entryway of this hotel, which is among the largest in the city. The luxurious rooms are contained in two 26-story towers. Most are decorated with upscale contemporary furniture. Lots of fine dining options are available. **www.ballyslasvegas.com**

Candlewood Suites

$$$

4034 Paradise Rd, 89109 **Tel** *(702) 836-3660* **Fax** *(702) 836-3661* **Rooms** *276*   **Map** *4 D3*

Ideal for business travelers and those making a long stay in Las Vegas, this hotel offers rooms with several facilities. These include modem ports and fully-equipped kitchens with a microwaves, refrigerators, and coffeemakers. Guests can also enjoy the extensive video and CD library. **www.candlewoodsuites.com**

Carriage House

$$$

105 E Harmon Ave, 89109 **Tel** *(702) 798-1020* **Fax** *(702) 798-1020 ext 112* **Rooms** *154*   **Map** *3 C4*

This non-gaming resort is located between MGM Grand and Planet Hollywood with various attractions within walking distance. All the rooms and suites are decorated in bright colors and have overstuffed sofas and dark wood furniture. Many of the rooms offer sweeping views of the Strip. **www.carriagehouselasvegas.com**

Clarion Hotel & Suites Emerald Springs

$$$

325 E Flamingo Rd, 89109 **Tel** *(702) 732-9100* **Fax** *(702) 731-9784* **Rooms** *150*   **Map** *3 C3*

A very comfortable and stylish non-gaming hotel just a few blocks from the Strip. The lobby is dominated by a massive staircase and has an excellent seating area. Spacious rooms offer amenities such as refrigerators and wet bars. The hotel's Veranda Café serves superb meals. **www.clarionlasvegas.com**

Embassy Suites Hotel

$$$

3600 Paradise Rd, 89109 **Tel** *(702) 893-8000* **Fax** *(702) 893-0378* **Rooms** *286*   **Map** *4 D3*

Modern accommodations close to the Las Vegas Convention Center and Strip. The two-room suites have a private bedroom, living area, and other conveniences such as wet bars, microwaves, refrigerators, and high-speed Internet access facilities. Breakfast is included in the room charge. **www.eslvcc.com**

Fairfield Inn

$$$

3850 Paradise Rd, 89109 **Tel** *(702) 791-0899* **Fax** *(702) 791-2705* **Rooms** *129*   **Map** *4 D3*

A property of the Marriott group of hotels, Fairfield pampers its guests with a complimentary Continental breakfast and airport shuttle service. The rooms are large with well-lit work areas. Some suites have individual living, sleeping, and working rooms, as well as whirlpool tubs. **www.fairfieldinn.com**

Flamingo Las Vegas

$$$

3555 Las Vegas Blvd S, 89109 **Tel** *(702) 733-3111* **Fax** *(702) 733-3353* **Rooms** *3,565*   **Map** *3 C3*

True to its Miami Moderne image, the Flamingo's decor is heavily inundated with tropical pink, magenta, and tangerine neon accents. The lush tropical grounds are populated with live Chilean flamingoes, fish ponds, and water-falls. The hotel spa offers a wide range of pampering treatments. **www.flamingolasvegas.com**

Hampton Inn Tropicana

$$$

4975 Industrial Rd, 89118 **Tel** *(702) 948-8100* **Fax** *(702) 948-8101* **Rooms** *320*   **Map** *3 B4*

Spacious rooms feature a Southwestern decor and provide amenities such as daily newspapers, coffeemakers, hair dryers, irons, and modem connections. This non-gaming hotel offers a complimentary Continental breakfast also. Children below the age of 18 can share a room with their parents for free. **www.hamptoninntropicana.com**

Hyatt Place Las Vegas

$$$

4520 S Paradise Rd, 89109 **Tel** *(702) 369-3366* **Fax** *(702) 369-0009* **Rooms** *202*   **Map** *4 D4*

This all-suite resort is close to both McCarran International Airport and Las Vegas Convention Center. The rooms are equipped with amenities that include refrigerators, microwaves, coffeemakers, irons, and cable television. A complimentary Continental breakfast is served every morning. **www.amerisuites.com**

Imperial Palace
$($$$)$$ $(\$)(\$)(\$)$

3535 Las Vegas Blvd S, 89109 **Tel** *(702) 731-3311* **Fax** *(702) 735-8578* **Rooms** *2,700*   **Map** *3 C3*

The tiny blue-roof pagoda in front is just the tip of this sprawling property. A favorite with tour groups, the resort features Asian-themed rooms and common areas. The highlight here is the automobile museum, displaying a selection of classic and collectible cars, all of which are for sale. **www.imperialpalace.com**

La Quinta Inn Las Vegas Airport/Convention Center
$(\$)(\$)(\$)$

3970 Paradise Rd, 89109 **Tel** *(702) 796-9000* **Fax** *(702) 796-3537* **Rooms** *251*   **Map** *3 B4*

The decor here is modern and contemporary. The split-level lobby resembles a Swiss chalet. Rooms are large and comfortable with separate sitting areas, whirlpool tubs, refrigerators, and lavish bathrooms with tiled floors and angled mirrors. A complimentary Continental breakfast is served daily. **www.lq.com**

Luxor
$(\$)(\$)(\$)$

3900 Las Vegas Blvd S, 89119 **Tel** *(702) 262-4000* **Fax** *(702) 262-4977* **Rooms** *4,408*   **Map** *3 C5*

This opulent Egyptian-themed hotel is designed to resemble a 30-story tall pyramid. The rooms, decorated in tastefully muted tones, have sloping ceilings, and the elevators, also known as "inclinators," move at a 39-degree angle. The resort also has two popular exhibits; Titanic and Bodies. **www.luxor.com**

Palms Casino Resort
$(\$)(\$)(\$)$

4321 W Flamingo Rd, 89103 **Tel** *(702) 942-7777* **Fax** *(702) 942-7001* **Rooms** *425*   **Map** *3 A3*

The biggest rival to the Hard Rock Hotel for the 20- and 30-something partygoers, the Palms hosts the Rain nightclub and Ghost Bar *(see p150)*, restaurants, and a massive movie theater center. Rooms offer breathtaking views of the Strip and reflect a California modern motif with colorful art and light wood furniture. **www.palms.com**

Paris Las Vegas
$(\$)(\$)(\$)$

3655 Las Vegas Blvd S, 89109 **Tel** *(702) 946-7000* **Fax** *(702) 946-4405* **Rooms** *2,916*   **Map** *3 C3*

A superb half-sized replica of the Eiffel Tower stands in front of this Paris-themed hotel. Other accurate reproductions of the French city include a cobblestone street that meanders through the casino and restaurants. The charming rooms are modeled on 18th-century Paris and have stylish bathrooms. **www.parislasvegas.com**

Planet Hollywood Resort & Casino
$(\$)(\$)(\$)$

3667 Las Vegas Blvd S, 89109 **Tel** *(702) 785-5555* **Fax** *(702) 785-5558* **Rooms** *2,567*   **Map** *3 C4*

This resort features fine restaurants, lounges, nightclubs, a full service spa, and 100,000 sq ft (9,200 sq m) of gaming. One of the highlights is the vast Miracle Mile shopping and entertainment complex *(see p137)* which encircles the hotel. **www.planethollywoodresort.com**

Tropicana Resort & Casino
$(\$)(\$)(\$)$

3801 Las Vegas Blvd S, 89109 **Tel** *(702) 739-2222* **Fax** *(702) 739-3648* **Rooms** *1,878*   **Map** *3 C4*

This venerable tropical-themed resort has a lush pool area with waterfalls and rich landscaping. During summer, guests can play blackjack at "swim-up" tables or soak in any one of its three outdoor Jacuzzis. Entertainment options include *Xtreme Magic* starring Dirk Arthur. **www.tropicanalv.com**

Alexis Resort & Villas
$(\$)(\$)(\$)(\$)$

375 E Harmon Ave, 89109 **Tel** *(702) 796-3300* **Fax** *(702) 796-4334* **Rooms** *500*   **Map** *3 C4*

This all-suite, non-gaming resort has landscaped grounds, fountains, three pools, a day spa, fitness center, and a salon. The suites are large with saunas, bars, refrigerators, and Internet access facilities. The hotel's convention center caters to the business traveler. **www.alexispark.com**

Bellagio
$(\$)(\$)(\$)(\$)$

3600 Las Vegas Blvd S, 89109 **Tel** *(702) 693-7111* **Fax** *(702) 693-8546* **Rooms** *4,000*   **Map** *3 C3*

One of the most sophisticated resorts in Las Vegas, Bellagio's elegant rooms are set in an opulent, Tuscan setting with imported Carrara marble bathrooms and silk furnishings. Exquisite works of art are displayed throughout the lobby, and the beautiful conservatory is an attraction by itself. **www.bellagio.com**

Bill's Gamblin' Hall & Saloon
$(\$)(\$)(\$)(\$)$

3595 Las Vegas Blvd S, 89109 **Tel** *(702) 737-2100* **Fax** *(702) 894-9954* **Rooms** *200*   **Map** *3 C3*

The motif here is 19th-century San Francisco. This intimate hotel has beautifully decorated rooms with Victorian-style furnishings, etched glass mirrors, lace curtains, and four poster beds. Offers excellent dining options, as well as the after-hours nightclub Drai's *(see p150)*. **www.billslasvegas.com**

Caesars Palace
$(\$)(\$)(\$)(\$)$

3570 Las Vegas Blvd S, 89109 **Tel** *(702) 731-7110* **Fax** *(702) 967-3890* **Rooms** *3,350*   **Map** *3 B3*

This stylish resort with a Roman theme is famous for its plush rooms and suites, all with marbled bathrooms. The Forum Shops are a must-see attraction here, as are the world-class entertainments that take place in the Colosseum theater. The Garden of the Gods complex has European-style pools. **www.caesarspalace.com**

Courtyard Las Vegas
$(\$)(\$)(\$)(\$)$

3275 Paradise Rd, 89109 **Tel** *(702) 791-3600* **Fax** *(702) 796-7981* **Rooms** *149*   **Map** *4 D3*

A Marriott International property that has been designed specifically for the business traveler. The tastefully decorated rooms are well equipped with conveniences such as fax machines, meeting rooms, and large work desks with appropriate lighting. Some of the suites resemble a town house. **www.courtyard.com**

Key to Price Guide *see p112* **Key to Symbols** *see back cover flap*

Excalibur

🏨 🍴 ♿ 📶 🏋 🎵 24 🍸 $$$$

3850 Las Vegas Blvd S, 89109 **Tel** *(702) 597-7777* **Fax** *(702) 597-7009* **Rooms** *4,008*   *Map 3 C4*

Cross the moat and drawbridge and return to the days of King Arthur. The kitsch medieval theme is evident throughout the hotel and the showroom, which hosts the *Tournament of Kings* show, is complete with sword play and jousting. All the rooms have a modern decor. **www.excalibur.com**

Hard Rock Hotel & Casino

🏨 🍴 ♿ 📶 🏋 🎵 24 🍸 $$$$

4455 Paradise Rd, 89109 **Tel** *(702) 693-5000* **Fax** *(702) 693-5588* **Rooms** *670*   *Map 4 D4*

A shrine to rock 'n' roll music, the hotel showcases a vast collection of memorabilia and musical instruments. Outstanding features include the Beach Club, Body English nightclub, the Joint concert venue, many high-class restaurants, cocktail lounges, and the Rock Spa. **www.hardrockhotel.com**

Mandalay Bay

🏨 🍴 ♿ 📶 🏋 🎵 24 🍸 $$$$

3950 Las Vegas Blvd S, 89119 **Tel** *(702) 632-7777* **Fax** *(702) 632-7228* **Rooms** *3,400*   *Map 3 C5*

Built around a sprawling lagoon area with landscaping, fountains, and sculptures, this hotel's rooms are elegant with upscale furnishings, as well as various modern amenities. The pool area has a "beach" and a gently-flowing "river," where guests may enjoy a leisurely swim. **www.mandalaybay.com**

MGM Grand

🏨 🍴 ♿ 📶 🏋 🎵 24 🍸 $$$$

3799 Las Vegas Blvd S, 89109 **Tel** *(702) 891-1111* **Fax** *(702) 891-3036* **Rooms** *5,304*   *Map 3 C4*

The Grand has a relaxed and friendly atmosphere. It boasts a particularly luxurious spa and has more restaurants than most small cities. Guests can also watch new TV shows at the CBS research center or view magnificent lions at the Lion Habitat. **www.mgmgrand.com**

Monte Carlo

🏨 🍴 ♿ 📶 🏋 🎵 24 🍸 $$$$

3770 Las Vegas Blvd S, 89109 **Tel** *(702) 730-7777* **Fax** *(702) 730-7250* **Rooms** *3,014*   *Map 3 C4*

Chic European architecture, Renaissance sculptures, and gushing fountains set the stage for lavish accommodations and a superb range of amenities. The rooms and suites are large with stylish decor and furnishings. On the top floor is HOTEL32, a stylish, 50-room hotel within a hotel. **www.montecarlo.com**

Rio

🏨 🍴 ♿ 📶 🏋 🎵 24 🍸 $$$$

3700 W Flamingo Rd, 89103 **Tel** *(702) 777-7777* **Fax** *(702) 252-7611* **Rooms** *2,520*   *Map 3 B3*

The Brazilian carnival is the theme here along with elements of a Mardi Gras party. Offers spacious suites with festive furnishings and all modern amenities. One of the highlights is the World Series of Poker competition *(see p31)*. The pool area with its tropical lagoon and sand beach is one of nicest in town. **www.playrio.com**

Westin Casuarina

🏨 🍴 ♿ 📶 🏋 🎵 24 🍸 $$$$

160 E Flamingo Rd, 89109 **Tel** *(702) 836-5900* **Fax** *(702) 836-9776* **Rooms** *825*   *Map 3 C3*

Formerly known as the Maxim Hotel, Westin upgraded the property with bright, California-chic rooms and uncasino-like common areas that have comfortable club chairs, tables, and open windows. Amenites in the rooms include minibars, refrigerators, safes, coffeemakers, and fine linens. **www.westin.com/lasvegas**

Four Seasons Hotel

🏨 🍴 ♿ 📶 🏋 🎵 24 🍸 $$$$$

3960 Las Vegas Blvd S, 89109 **Tel** *(702) 632-5000* **Fax** *(702) 632-5195* **Rooms** *424*   *Map 3 C5*

Located within the Mandalay Bay resort, but not part of it, Four Seasons has some of the Strip's finest rooms. The guest services here are extensive, including twice-daily housekeeping, pressing, dry cleaning, and children's services. The hotel's tranquil atmosphere is one of its main attractions. **www.fourseasons.com**

NORTH STRIP

Circus Circus

🏨 🍴 ♿ 📶 🏋 🎵 24 🍸 $

2880 Las Vegas Blvd S, 89109 **Tel** *(702) 734-0410* **Fax** *(702) 734-5897* **Rooms** *3,774*   *Map 3 C2*

A favorite with families traveling with small children, attractions here include free circus acts, carnival games, and the exciting Adventuredome theme park, which features thrilling rides such as the Canyon Blaster roller coaster. A wide range of dining options are also available. **www.circuscircus.com**

Palace Station

🏨 🍴 ♿ 📶 🏋 🎵 24 🍸 $

2411 W Sahara Ave, 89102 **Tel** *(702) 367-2411* **Fax** *(702) 221-6510* **Rooms** *1,028*   *Map 3 B1*

Originally known as the Bingo Palace, this casino opened in the 1960s and still reigns as one of most popular gathering spots for the general population. Offers expansive rooms and good food, all at affordable prices. Kids below the age of 17 can share a room with an adult family member for free. **www.palacestation.com**

Blue Moon Resort

🏨 🍴 ♿ $$

2651 Westwood Dr, 89109 **Tel** *(702) 361-9099* **Fax** *(702) 361-9110* **Rooms** *45*   *Map 3 C1*

The only Las Vegas hotel that is aimed specifically at gay and lesbian travelers. The rooms are comfortable and equipped with basic amenities, and the decor suggests a Spanish theme. The resort has a lagoon-style pool along with a sundeck, steam room, and a Jacuzzi that is set amid waterfalls. **www.bluemoonlv.com**

Greek Isles Hotel & Casino 🄼 🆕 ⛵ 🛏 🔊 🎵 24 🍸 ⑤⑤

305 Convention Center Dr, 89109 **Tel** *(702) 952-8000* **Fax** *(702) 952-8100* **Rooms** *202* **Map** *4 D2*

Ideal for business travelers, this hotel is just a short walk from the Las Vegas Convention Center. Rooms offer amenities such as refrigerators, two-line phones, and computer ports. The two- and three-room suites have separate living room areas, microwaves, and wet bars. Also provides a 24-hour heated spa. **www.greekislesvegas.com**

Harrah's 🄼 🆕 ⛵ 🛏 🔊 🎵 24 🍸 ⑤⑤

3475 Las Vegas Blvd S, 89109 **Tel** *(702) 369-5000* **Fax** *(702) 369-6014* **Rooms** *2,579* **Map** *3 C3*

This friendly hotel has comfortable rooms. Guests can also play keno through their room's TV set. The basic suites even have a television in the bathrooms. The casino specializes in entertainment offerings that include the Improv comedy club *(see p146)*. **www.harrahs.com**

Riviera 🄼 🆕 ⛵ 🛏 🔊 🎵 24 🍸 ⑤⑤

2901 Las Vegas Blvd S, 89109 **Tel** *(702) 734-5110* **Fax** *(702) 794-9451* **Rooms** *2,075* **Map** *3 C2*

This is one of the Strip's oldest hotels. The rooms are agreeable, try to book one in the new tower. They're slightly smaller but better furnished than the rooms in the main building. Also features a wide variety of entertainment options, including the Riviera Comedy Club *(see p146)*. **www.rivierahotel.com**

Sahara 🄼 🆕 ⛵ 🛏 🔊 🎵 24 🍸 ⑤⑤

2535 Las Vegas Blvd S, 89109 **Tel** *(702) 737-2111* **Fax** *(702) 791-2027* **Rooms** *1,720* **Map** *4 D1*

This Moroccan-themed hotel has undergone numerous face-lifts. Offers large, pleasant rooms at affordable prices. A wide selection of dining options includes NASCAR Café, a favorite among racing fans. Guests can also ride Speed, the roller coaster, or drive virtual reality stock cars at the Cyber Speedway. **www.saharalasvegas.com**

Stratosphere 🄼 🆕 ⛵ 🛏 🔊 🎵 24 🍸 ⑤⑤

2000 Las Vegas Blvd S, 89104 **Tel** *(702) 380-7777* **Fax** *(702) 383-5334* **Rooms** *2,444* **Map** *4 D1*

Located at the northern end of the Strip, this hotel features the country's highest observation tower, and has some of the most magnificent views of the city. The top floor also hosts a restaurant, and a handful of extremely thrilling rides. The rooms here are tastefully furnished with basic amenities. **www.stratospherehotel.com**

Artisan Hotel 🄼 🆕 🛏 ⑤⑤⑤

1501 W Sahara Ave, 89102 **Tel** *(702) 214-4000* **Fax** *(702) 733-1571* **Rooms** *65* **Map** *3 B1*

True to its name, the Artisan showcases artworks by several world-renowned artists, including Salvador Dali, Edgar Degas, Paul Gauguin, and Pablo Picasso, in the lobby and other common areas throughout the hotel. In addition, the Art Deco-style rooms showcase works by local artists. **www.artisanhotel.com**

Las Vegas Hilton 🄼 🆕 ⛵ 🛏 🔊 🎵 24 🍸 ⑤⑤⑤

3000 Paradise Rd, 89109 **Tel** *(702) 732-5111* **Fax** *(702) 262-5089* **Rooms** *3,174* **Map** *4 D2*

Just a block from the Strip and situated next door to the Las Vegas Convention Center. The Hilton offers luxurious rooms and suites, including the Classic Theme suites designed to re-create an African safari, the Bahamas, or 1920s Hollywood. Tennis courts, a jogging track, and a spa are also available. **www.lvhilton.com**

The Mirage 🄼 🆕 ⛵ 🛏 🔊 🎵 24 🍸 ⑤⑤⑤

3400 Las Vegas Blvd S, 89109 **Tel** *(702) 791-7111* **Fax** *(702) 791-7446* **Rooms** *3,044* **Map** *3 C3*

An exploding volcano at the front announced a new era of mega resorts when it first erupted in 1989. Conveniently based at the center of the Strip, the Mirage is famous for its tropical atrium, beautiful pool area, and the white tigers habitat. Rooms are well furnished and have a stylish decor. **www.mirage.com**

Treasure Island – TI 🄼 🆕 ⛵ 🛏 🔊 🎵 24 🍸 ⑤⑤⑤

3300 Las Vegas Blvd S, 89109 **Tel** *(702) 894-7111* **Fax** *(702) 894-7446* **Rooms** *2,885* **Map** *3 C2*

The luxurious guest rooms at this mid-Strip hotel and casino all feature floor-to-ceiling windows with a view of the mountains, the tropical pool area or the sirens' cove on the Strip. The hotel is home to a spectacular production by Cirque du Soleil, *Mystère*, and a free pirate show, *Sirens of TI*. **www.treasureisland.com**

Renaissance Las Vegas 🄼 🆕 ⛵ 🛏 🔊 24 🍸 ⑤⑤⑤⑤

3400 Paradise Rd, 89169 **Tel** *(702) 784-5700* **Fax** *(702) 735-3130* **Rooms** *548* **Map** *4 D2*

Since it opened in 2004, this hotel has become with popular with business travelers due to its location adjacent to the Las Vegas Convention Center. The rooms have been decorated in a sophisticated style and there is complimentary internet access. The restaurant ENVY serves traditional steakhouse cuisine. **www.renaissancelasvegas.com**

Residence Inn – Convention Center 🄼 ⛵ 🛏 🔊 ⑤⑤⑤⑤

3225 Paradise Rd, 89109 **Tel** *(702) 796-9300* **Fax** *(702) 796-9562* **Rooms** *192* **Map** *4 D2*

A property of the Marriott International chain of hotels. Ideal for the business traveler as it is located across the street from the Las Vegas Convention Center. The rooms are built like town houses, with separate living and sleeping areas, as well as kitchens with refrigerators, microwaves, and coffeemakers. Also has suites. **www.residenceinn.com**

Palazzo Las Vegas 🄼 🆕 ⛵ 🎵 🛏 🔊 24 🍸 ⑤⑤⑤⑤⑤

3325 Las Vegas Blvd S, 89109 **Tel** *(702) 607-7777* **Rooms** *3,066* **Map** *3 C2*

Palazzo has a modern European feel with an Italian interior. Located at the heart of the Strip adjacent to the Venetian, amenities include a shopping mall with sixty high end and mid-range shops and fourteen restaurants with renowned chefs at the helm. **www.palazzolasvegas.com**

Key to Price Guide *see p112* **Key to Symbols** *see back cover flap*

Trump International Hotel and Tower Las Vegas $$$$$$

2000 Fashion Show Dr, 89109 **Tel** *(702) 476-7339* **Rooms** *1,282*   **Map** *3 C2*

The luxurious Trump International Hotel and Tower was completed in 2008. The 64-story tower offers panoramic views of Las Vegas. Amenities include two restaurants, a spa and health club. The hotel enjoys a prime location next to the Fashion Show Mall and the Las Vegas Strip. **www.trumplasvegashotel.com**

Venetian $$$$$$

3355 Las Vegas Blvd S, 89109 **Tel** *(702) 414-1000* **Fax** *(702) 414-4805* **Rooms** *4,049*   **Map** *3 C3*

A beautifully executed Venice theme showcases several of the Italian city's architectural landmarks, such as St. Marks Square and the Rialto Bridge. Rooms are all opulent suites with elegantly appointed Italian marble, armoires, high ceilings, two flat-screen TVs, and more. Also has various shops and gondola rides. **www.venetian.com**

Wynn Las Vegas $$$$$$

3131 Las Vegas Blvd S, 89109 **Tel** *(702) 770-7100* **Fax** *(702) 770-5800* **Rooms** *2,700*   **Map** *3 C2*

Opened in 2005, this mega resort is the creation of the famous hotelier Steve Wynn. Exclusive and refined, the amenities, hotel services, and guest rooms set new standards in Vegas. Features a championship golf course, a Ferrari-Maserati car dealership, and a theater production, *Le Rêve*, created by Franco Dragone. **www.wynnlasvegas.com**

DOWNTOWN & FREMONT STREET

El Cortez $

600 E Fremont St, 89101 **Tel** *(702) 385-5200* **Fax** *(702) 474-3626* **Rooms** *402*   **Map** *2 E3*

The venerable El Cortez has been a downtown landmark since the 1940s. The original walk-up rooms are slightly worn but clean. The nicer rooms are in the hotel's tower. El Cortez has one of the city's largest casinos and a vast collection of slot machines. The coffee shop provides breakfast for just a dollar. **www.elcortezhotelcasino.com**

Four Queens $

202 E Fremont St, 89101 **Tel** *(702) 385-4011* **Fax** *(702) 387-5160* **Rooms** *690*   **Map** *2 D3*

Built in 1966, the Four Queens is the Grand Old Dame of downtown Las Vegas. Its impressive glittering façade retains the glamorous atmosphere of old Vegas. The decor suggests New Orleans's French Quarter with a carved-wood registration desk and a hurricane lamp chandelier in the lobby. **www.fourqueens.com**

Fremont Hotel $

200 E Fremont St, 89101 **Tel** *(702) 385-3232* **Fax** *(702) 385-2600* **Rooms** *447*   **Map** *2 D3*

Built in 1956, the Fremont was downtown's first "carpet joint," a non-saloon-style gambling hall as opposed to the other sawdust-floor casinos. Singer Wayne Newton made his Vegas debut here. Like California Hotel, many of the visitors here are Hawaiian tourists. The rooms are pleasant. **www.fremontcasino.com**

Main Street Station $

200 N Main St, 89101 **Tel** *(702) 387-1896* **Fax** *(702) 388-2600* **Rooms** *406*   **Map** *2 D3*

Following a Victorian theme, this hotel houses an enviable collection of antiques and memorabilia. These include President Theodore Roosevelt's Pullman railroad car, a chandelier from the Figaro Opera House, a fireplace from Scotland's Preswick castle, and a portion of the Berlin wall. **www.mainstreetcasino.com**

The Plaza $

1 Main St, 89101 **Tel** *(702) 386-2110* **Fax** *(702) 386-2378* **Rooms** *1,200*   **Map** *2 D3*

Pioneering hotelier Jackie Gaughan sold this and most of his holdings to Barrick Corporation in 2004. Since then, the property has been upgraded and now features an expanded poker parlor in the casino and a renovated race and sports book. The rooms offer great views of the Fremont Street Experience. **www.plazahotelcasino.com**

Binion's $$

128 E Fremont St, 89101 **Tel** *(702) 382-1600* **Fax** *(702) 384-1574* **Rooms** *366*   **Map** *2 D3*

This casino retains a touch of old Las Vegas with its Western-themed decor that includes quilted spreads, brass beds, velvet headboards, and Victorian wallpaper in the rooms. The hotel is also known for its Ranch Steakhouse restaurant, which consistently serves excellent steak and seafood dishes. **www.binions.com**

California Hotel $$

12 Ogden Ave, 89101 **Tel** *(702) 385-1222* **Fax** *(702) 388-2660* **Rooms** *781*   **Map** *2 D3*

Contrary to its name, this hotel is actually a very popular destination with Hawaiian tourists. Hawaiian goods and cuisine are the specialty here, and even the hotel staff dresses in aloha shirts. The guest rooms are spacious and affordably priced. The hotel is also home to several gift and food shops. **www.thecal.com**

Fitzgeralds $$

301 E Fremont St, 89101 **Tel** *(702) 388-2400* **Fax** *(702) 388-2181* **Rooms** *638*   **Map** *2 D3*

Every day is St. Patrick's Day at this Irish-themed, 34-story hotel. The hotel operated as a Holiday Inn property until 2003 and has several modern amenities. The rooms are tastefully decorated and many of them offer spectacular views across the city to the mountains. **www.fitzgeralds.com**

Golden Gate Hotel

1 Fremont St, 89101 **Tel** *(702) 385-1906* **Fax** *(702) 382-5349* **Rooms** *106*   **Map** *2 D3*

Originally built in 1906, this is Las Vegas's most historic hotel. The rooms are modest but now offer basic, modern amenities such as in-room bathrooms and air conditioning. The shrimp cocktail, which is believed to have made its debut in the city in1955, is still served in a tulip glass with a slice of lemon. **www.goldengatecasino.net**

Vegas Club

18 E Fremont St, 89101 **Tel** *(702) 385-1664* **Fax** *(702) 386-2318* **Rooms** *410*   **Map** *2 D3*

Originally known as the Las Vegas Club, this hotel is within walking distance of all downtown attractions. A sports theme runs through the casino, which showcases an interesting collection of baseball memorabilia. Offers spacious rooms at affordable prices. Opulent suites are also available. **www.vegasclubcasino.net**

Golden Nugget

129 Fremont St, 89101 **Tel** *(702) 385-7111* **Fax** *(702) 386-8244* **Rooms** *2,330*   **Map** *2 D3*

Recognized as one of the most luxurious hotels in downtown and winner of the AAA Four Diamond Award for excellence for 32 consecutive years. The tastefully furnished rooms are decorated in pleasant shades of gold, brown, and beige. Marble sculptures and ornate fixtures line the lobby and the pool terrace. **www.goldennugget.com**

FARTHER AFIELD

BONNIE SPRINGS Bonnie Springs Motel

1 Gunfighter Lane, Bonnie Springs, NV, 89004 **Tel** *(702) 875-4191* **Fax** *(702) 875-4424* **Rooms** *30*

This Wild West-themed motel is popular with families. The rooms have electric fireplaces and hot tubs. Suites with attached kitchenettes are also available. The adjoining ranch features a petting zoo, horseback riding, and Old Nevada's re-creation of a frontier town, complete with mock gunfights. **www.bonniesprings.com**

BOULDER CITY Best Western Lake Mead Inn

110 Ville Dr, Boulder City, NV, 89005 **Tel** *(702) 293-6444* **Fax** *(702) 293-6547* **Rooms** *70*

Perched on a hill overlooking Lake Mead, this inn is just a short drive from Las Vegas. The rooms offer a beautiful view of the lake. Guests can choose from a range of outdoor activities including swimming, fishing, hiking, waterskiing, and sightseeing trips to nearby attractions such as Hoover Dam. **www.bestwestern.com**

BOULDER CITY Boulder Dam Hotel

1305 Arizona St, Boulder City, NV, 89005 **Tel** *(702) 293-3510* **Fax** *(702) 293-3093* **Rooms** *22*

Earmarked as a Historic District by the National Register of Historic Places, this hotel was originally built to house dignitaries overseeing the construction of Hoover Dam in 1933. The resort is home to an attractive lobby with antique furniture, basement lounge, country-style restaurant, and gift shops. **www.boulderdamhotel.com**

BOULDER CITY Sands Motel

809 Nevada Hwy, Boulder City, NV, 89005 **Tel** *(702) 293-2589* **Fax** *(702) 294-0160* **Rooms** *26*

Located in the heart of Boulder City, the hotel is at an easy distance, (10 miles/16 km), from Hoover Dam and Lake Mead. The simply furnished rooms are well maintained and clean. All offer basic conveniences that include refrigerators among other things. Some even have attached kitchenettes. **www.sandsmotelbouldercity.com**

HENDERSON Railroad Pass Hotel & Casino

2800 S Boulder Hwy, Henderson, NV, 89015 **Tel** *(702) 294-5000* **Fax** *(702) 294-0129* **Rooms** *120*

This is the closest casino-resort to Boulder City. Its also within a convenient driving distance from Hoover Dam and Lake Mead. The rooms are nicely furnished with a Southwestern decor. Besides slot machines and table games, the hotel also has buffet dining, a steakhouse, and a 24-hour coffee shop. **www.railroadpass.com**

HENDERSON Sam's Town

5111 Boulder Hwy, Henderson, NV, 89122 **Tel** *(702) 456-7777* **Fax** *(702) 454-8107* **Rooms** *646*

Situated at the intersection of Boulder Highway and Flamingo Avenue. The rooms are located around a nine-story atrium, which is lined with trees and waterfalls. Also features a nightly water and laser show. The hotel is a Mecca for the local population with its bowling alley, movie theater, and casino. **www.samstownlv.com**

HENDERSON Sunset Station

1301 W Sunset Rd, Henderson, NV, 89014 **Tel** *(702) 547-7777* **Fax** *(702) 547-7744* **Rooms** *457*

Only a 20-minute drive from the Las Vegas Strip, this popular "locals" hotel has newly-renovated rooms, accented with Southwestern design elements and colors. Like other Station Casinos properties, the casino here is massive. The hotel also offers many good dining options. **www.sunsetstation.com**

HENDERSON Green Valley Ranch Resort

2300 Paseo Verde Pkwy, Henderson, NV, 89052 **Tel** *(702) 617-7777* **Fax** *(702) 617-7748* **Rooms** *490*

This Station Casinos flagship hotel is a winner of the AAA Four Diamond Award. Rooms contain minibars, terry robes, down comforters, twice-daily turndown service, and much more. Dining options are excellent and Quinn's Irish Pub has a good range of Irish and European beers. **www.greenvalleyranchresort.com**

Key to Price Guide *see p112* **Key to Symbols** *see back cover flap*

HENDERSON Residence Inn
☒ �📶 🅱 $$$$

2190 Olympic Ave, Henderson, NV, 89014 **Tel** *(702) 434-2700* **Fax** *(702) 434-3999* **Rooms** *126*

A property of the Marriott International chain of hotels and a great place for an extended stay. The suites offer separate living and sleeping areas, fully-equipped kitchens with refrigerators, microwaves, dishwashers, coffeemakers, china, and other utensils. Also provides free high-speed Internet access in the rooms. **www.residenceinn.com**

HENDERSON Loews Lake Las Vegas
📶 🅪 ☒ 📶 🅱 ☒ 🅈 $$$$$

101 MonteLago Blvd, Henderson, NV, 89011 **Tel** *(702) 567-1234* **Fax** *(702) 567-6067* **Rooms** *496*

Bordering the shores of a beautiful private lake, this Mediterranean-style hotel is located about 17 miles (27 km) from the Strip. The rooms and suites offer spectacular views of the lake and surrounding mountains. Two championship golf courses are also available. **www.loewshotels.com/lakelasvegas**

HENDERSON Ritz-Carlton, Lake Las Vegas
📶 🅪 ☒ 📶 🅱 ☒ 🅈 $$$$$

1610 Lake Las Vegas Pkwy, Henderson, NV, 89011 **Tel** *(702) 567-4700* **Fax** *(702) 567-4777* **Rooms** *349*

This Mediterranean-style hotel overlooks Lake Las Vegas and is about 17 miles (27 km) from the Strip. The rooms and suites are lavishly appointed with Frette linen and marble bathrooms. Winner of the AAA Four Diamond Award, the resort has several fine restaurants and shops. **www.ritzcarlton.com/resorts/lake_las_vegas/**

LAS VEGAS Arizona Charlie's Boulder
📶 🅪 ☒ 🎵 ☒ 🅈 $

4575 Boulder Hwy, Las Vegas, NV, 89121 **Tel** *(702) 951-9000* **Fax** *(702) 383-5334* **Rooms** *301*

The rooms at this resort are agreeable with modern furnishings and conveniences such as alarm clocks, hair dryers and on-command movies. The dining choices here are excellent with a fine steakhouse and bargain-priced coffee shop. The hotel also has a well-equipped RV park open throughout the year. **www.azcharlies.com**

LAS VEGAS South Point Hotel &Casino
📶 🅪 ☒ 📶 🅱 🎵 ☒ 🅈 $$

9777 S Las Vegas Blvd, Las Vegas, NV, 89123 **Tel** *(702) 796-7111* **Fax** *(702) 796-7111* **Rooms** *1350*

This hotel is the only one in the US to have an equestrian center attached to it. The center has a 4,400 seat arena, a veterinary clinic, feed store, and 1,200 climate-controlled horse stalls. Other amenities include a 16-screen movie theater complex, a 64-lane bowling center, and several restaurants. **www.southpointcasino.com**

LAS VEGAS Suncoast Hotel & Casino
📶 🅪 ☒ 📶 🅱 🎵 ☒ 🅈 $$

9090 Alta Dr, Las Vegas, NV, 89145 **Tel** *(702) 636-7111* **Fax** *(702) 636-7288* **Rooms** *440*

Based in the upscale suburb of Summerlin, Suncoast is also a much-liked community center with its movie theater complex, bowling alley, and range of dining options. The rooms are pleasant and offer several amenities. Golf stay and play packages are available. A free shuttle to the Strip or airport is offered. **www.suncoastcasino.com**

LAS VEGAS Silverton Casino Hotel
📶 🅪 ☒ 📶 🅱 🎵 ☒ 🅈 $$$

3333 Blue Diamond Rd, Las Vegas, NV, 89139 **Tel** *(702) 263-7777* **Fax** *(702) 896-5635* **Rooms** *300*

Following its Adirondak Lodge theme, Silverton opened a Bass Pro Shops Outdoor World store for sports and outdoor enthusiasts. The shop offers a variety of equipment, including fishing boats, golf products, and climbing and hunting gear to name a few. The hotel also has a massive aquarium. **www.silvertoncasino.com**

LAS VEGAS JW Marriott Las Vegas Resort, Spa & Golf
📶 🅪 ☒ 📶 🅱 🎵 ☒ 🅈 $$$$

221 N Rampart Blvd, Las Vegas, NV, 89128 **Tel** *(702) 869-7777* **Fax** *(702) 869-7339* **Rooms** *541*

Located in Summerlin community, JW Marriott is just a 20-minute drive from the neon Strip. Features Mediterranean-style architecture and lovely grounds with landscaping and waterfalls. The rooms are spacious and have refrigerators, minibars, coffeemakers, and whirlpool tubs. **www.marriott.com**

LAS VEGAS Red Rock Resort
📶 🅪 ☒ 📶 🅱 🎵 ☒ 🅈 $$$$

11011 W Charleston Blvd, Las Vegas, NV, 89135 **Tel** *(702) 797-7777* **Fax** *(702) 240-9752* **Rooms** *462*

Just outside of Las Vegas city center, Red Rock is an upscale resort with attractively decorated rooms, some of which have spectacular views over Red Rock Canyon. Basic room amenities include a plasma screen TV, an iPod, and in-room spa services. There is also a good child care center, Kid Quest. **www.redrocklasvegas.com**

MOUNT CHARLESTON Mount Charleston Hotel
📶 🅪 🎵 🅈 $$$$

2 Kyle Canyon Rd., Mount Charleston, NV, 89124 **Tel** *(702) 872-5500* **Fax** *(702) 872-5685* **Rooms** *54*

Although located below the timber line, this romantic retreat provides sweeping, panoramic views of the canyon. The best rooms are situated on the top floor and have peaked, exposed ceilings and wood-burning fireplaces. The dining room has Ponderosa pine pillars and an open-pit fireplace. **www.mtcharlestonhotel.com**

MOUNT CHARLESTON Mount Charleston Lodge
🅪 🎵 🅈 $$$$

1200 Old Park Rd, Mount Charleston, NV, 89124 **Tel** *(702) 872-5408* **Fax** *(702) 872-5403* **Rooms** *24*

Lush green pine trees and breathtaking views are on offer at this intimate lodge located at the top of the mountain. The log cabins are comfortable, each with whirlpool tubs and attached kitchenettes; but no phones. An ideal choice for honeymooners. Condo-style units are also available. **www.mtcharlestonlodge.com**

OVERTON Overton Motel
$

137 N Moapa Valley Blvd, Overton, NV, 89040 **Tel** *(702) 397-2463* **Rooms** *19*

This small non-gaming motel is located at a convenient distance from the Valley of Fire State Park and the Lost City Museum. Guests can choose from a range of recreational activities available at the nearby Lake Mead. Offers clean accommodations with few on-site amenities.

OVERTON Best Western Northshore Inn $$

520 N Moapa Valley Blvd, Overton, NV, 89040 **Tel** *(702) 397-6000* **Fax** *(702) 397-6008* **Rooms** *28*

Located on the picturesque north shore of Lake Mead, near the Valley of Fire State Park and Lost City Museum. The adobe-style buildings of this charming inn have rooms that are decorated with Southwest and Native American designs. The scenic surroundings offer excellent photographic opportunities. **www.bestwestern.com**

BEYOND LAS VEGAS

BRYCE CANYON Best Western Ruby's Inn $$

Hwy 63, Bryce, UT, 84764 **Tel** *(435) 834-5341* **Fax** *(435) 834-5265* **Rooms** *368*

Part of the Best Western chain of hotels, this family-run resort was set up in 1915 and offers friendly service. Located near Bryce Canyon National Park, the full-service inn has its own general store, liquor store, helicopter pad, riding stables, gas station, and post office. The rooms follow a Southwestern motif. **www.bestwestern.com**

BRYCE CANYON Bryce Canyon Lodge $$$

Bryce Canyon National Park, UT, 84717 **Tel** *(435) 834-5361; (888) 297-2757* **Fax** *(435) 834-5464* **Rooms** *115*

This country-western-themed classic resort is a short distance from the rim of Bryce Canyon. Provides elegant period decor, cabins with fireplaces, as well as suites and rooms with a tasteful Southwestern atmosphere. Closed from November 1 to March 31, but open for reservations throughout the year. **www.brycecanyonlodge.com**

CEDAR CITY Crystal Inn $$

1575 W 200 N, Cedar City, UT, 84720 **Tel** *(435) 586-8888* **Fax** *(435) 586-1010* **Rooms** *100*

Property of the Crystal Inn chain of hotels, this inn is located close to the Bryce Canyon and Zion National Parks, Cedar City Regional Airport, and Southern Utah University. The large, modern rooms are among the best in the city. Guests can also enjoy skiing at the Brianhead Ski Resort nearby. **www.crystalinns.com/cdc.html**

DEATH VALLEY Amargosa Opera House & Hotel $$

P.O. Box 8, Death Valley Junction, CA, 92328 **Tel** *(760) 852-4441* **Fax** *(760) 852-4138* **Rooms** *14*

This 1920s hotel situated in an old mining town known as Death Valley Junction was refurbished by Marta Becket, a former ballerina who performs cabaret shows in the small theater. In keeping with the rustic ambience, the rooms have no TVs or telephones and are decorated with colorful murals. **www.amargosa-opera-house.com**

DEATH VALLEY Furnace Creek Ranch $$$

1 Main St, Death Valley, CA, 92328 **Tel** *(760) 786-2345* **Fax** *(760) 786-2514* **Rooms** *224*

Based within the Death Valley National Park, this resort was originally built as a working ranch. Offers deluxe motel-like rooms or cabins. Facilities sprawl across several acres and include three restaurants, a saloon, general store, and an airstrip. Activities such as hiking and horseback riding are also available. **www.furnacecreekresort.com**

DEATH VALLEY Stovepipe Wells Village $$$

Stove Pipe Wells, CA, 92328 **Tel** *(760) 786-2387* **Fax** *(760) 786-2389* **Rooms** *83*

The scenic beauty of Death Valley National Park presents a serene backdrop to the accommodations here. The rooms are within walking distance from the main facility – which features a restaurant, saloon and gift shop – and have private bathrooms, but do not have any telephones. Also has a RV park. **www.stovepipewells.com**

DEATH VALLEY Furnace Creek Inn $$$$$

1 Main St, Death Valley, CA, 92328 **Tel** *(760) 786-2345* **Fax** *(760) 786-2514* **Rooms** *66*

Open from mid-October through mid-May, the Spanish-Moorish-themed inn is the jewel of Death Valley resorts. Most rooms have decks or terraces, and some even have spa tubs. Facilities include a spring-fed pool, tennis courts, and a massage therapy service. Also hosts a lovely oasis garden with palm trees. **www.furnacecreekresort.com**

GRAND CANYON Bright Angel Lodge $$

Grand Canyon South Rim, AZ, 86023 **Tel** *(303) 297-2757* **Fax** *(303) 297-3175* **Rooms** *89*

This rustic log-and-stone lodge is very popular with hikers and those who enjoy horseback riding. The rooms are available at bargain prices and are located in the main lodge. It also has cabins that are located on the rim of the Grand Canyon. Some have fireplaces and are slightly more expensive. **www.grandcanyonlodges.com**

GRAND CANYON Phantom Ranch $$

Grand Canyon, AZ, 86023 **Tel** *(303) 297-2757* **Fax** *(303) 297-3175* **Rooms** *40*

Situated on the floor of the Grand Canyon among cottonwood trees and chaparral, the lodge has small rooms and dormitory-style accommodations for those on a budget. The timber cabins are ideal for outdoor enthusiasts as they put visitors in the heart of the wilderness. Offers basic conveniences. **www.grandcanyonlodges.com**

GRAND CANYON El Tovar Hotel $$$$

Grand Canyon South Rim, AZ, 86023 **Tel** *(303) 297-2757* **Fax** *(303) 297-3175* **Rooms** *78*

This historic hotel is a Registered National Historic Landmark. Amenities here include a dining room, lounge, and curio shop. The lobby has a large fireplace and wood ceiling beams. The rooms are nicely furnished and offer basic conveniences as well as a sitting room. Some even have a porch or balcony. **www.grandcanyonlodges.com**

Key to Price Guide *see p112* **Key to Symbols** *see back cover flap*

LAUGHLIN Colorado Belle Hotel & Casino $

2100 S Casino Drive, Laughlin, NV, 89029 **Tel** *(702) 298-4000* **Fax** *(702) 298-2597* **Rooms** *1,217*

Located on the shores of the Colorado River, this is one of the most unusual casinos in Laughlin. The main building is a replica of a 19th-century Mississippi paddlewheel riverboat, with further accommodation provided in the two adjacent towers. Room service is only available for Continental breakfasts from 6am to noon. **www.coloradobelle.com**

LAUGHLIN Harrah's Laughlin $

2900 S Casino Drive, Laughlin, NV, 89029 **Tel** *(702) 298-4600* **Fax** *(702) 298-6802* **Rooms** *1,561*

The three towers of this resort have been decorated in south-of-the-border style, a theme that is seen in some of the hotel's many restaurants and bars. The casino is particularly pleasant, with large windows looking out over the Colorado River. The pools and private sandy beach are open to guests only. **www.harrahs.com**

LAUGHLIN Tropicana Express Hotel & Casino $

2121 S Casino Drive, Laughlin, NV, 89029 **Tel** *(702) 298-4200* **Fax** *(702) 298-6403* **Rooms** *1,500*

The rooms and suites at this hotel were renovated in 2008. Guests can take a dip in the pool or shelter in one of the private cabanas. There is a range of boutiques onsite, as well as a spa. Other attractions include Old No 7, Laughlin's only working railroad which travels around all 27 acres of the resort. **www.tropicanax.com**

LAUGHLIN Don Laughlin's Riverside Resort $$

1650 S Casino Drive, Laughlin, NV, 89029 **Tel** *(702) 298-2535* **Fax** *(702) 298-2695* **Rooms** *1,400*

This expansive resort consists of a comfortable hotel and an RVpark with 740 hook-up spaces, showers, laundry services, and 24-hour security. Other amenities include a classic auto showroom, an antique slot machine display, and cruises on the USS *Riverside*. All rooms have either river or mountain views. **www.riversideresort.com**

LAUGHLIN Golden Nugget Riverside $$

2300 S Casino Drive, Laughlin, NV, 89028 **Tel** *(702) 298-7111* **Fax** *(702) 298-7122* **Rooms** *300*

A beautiful atrium filled with cascading waterfalls, palm trees, and 300 species of tropical plants sets the decor for this hotel. Rooms are well kept and attractively designed, with king-size beds and internet access for a small surcharge. Water sports equipment is available nearby, as is a good golf course. **www.gnlaughlin.com**

RHYOLITE Exchange Club Motel $

119 W Main St, Beatty, NV, 89003 **Tel** *(775) 553-2333* **Rooms** *44*

At the Exchange Club Motel guests should expect a clean and relaxing stay here. Basic rooms feature a refrigerator, television and air-conditioning, but if looking for upgraded accommodation, it is advisable to reserve the Jacuzzi Suite in advance. The motel also offers a laundry facility.

RHYOLITE Motel 6 $

550 U.S. 95 North, Beatty, NV, 89003 **Tel** *(775) 553-9090* **Rooms** *69*

Motel 6 offers simple and clean rooms, and is conveniently located to Death Valley. The motel offers comfortable accommodation for the value price, although it can be a little noisy at times. Guests will find a swimming pool (located down the street) and high-speed internet access. Children under 17 stay free with paying adults.

RHYOLITE Phoenix Inn $

U.S. 95 at First St, Beatty, NV, 89003 **Tel** *(775) 553-2250* **Rooms** *54*

Phoenix Inn offers a comfortable respite to tourists visiting the nearby attractions, which include Death Valley and Rhyolite Ghost Town. Each room has amenities such as a phone, microwave, coffeemaker, refrigerator, and iron; complimentary coffee is available to guests. There has been a recent remodeling of the inn's interior furnishings.

RHYOLITE Stagecoach Inn & Casino $$

Hwy 95, Beatty, NV, 89003 **Tel** *(775) 553-2419* **Fax** *(775) 553-9054* **Rooms** *80*

The Wild West is alive and well at this hotel close to the eastern entrance to Death Valley. The well-maintained rooms provide amenities that include refrigerators and hair dryers; some have hot tubs as well. The casino has slot machines and table games, while the restaurant has a Western-style barbecue. **www.nationalparkreservations.com**

ST. GEORGE Knights Inn $$

1140 S Bluff St, St. George, UT, 84770 **Tel** *(435) 628-6699* **Fax** *(435) 673-8705* **Rooms** *61*

Conveniently located within easy access to the town's antiques shops and fine restaurants, the Bluffs Inn features modern rooms with cable TV, telephones, and a hot tub. Some even have attached kitchenettes. One-bedroom apartments are also available. Also offers a complimentary Continental breakfast. **www.knightsinn.com**

ST. GEORGE Seven Wives Inn $$$

217 N 100 W, St. George, UT, 84770 **Tel** *(435) 628-3737* **Fax** *(435) 628-5646* **Rooms** *13*

This charming bed-and-breakfast consists of two homes built in the 1870s, a main Victorian home and a smaller cottage known as the President's House. All the rooms follow a theme and are tastefully furnished. The best rooms are in the main house and are named after the original innkeeper's seven wives. **www.sevenwivesinn.com**

ZION NATIONAL PARK Best Western Zion Park Inn $$$

1215 Zion Park Blvd, Springdale, UT, 84767 **Tel** *(435) 772-3200* **Fax** *(435) 772-2449* **Rooms** *120*

Tucked among the towering red rock cliffs of Zion National Park, the inn offers spectacular views. Rooms are equipped with modern features, including data ports, interactive games, and pay-per-view movies. Also hosts a fine restaurant, liquor store, and a charming gift shop. **www.zionparkinn.com**

WHERE TO EAT

Steak at
Excalibur hotel

The consumption of food and drink has always been a cornerstone of Las Vegas's resort industry. Until recently, most hotel dining rooms were known mainly for the inexpensive food they served – the $10 all-you-can-eat buffets and the 99-cent breakfasts. However, over the past decade, resorts have added a wider and more eclectic selection of dining choices, including designer restaurants hosted by celebrity chefs and international restauranteurs. The first of these master chefs was Wolfgang Puck, who set up a branch of his trendy Spago at Caesars Palace in 1992. The success of Spago paved the way for the likes of Joël Robuchon and his two restaurants at MGM Grand and several other eateries that offer innovative and oftentimes award-winning cuisine. Today, Las Vegas can rival any city in the country for the quaity of ingredients and variety of cuisine available, with ambiences ranging from the rustic to the romantic. In addition to these upscale restaurants, the city hosts a vast array of diners, steakhouses, cafés, and snack bars. See the listings on pages 124–133.

The romantic ambience of Spago at Caesars Palace *(see p128)*

EATING HOURS

The city that never sleeps lives up to its 24-hour culture by offering numerous dining options at any time of the day and night. The coffee shops in most hotels are open around the clock and many serve a complete menu all through the night. The choices at most other eateries are, however, limited to the "regular" breakfast, lunch, and dinner schedules. Some of the larger resorts have several restaurants – MGM Grand for instance has as many as 20. But most of the dining rooms are open just for dinner, from about 5pm to 10pm, while a few others are open for lunch as well. Las Vegas's popular all-you-can-eat buffets usually offer breakfast from about 6am to 11am, lunch from 11:30am to 4pm, and dinner from 4:30pm to about 10pm.

PRICES AND TIPPING

Las Vegas is famous for its affordable dining. A wide variety of coffee shops, chain restaurants, and the ubiquitous all-you-can-eat buffets offer inexpensive yet tasty meals. The city features several fine dining choices as well. Patrons can end up spending $60–120 per person for a three-course meal and a bottle of wine at any of these upscale eateries.

The standard tip is 15 percent of the bill before sales taxes, though tipping should always be based on service. Bartenders and cocktail servers also expect to be tipped for each round of drinks.

TYPES OF FOOD AND RESTAURANTS

Dining establishments in Las-Vegas come in a range of shapes and sizes from small and friendly diners offering hearty burgers and snacks to gourmet restaurants serving the latest Southwestern and fusion cuisine. Lavish dining rooms can be found in some of the city's top resorts.

Starting at the lower end of the scale, an extensive collection of fast food outlets can be found throughout the city. They serve the usual inexpensive variations on burgers, fries, and soft drinks. Pizza chains are also plentiful.

The mid-range restaurants include a range of ethnic cuisine, such as Italian, Greek, Chinese, Japanese, Mexican, and Indian food. Many good restaurants of this type can be found at the shopping malls.

Southwestern cuisine – a fusion of Native American, Hispanic, and international influences – is also growing in popularity and is increasingly showcased in the city's finest restaurants.

The chic and exclusive Picasso restaurant in Bellagio *(see p128)*

The rustic yet charming setting of the buffet at Paris Las Vegas *(see p114)*

Most of Las Vegas's upscale restaurants are headed by celebrity chefs such as Joël Robuchon's restaurant of the same name *(see p126)* in MGM Grand and Julian Serrano's Picasso *(see p128)* in Bellagio.

THE ALL-YOU-CAN-EAT BUFFET

Virtually every hotel in Las Vegas has a buffet. Even though some may be fancier and pricier, and might serve better food than others – they all operate the same way: one price, sometimes as low as $7.99, for all-you-can-eat. The concept of the buffet started in the early 1940s at the original El Rancho hotel, where the owner was searching for ways to tempt patrons to stay on at the hotel after its late stage show came to an end. He ultimately dreamed up the "Midnight Chuckwagon Buffet – all you can eat for a dollar." The idea of treating guests to an elaborate feast for a small price was copied by other hotels and the Vegas buffet boom was born.

Today, the average dinner buffet features about 45 food selections that include salads, fruits, roast beef, baked ham, roast turkey, fried chicken, vegetables, potatoes, rolls, coffee, and all the desserts imaginable. Some hotels also offer international choices such as Mexican, Brazilian, Chinese, and Italian

Todai Seafood and Sushi Bar *(see p124)*

specialties served at specific food stations. In addition to breakfast, lunch, and dinner buffets, many resorts feature weekend champagne brunch buffets for a slightly higher price. Others offer theme-based buffets highlighting different cuisines such as seafood, Italian, or Greek food, usually on different days of the week.

Though buffet prices can vary depending on the scale of the hotel, they usually average about $12 per person for breakfast to $17 for lunch, and $22 for dinner at the major resorts. Some of the nicer buffets, such as the Spice Market Buffet at Planet Hollywood or the buffet at Paris Las Vegas, charge more, but the quality of food is also better. Here breakfast can be as high as $15, with lunch at $20, and dinner costing $28.

VEGETARIAN

Even the steakhouses in Las Vegas offer something for the vegetarian – a variety of salads and hot vegetable platters consisting of freshly steamed vegetables and rice or potatoes. In addition, many of the ethnic styles of cooking, such as Asian, Middle Eastern, and Italian, offer vegetarian specialties. And the all-you-can-eat buffets usually feature massive salad bars with enough options to satisfy virtually any appetite.

DISABLED FACILITIES

All restaurants in the city are required to provide wheelchair access and a ground-level restroom by law.

CHILDREN

Most of the eating places in Las Vegas are child-friendly. Except for the more exclusive dining rooms, restaurants usually feature a child's menu that lists simple dishes, served in smaller portions and at greatly reduced prices. Most eateries also provide either high chairs or booster seats.

DRESS CODES

Dining is casual throughout Las Vegas except at the upscale, ultra-deluxe dining rooms, which might require jacket, tie, and other formal dress. Elsewhere, jeans, Bermuda shorts, sneakers, and T-shirts are all accepted, so you can expect to be seated nearly everywhere.

Preparing a meal at a Japanese Steakhouse

Choosing a Restaurant

These restaurants have been selected for their good food, value, and location. This chart highlights factors that may influence your choice. All restaurants are wheelchair accessible and are non-smoking. Entries are listed by area, and alphabetically within each price category. For map references, see pages 192–5.

PRICE CATEGORIES
For a three-course dinner for one, including half a bottle of wine and tax:

$ under $25
$$ $25–$35
$$$ $35–$50
$$$$ $50–$70
$$$$$ over $70

SOUTH STRIP

Battista's Hole in the Wall
$$

4041 Audrie Lane, 89109 **Tel** *(702) 732-1424* **Map** *3 C3*

This is a fun, friendly place with a wandering accordion player who guarantees he can play a tune from anyone's home town. Serves mouthwatering Italian cuisine. The homemade specialties include meat cannelloni, cheese manicotti, lasagna, ravioli, eggplant parmigiana, and veal dishes. Open daily from 4:30pm onwards.

Cypress Street Marketplace
$$

At Caesars Palace, 3570 Las Vegas Blvd S, 89109 **Tel** *(702) 731-7110* **Map** *3 C3*

This restaurant proffers the newest concept in food courts. Patrons get a smart card and can swipe it at any of the nine serving stations they choose to take dishes from. A myriad of food choices are prepared to order, unlike traditional all-you-can-eat buffets. Hours vary for each station but all are open from 11am to 11pm.

ESPN Zone
$$

At New York-New York, 3790 Las Vegas Blvd S, 89109 **Tel** *(702) 740-6969* **Map** *3 C4*

Features the Studio Grill, a sports-themed restaurant that serves American favorites, including barbecued ribs, steaks, burgers, and fries. Also houses a huge screening room with TV screens and monitors, where sports events, shows, and specials are aired continuously. There's also a shop of ESPN souvenirs. Opens at 11am.

Todai Seafood and Sushi Bar
$$

At Planet Hollywood Resort & Casino, 3663 Las Vegas Blvd S, 89109 **Tel** *(702) 892-0021* **Map** *3 C3*

This fast-paced Asian buffet has about eight sushi chefs preparing a wide range of mouthwatering sushi and sashimi dishes. Guests can also choose from traditional favorites that include tempura, teppanyaki, and grilled fish. Also offers a variety of salads and desserts.

Cozymel's Coastal Mexican Grill
$$$

355 Hughes Center Dr, 89109 **Tel** *(702) 732-4833* **Map** *4 D3*

The large and open dining room has a coastal ambience with weathered wood decor. Fresh fish is flown in from the Yucatan peninsula and prepared with a south of the border accent. Chef favorites include grilled ahi tuna in citrus marinade, lamb fajitas, and pork *tamale*. Open from 11am onwards.

Crown & Anchor
$$$

1350 E Tropicana Ave, 89109 **Tel** *(702) 739-8676* **Map** *4 D4*

This British-style pub and restaurant is a haven for expatriates. Wooden staircases and furnishings as well as a selection of nautical artifacts enhance the ambience. Offers plenty of beers, ales, and stouts, plus classic dishes such as fish and chips, steak and kidney pie, Lancashire hot pot, and bangers and mash. Open 24-hours daily.

Don Miguel's
$$$

At the Orleans, 4500 W Tropicana Ave, 89103 **Tel** *(702) 365-7111* **Map** *3 A4*

This bright and festive dining room serves traditional Mexican favorites as well as unique creations that include salmon Yucatan *tamales* and jumbo shrimp stuffed with spinach and wrapped in bacon. Also features a tortilla cooking display and a margarita bar. Open from 4pm.

Dragon Noodle Company
$$$

At the Monte Carlo, 3770 Las Vegas Blvd S, 89109 **Tel** *(702) 730-7965* **Map** *3 C4*

Authentic Cantonese and Hong Kong-style cuisine is served in a soothing Oriental atmosphere. The decor has been designed in accordance with the practice of feng shui. Rare dim sum is the house favorite along with helpings of soup, noodles, and fresh fish, meat, chicken, and duck. The Tea Bar features specialty teas. Open from 11am onwards.

Garduno's
$$$

At the Palms Casino Resort, 4321 W Flamingo Rd, 89103 **Tel** *(702) 942-7777* **Map** *3 A3*

A New Mexico-based cantina serving flavorful and authentic Mexican specialties. Many dishes have a Southwestern touch and tend to be on the fiery side, so ask for mild seasonings if you are not comfortable with spicy hot cuisine. Cascading waterfalls form part of the decor. Guests can also choose from a wide selection of margaritas.

Key to Symbols *see back cover flap*

Gaylord India Restaurant

At the Rio, 3700 W Flamingo Rd, 89103 **Tel** *(702) 252-7777* **Map** *3 C2*

A branch of the famous San Francisco restaurant, Gaylord brings tandoori and Mughlai-style dishes to Las Vegas. Eclectic selections include assorted kebabs, fragrant curries, savory rice dishes, homemade breads, tandoori chicken, lamb samosa, and a range of vegetarian dishes. Brunch buffets are available on Saturday and Sunday.

Hofbrauhaus Las Vegas

4510 Paradise Rd, 89109 **Tel** *(702) 853-2337* **Map** *4 D4*

Patterned after the famous beer hall in Munich, this restaurant serves quality Bavarian cuisine and a vast range of imported German and Bavarian beers. A live band serenades patrons. The menu may be meat-centric but vegetarians are also catered for. Open from 11am onwards. Service here is efficient.

Joe's Seafood, Prime Steak and Stone Crab

At the Forum Shops at Caesars Palace, 3500 Las Vegas Blvd. S, 89109 **Tel** *(702) 792-9222* **Map** *3 C2*

Excellent steak and seafood served by tuxedoed waiters in this renowned steakhouse. The main draw here is the stone crabs, available in a variety of sizes, and which are served with Joe's mustard sauce. The sweet stone crab bisque is delicious. Patio seating is available. Open from 11:30am.

McCormick & Schmick's

335 Hughes Center Dr, 89109 **Tel** *(702) 836-9000* **Map** *4 D3*

The club-like dining room is decorated with stained-glass skylights, mosaic flooring, hardwood tables, and hand-crafted chandeliers. Serves fresh seafood with a Pacific Northwest flavor. Some of the specialties here are Alaska king salmon, Oregon petrale sole, and Northwest oysters. Open daily for dinner; open for lunch from Monday to Friday.

Marrakech

3900 Paradise Rd, 89109 **Tel** *(702) 736-7655* **Map** *4 D3*

This dining room is designed to resemble a Moroccan tent, complete with oak and etched glass doors and tables set amid cushions. A six-course meal includes lamb shish kebab, hummus, shrimp, homemade lentil soup, and more. Accompanying the meal are belly dancers. Open only for dinner.

Pink Taco

At the Hard Rock Hotel, 4165 Paradise Rd, 89109 **Tel** *(702) 693-5000* **Map** *4 D4*

This trendy and colorful cantina is popular with visiting rock stars and sports celebrities. House favorites include New Wave versions of pork tacos, beef and bean burritos, quesadilla, enchiladas, and chimichangas. Features an excellent selection of tequilas and an impressive variety of *cerveza* and margaritas.

Smith & Wollensky

3767 Las Vegas Blvd S, 89109 **Tel** *(702) 862-4100* **Map** *3 C4*

This three-story restaurant has a cut of beef for every meat-lover. All meat is dry-aged to perfection. Popular dishes include filet mignon, sirloin, prime rib, and a gourmet hamburger. Seafood lovers will enjoy the grilled Atlantic salmon, and all should save room for the signature coconut cake. Open for lunch and dinner.

Sushi Roku

At the Forum Shops, Caesars, 3500 South Las Vegas Blvd, 89103 **Tel** *(702) 733-7373* **Map** *3 C3*

Opened in 2008, this Japanese restaurant is one of Las Vegas' best looking restaurants. Sushi is the obvious choice but a range of hot dishes is also served. Choose between the Garden, Sea or Farm menus and wash it all down with one of the three grades of Sake. The octopus sashimi, tempura, and seafood ceviche are particularly recommended.

Border Grill

At Mandalay Bay, 3950 Las Vegas Blvd S, 89109 **Tel** *(702) 632-7777* **Map** *3 C5*

Owned by the popular TV celebrities Mary Sue Milliken and Susan Feniger of the TV Food Network, this bright and airy restaurant serves upscale Southwestern and Mexican cuisine accented with bold and flavorful spices. Open for lunch and dinner. It would be a good idea to make advance reservations.

Buzio's Seafood Restaurant

At the Rio, 3700 W Flamingo Rd, 89103 **Tel** *(702) 252-7777* **Map** *3 B3*

This charming restaurant has a nautical theme and overlooks the hotel's Ipanema Beach and the beautiful pool area. Specialties here include steamed mussels, clams and shrimp, *cioppino*, and *bouillabaisse*. Also features an oyster bar. A private dining area that seats up to 100 people is also available. Open only for dinner Wednesday to Sunday.

Hard Rock Café

4475 Paradise Rd, 89169 **Tel** *(702) 733-8400* **Map** *4 D4*

Memorabilia and collectibles line the walls of this shrine to rock 'n' roll. A 77-ft (23-m) tall Gibson guitar marks the entrance and loud rock music plays constantly. Tasty specialties include hickory-smoked pork sandwich, charbroiled burgers, piled-high sandwiches, and spinach salad. Open from 11am onwards.

Hyakumi

At Caesars Palace, 3570 Las Vegas Blvd S, 89109 **Tel** *(702) 731-7731* **Map** *3 C3*

Elegant dining in a Far Eastern setting. Specialties include fresh sushi and sashimi, along with dishes prepared in teppanyaki-style cooking. Offers a wide assortment of Japanese beers as well as sake and wine by the glass. Open only for dinner. The sushi bar and an Asian noodle kitchen is open for lunch.

Lawry's the Prime Rib ⓣⓘⓙⓓⓨ $$$$
4043 Howard Hughes Pkwy, 89109 **Tel** *(702) 893-2223*   **Map** *3 C3*

A branch of the original restaurant in Los Angeles, Lawry's specialty is prime rib in a variety of cuts. Non meat-eaters can try the lobster tails or grouper. The side dishes are famous and include the spinning salad bowl, fresh potatoes, and Yorkshire pudding. Advance reservations are necessary.

Les Artistes Steakhouse $$$$
At Paris Las Vegas, 3645 Las Vegas Blvd S, 89109 **Tel** *(702) 967-7999*   **Map** *3 C3*

Often called the most beautiful dining room in Las Vegas because of its stunning architecture and Impressionist art, Les Artistes Steakhouse's menu is as equally impressive. Typical of the menu is bone-in filet mignon, salt-crusted prime rib, and an array of seafood dishes. Open only for dinner.

Little Buddha ⓓⓨ $$$$
At Palms Casino Resort, 4321 W Flamingo Rd, 89103 **Tel** *(702) 942-7778*   **Map** *3 A3*

A serene and relaxing environment that is both soothing and opulent. There are approximately 200 Buddha statues incorporated into the decor. The food combines Asian fusion cuisine with a dash of French influence. There is also a full-service sushi bar and a patio overlooking the pool area. Opens at 5:30pm.

Mon Ami Gabi ⓨ $$$$
At Paris Las Vegas, 3645 Las Vegas Blvd S, 89109 **Tel** *(702) 944-4224*   **Map** *3 C3*

This stylish Parisian-style café serves classic French fare such as steak frites, onion soup, shallot steak with *pommes frites*, a variety of quiche and traditional cassoulet, and delicious salads and desserts. The waiters are attired in white aprons and black bow ties. It is also one of the few Vegas restaurants whose terrace overlooks the Strip.

Pampas $$$$
Miracle Mile Shops, 3663 Las Vegas Blvd, 89103 **Tel** *(702) 737-4748*   **Map** *3 C3*

Pampas offers spit roasted Brazilian-style food in a casual setting. The Rodizio is an all-you-can-eat option, where a range of skewered meats is carved at your table. Accompany this with a selection of hot and cold starters, side dishes, and a cocktail. Open daily for lunch and dinner.

Paymon's Mediterranean Café ⓙⓓⓨ $$$$
4147 S Maryland Pkwy, 89109 **Tel** *(702) 731-6030*   **Map** *4 E3*

Located two blocks from the University of Nevada, Las Vegas campus, this is the best Mediterranean restaurant in town. Specialties made from freshest ingredients include baba ganoush, hummus, *tabouli*, *kibbe*, kebabs, and more. Also has an adjoining grocery store for packaged goods.

Planet Hollywood ⓓⓨ $$$$
At the Forum Shops, 3500 Las Vegas Blvd S, 89109 **Tel** *(702) 791-7827*   **Map** *3 C3*

Part of an international chain of restaurants, this is an interesting place to eat, drink, people watch, or even purchase a leather bomber jacket. The California chic cuisine has elements of Asian, Mexican, and Italian foods. Favorites includes pot stickers, gourmet pizzas, ribs, and a chocolate mousse to die for. Opens at 8am daily.

Prime Rib Loft ⓨ $$$$
At the Orleans, 4500 W Tropicana Ave, 89103 **Tel** *(702) 365-7111*   **Map** *3 A4*

Las Vegas-style murals line the walls of this pleasant room overlooking the sprawling Orleans casino. True to its name, aged prime rib of beef is the specialty, along with medallions of beef, beef stroganoff, and the jambalaya pasta. Also serves a variety of delicious salads and desserts. Open only for dinner.

rare 120° ⓨ $$$$
At the Hard Rock Hotel & Casino, 4455 Paradise Rd, 89169 **Tel** *(702) 693-5500*   **Map** *4 D2*

Diners enjoy classic steakhouse cuisine with a modern twist in a sleek, contemporary atmosphere with gleaming exotic wood finishes, brushed stainless steel, plush, Italian leather banquettes, and mesmerizing "living wallpaper." There is also a spacious lounge. Closed on Monday and Tuesday.

Steakhouse at Bill's ⓓⓨ $$$$
At Bill's Gamblin' Hall & Saloon, 3595 Las Vegas Blvd S, 89109 **Tel** *(702) 737-2100*   **Map** *3 C3*

Expect intimate dining in the comfortable environment of Steakhouse at Bill's, specializing in steak and chops – mesquite-grilled to perfection – and seafood, plus chicken and pasta. Enjoy tableside preparations of Caesar and spinach salads, cherries jubilee and bananas Foster.

Strip House ⓨ $$$$
At Planet Hollywood Resort and Casino, 3667 Las Vegas Blvd S, 89109 **Tel** *(702) 785-5555*   **Map** *3 C3*

John Schenk brings his culinary expertise to this Planet Hollywood steakhouse where patrons can dine in an atmosphere designed by the acclaimed David Rockwell. The menu offers prime cuts of beef and creative presentation in a luxury interior with bright red walls and rosy lighting. Opens at 5pm.

Tender Steak and Seafood ⓣⓓⓨ $$$$
At the Luxor, 3900 Las Vegas Blvd S, 89109 **Tel** *(702) 262-4000*   **Map** *3 C3*

A steakhouse with a comfortable modern atmosphere, which pays homage to the American West with old, reclaimed barn wood, Longhorn chandeliers, and black and white photographs of rustic American landscapes. Exotic meats such as antelope, bison, and Rocky Mountain elk are served alongside traditional cuts. Opens at 5pm.

Key to Price Guide *see p124* **Key to Symbols** *see back cover flap*

Trevi
🍴 $$$$

At the Forum Shops, 3500 Las Vegas Blvd S, 89109 **Tel** *(702) 735-4663* **Map** *3 C3*

Diners can dine in a club-style dining room or on an alfresco-type patio next to fountains and waterfalls. Serves a wide range of delicious risottos, wood-fired pizzas, fish, fresh pastas, handmade gelatto, and sorbet. Open from 11am onwards.

Verandah
🍴 $$$$

At the Four Seasons, 3960 Las Vegas Blvd S, 89109 **Tel** *(702) 632-5000* **Map** *3 C5*

Overlooking the hotel's beautiful pool area, the elegant and comfortable Verandah serves upscale dishes. House specialties range from a delicious *foie gras* and filet of sea bass to an appetizing meat loaf and chicken pot pie. Diners can even create their own entrées. Opens 6:30am onwards.

Alizé
🍴🍴 $$$$$

At the Palms Casino Resort, 4321 W Flamingo Rd, 89109 **Tel** *(702) 951-7000* **Map** *3 A3*

Brainchild of master chef Andre Rochat, this penthouse-style dining room combines classic French cuisine with breathtaking views of the Strip. A two-story glass wine cellar reveals 6,000 bottles of wine from all over the world, and a collection of port, Armagnac, and cognac dating to 1777. Open only for dinner.

Andre's
🍴🍴 $$$$$

At the Monte Carlo, 3770 Las Vegas Blvd S 89109 **Tel** *(702) 385-5016* **Map** *3 C3*

This converted house has several dining rooms furnished with country antiques. Their wine cellar is one of the city's finest. Acclaimed chef Andre Rochat serves specialties such as duck *foie gras, escargots de Bourgogne*, black truffle terrine, and sea scallops wrapped in a macadamia nut crust. Open only for dinner and closed on Monday.

Aureole
🔲🍴 $$$$$

At Mandalay Bay, 3950 Las Vegas Blvd S, 89109 **Tel** *(702) 632-7401* **Map** *3 C5*

Famous New York chef Charlie Palmer produces contemporary American cuisine. In addition to seasonal dishes prepared to perfection, Aureole has an ingenious four-story wine tower made of glass. The stewards strap on harnesses and are hoisted up the tower to make their selections. Open only for dinner.

BOA Steakhouse
$$$$$

At the Forum Shops Caesars, 3500 Las Vegas Blvd S, 89109 **Tel** *(702) 733-7373* **Map** *3 C3*

Located at the Forum Shops, BOA Steakhouse breaks the mould when it comes to steaks. All of the classic cuts of beef are served, along with the surf and turf menu, which is highly popular with diners. The contemporary and elegant setting of the restaurant enhances the dining experience greatly.

Bradley Ogden Restaurant
🔲🍴 $$$$$

At Caesars Palace, 3570 Las Vegas Blvd S, 89109 **Tel** *(702) 731-7731* **Map** *3 C3*

Famous chef Bradley Ogden offers seasonal fare that includes Alaskan ivory salmon, *Humboldt* fog blue cheese soufflé, slow roasted monkfish, and lobster *gremolata*. This is Ogden's first restaurant outside California. Open only for dinner; closed on Monday and Tuesday.

Charlie Palmer Steak
🍴 $$$$$

At Four Seasons, 3960 Las Vegas Blvd S, 89109 **Tel** *(702) 632-5123* **Map** *3 C5*

In addition to tender cuts of beef, renowned chef Charlie Palmer serves innovative seafood specialties such as apple-wood smoked Atlantic salmon, ahi tuna, and Dover sole. The restaurant has a comfortable and club-like atmosphere. A quiet private room seats up to 20 people. Open only for dinner from 5:30pm to 10:15pm.

China Grill
🍴 $$$$$

At Mandalay Bay, 3950 Las Vegas Blvd S, 89109 **Tel** *(702) 632-7404* **Map** *3 C5*

The dining room is artistically decorated with colorful shapes projected on to the high ceilings. Asian specialties are prepared with the freshest ingredients, and include tangy barbecued salmon and tempura ahi tuna in a creamy hot mustard sauce. The portions are extremely generous and are served artistically. Open only for dinner.

Diego
🍴 $$$$$

At the MGM Grand, 3799 Las Vegas Blvd S, 89109 **Tel** *(702) 891-3200* **Map** *3 C4*

Award-winning chef Vincent Wolf creates dishes influenced by the streetfood of urban Mexico as well as the area's traditional home-fire cooking. Also offers a range of vegetarian dishes and salads. Be sure to try the mobile salsa cart, frozen margarita popsicles and tequila sorbet shooters. Open only for dinner.

Eiffel Tower Restaurant
🔲🍴 $$$$$

At Paris Las Vegas, 3655 Las Vegas Blvd S, 89109 **Tel** *(702) 948-6937* **Map** *3 C3*

Chef J. Joho serves conservative and flavorful cuisine, such as braised *ballotine* of boneless quail, roasted rack of lamb Provençale, and tournedos Rossini in truffle sauce. Located at the top of the tower, the restaurant offers splendid views of the Strip. Open for lunch and dinner.

Emeril's New Orleans Fish House
🔲🍴 $$$$$

At MGM Grand, 3799 Las Vegas Blvd S, 89109 **Tel** *(702) 891-7374* **Map** *3 C4*

Celebrity chef and author Emeril Lagasse brings his signature New Orleans mix of Creole and Cajun cooking to Vegas. Favorites here include his famous barbecued shrimp, oyster stew, and tuna steak with *foir gras*. Save room for the mouthwatering banana cream pie with banana crust. Open for lunch and dinner.

Ferraro's
♫ ❱ 🍸 $$$$$

5900 W Flamingo Rd, 89103 **Tel** *(702) 364-5300*   **Map** 3 A3

This long-time Vegas eatery is fast reaching landmark status. The classic and elegant dining room has a piano bar and upscale furnishings. The specialty here is *osso buco*, along with other Italian favorites such as linguine *pomodoro*, veal *scaloppine*, homemade gnocchi, and a marvelous stuffed artichoke. Open only for dinner.

Fiamma Trattoria
❱ 🍸 $$$$$

At the MGM Grand, 3799 Las Vegas Blvd S, 89109 **Tel** *(702) 891-7600*   **Map** 3 C4

This classy restaurant earned a Three Star designation from The *New York Times* newspaper. Fiamma is a sleek, sexy trattoria serving signature pasta dishes and traditional Italian cuisine. Covering a massive area, it features a cozy bar, lounge, café, and a private screening room. Open only for dinner. Advance reservations recommended.

FIX
❱ 🍸 $$$$$

At the Bellagio, 3600 Las Vegas Blvd S, 89109 **Tel** *(702) 693-7111*   **Map** 3 C3

This lively dining room has a hip, yet elegant, atmosphere. The contemporary American fare includes tasty seafood, meat, and pasta dishes prepared on a wood-burning grill. The bread is freshly baked. Also offers a selection of designer cocktails and imported beverages, as well as some delectable desserts. Open only for dinner.

Joël Robuchon
🍴 🍸 $$$$$

At MGM Grand Hotel & Casino, 3799 Las Vegas Blvd S, 89109 **Tel** *(702) 891-7925*   **Map** 3 C4

Known as "Chef of the Century", legendary French chef Joël Robuchon has come out of retirement to open his first and only fine-dining restaurant in the U.S. Signature dishes include *La Noix de Saint-Jacques* (fresh scallop cooked in its shell with lemon and butter) and Brittany lobster. Reservations strongly recommended. Open only for dinner.

Le Cirque
🍴 🍸 $$$$$

At the Bellagio, 3600 Las Vegas Blvd S, 89109 **Tel** *(702) 693-8100*   **Map** 3 C3

A spin-off of the legendary Le Cirque in Manhattan, this chic restaurant overlooks a lake. Classic haute French cuisine is the specialty. Favorites here include Dover sole Grenobloise, *canard rôtie* and *poulet fermier*, *foie gras*, and *ravioli de truffle blanche*. Open only for dinner. Advance reservations are suggested. Closed on Monday.

N9NE
♫ ❱ 🍸 $$$$$

At the Palms Casino Resort, 4321 W Flamingo Rd, 89103 **Tel** *(702) 933-9900*   **Map** 3 A3

A slick, upscale dining room with an elegant yet cozy decor designed to create a relaxing atmosphere for its patrons. The restaurant serves Midwestern-style steaks and chops, as well as a nice selection of seafood and tartare prepared by master chefs. There's also a champagne and caviar bar. Service is efficient. Open only for dinner.

Nero's
🍸 $$$$$

At Caesars Palace, 3570 Las Vegas Blvd S, 89109 **Tel** *(702) 731-7731*   **Map** 3 C3

Chef Sean Griffin prepares creative dishes specializing in prime beef, fresh fish, seafood, and tender chops. Favorites include seared *foie gras* "sliders" with port poached rhubarb, slow baked salmon, Gorgonzola fondue, and roasted pecan crème brûlée. The desserts are worth trying too. Open only for dinner. Reservations are suggested.

Nobu
🍴 ♫ ❱ 🍸 $$$$$

At the Hard Rock Hotel & Casino, 4455 Paradise Rd, 89109 **Tel** *(702) 693-5090*   **Map** 4 D4

Celebrity chef and owner Nobu Matsuhisa, famous for his Los Angeles eatery, attracts an elite Hollywood crowd who love the innovative blend of Japanese, fusion and Peruvian cuisine. Fresh fish is flown in daily from the Tokyo fish market. The sushi bar here is one of the best in Las Vegas. Open only for dinner.

Picasso
🍴 🍸 $$$$$

At the Bellagio, 3600 Las Vegas Blvd S, 89109 **Tel** *(702) 693-7223*   **Map** 3 C3

Original masterpieces by renowned artist Pablo Picasso adorn the walls of this elegant dining room. The degustation menu is a nice way to experience the cuisine and may include *amuse-bouche*, warm lobster salad, and sautéed filet of black bass. Open only for dinner and closed on Tuesday.

Red Square
❱ 🍸 $$$$$

At Mandalay Bay, 3950 Las Vegas Blvd S, 89109 **Tel** *(702) 632-7407*   **Map** 3 C5

Inspired by a Moscow tearoom, Red Square offers more than 100 frozen vodkas and other Russian cocktails. Also serves a selection of caviar and perestroika-inspired specialties with American, French, and Italian flavors. These include Siberian nachos with smoked salmon and crab cakes. Open only for dinner.

Restaurant Guy Savoy
🍸 🍸 $$$$$

At Caesars Palace, 3570 Las Vegas Blvd S, 89109 **Tel** *(702) 731-7110*   **Map** 3 B3

This contemporary Parisian-style restaurant, directed by Michelin 3-star chef Guy Savoy, is located on the second floor of the Augustus Tower at Caesars Palace's. The menu is modern French, using fresh ingredients with delicacy and flair, while the ambience is elegant and intimate. Open only for dinner. Closed Monday and Tuesday.

Spago
❱ 🍸 $$$$$

At the Forum Shops, 3500 Las Vegas Blvd S, 89109 **Tel** *(702) 369-6300*   **Map** 3 C3

Acclaimed chef Wolfgang Puck's first venture into Vegas echoes its famous counterpart in Los Angeles. The menu changes on a day-to-day basis. Specialties here are duck sausage pizza, Peking duck spring roll, steamed Maine lobster, and ginger-crusted salmon. There's a café as well as a formal dining room. Open 11:30am daily.

Key to Price Guide *see p124* **Key to Symbols** *see back cover flap*

The Palm 🍽 $$$$$

At the Forum Shops, 3570 Las Vegas Blvd S, 89109 **Tel** *(702) 732-7256* **Map** *3 C3*

This New York-style steakhouse serves jumbo lobsters and large portions of prime beef among other American specialties. The atmosphere is comfortable and the walls showcase caricatures of several celebrities. A private dining room is also available. Open from 11:30am onwards.

NORTH STRIP

BLT Burger 🔲🍽 $$

3400 Las Vegas Blvd S, 89109 **Tel** *(702) 792-7888* **Map** *3 C2*

While the menu is heavy on beef burgers made with prime cuts of meat, non-beef choices include turkey breast, veggie falafel, and salmon. A large selection of milkshakes and draft beer accompany the extensive menu. BLT is located in the Mirage just steps from the room registration lobby. Open 11am onwards.

California Pizza Kitchen 🔲🍽 $$

At the Mirage, 3400 Las Vegas Blvd S, 89109 **Tel** *(702) 791-7223* **Map** *3 C3*

Features an enormous range of designer wood-fired pizzas such as Thai spice, barbecue shrimp, and portobello mushrooms. This open-air restaurant situated in the heart of the casino also serves pastas and delicious desserts. Salads such as walnuts and field greens are also prepared well. Open from 11am onwards.

Peppermill 🔲🍽 $$

2985 Las Vegas Blvd S, 89109 **Tel** *(702) 735-4177* **Map** *3 C2*

More than a coffee shop, the Peppermill is a throwback to days of old Las Vegas. The dining room offers great burgers, salads, steaks, and seafood dishes, but the real fun is in the adjoining lounge, where waitresses dressed in evening gowns serve customers seated on plush sofas around a fireplace. An enjoyable experience. Open 24 hours.

Benihana Village 🍴🔲🍽 $$$

At Las Vegas Hilton, 3000 Paradise Rd, 89109 **Tel** *(702) 732-5755* **Map** *4 D2*

This charming restaurant has two floors of dining rooms and is set amid lush gardens, meandering streams, fish ponds, and teahouses. Master chefs entertain guests as they prepare delectable dishes at the hibachi tables. Also houses a relaxing lounge. Open only for dinner. Advance reservations are suggested.

First Food and Bar 🍴🔲🍽 $$$

At the Palazzo, 3327 Las Vegas Blvd S, 89109 **Tel** *(702) 607-3478* **Map** *3 C2*

This eatery only closes for an hour or two each morning and offers dining in a casual atmosphere. There are leather couches in the bar, a large window with a view of the Strip, and walls covered with photos and posters. There is a wide selection of dishes on the menu for breakfast, lunch, and dinner. Opens at 7am.

Greek Island Deli 🎵🍽 $$$

At Greek Isles Hotel, 305 Convention Center Dr, 89109 **Tel** *(702) 952-8000* **Map** *4 D2*

This open and airy restaurant serves some traditional American meals with dishes such as breast of chicken or pork chops. New York steaks are also served. The decor is stylish and creates a comfortable atmosphere. Open from 10am daily.

Kahunaville 🎵🔲🍽 $$$

At Treasure Island – TI, 3300 Las Vegas Blvd S, 89109 **Tel** *(702) 894-7390* **Map** *3 C2*

Designed to resemble a tropical island, this is a fun place where the servers and bartenders put on a show and entertain the guests with dancing and "flair" bartending. Tasty dishes include coconut shrimp, Jamaican jerk chicken, and Hawaiian pork tenderloin. Poolside dining is also available at times. Open 8am onwards.

NASCAR Café 🍽 $$$

At the Sahara, 2535 Las Vegas Blvd S, 89109 **Tel** *(702) 737-2111* **Map** *4 D1*

Ideal for racing enthusiasts as diners are surrounded by stock car and racing memorabilia. No-frills entrées are served in large portions and include steak, catfish, baby back ribs, chicken and pasta dishes, pork chops, and many more. The decor includes large screen TVs showcasing NASCAR events and racing news. Open from 11:30am onwards.

Pamplemousse 🍴🍽 $$$

400 E Sahara Ave, 89109 **Tel** *(702) 733-2066* **Map** *4 D1*

This romantic hideaway is located in a converted house just a block from the Strip. There is a fixed menu for groups of 15 and over and the waiter recites the daily specials. The Riviera-style dinner starts with a basket of fresh veggies and a house vinaigrette. Favorites are escargots, shallots, scampi, Norwegian salmon and white veal. Dinner only.

Pho $$$

At Treasure Island – TI, 3300 Las Vegas Blvd S 89109 **Tel** *(702) 894 7111* **Map** *3 C2*

Located within the Coffee Shop at Treasure Island – TI, Pho specializes in noodle soups and traditional Vietnamese dishes. The restaurant is named for a signature Vietnamese dish, Pho, a rich beef broth with vermicelli noodles infused with spices and fresh herbs. It is the only Vietnamese restaurant on the Las Vegas strip. Open 11am onwards.

Piero's
355 Convention Center Dr, 89109 **Tel** *(702) 369-2305*
$$$ **Map** *4 D2*

Long established as a favored restaurant of local celebrities and dignitaries as well as the city's local population. Piero's resembles an upscale country club specializing in classic gourmet cuisine that includes veal chops in brandy sauce, mussels in tomato sauce, oysters Rockefeller, and lobster Thermidor. Open only for dinner.

Pinot Brasserie
At the Venetian, 3355 Las Vegas Blvd S, 89109 **Tel** *(702) 414-8888*
$$$ **Map** *3 C3*

This branch of the award-winning Los Angeles restaurant by celebrity chef Joachim Splichal is noted for offering French cuisine with a California twist. Serves steak, poultry, pastas, seafood, and wild game. Also hosts a rotisserie and oyster bar. Authentic French decor includes wooden French doors. Open for lunch and dinner.

Zeffirino Ristorante
At the Venetian, 3355 Las Vegas Blvd S, 89109 **Tel** *(702) 414-3500*
$$$ **Map** *3 C3*

Authentic Italian cuisine with a Genoa accent is served amid wooden furniture, wine cases, and a hand-crafted 40-ft (12-m) high bar. The romantic ambience is enhanced by the views of gondolas passing by on the Grand Canal outside. Features a collection of more than 300 wines. Open from 11:30am onwards.

Bartolotta Ristorante di Mare
At Wynn Las Vegas, 3131 Las Vegal Blvd S, 89109 **Tel** *(702) 770-7800*
$$$$ **Map** *3 C2*

The romantic setting of this seafood restaurant makes it a popular choice with couples. Chef Paul Bartolotta serves traditional Italian cuisine, using fresh seafood flown in daily. The best tables are the private cabanas, each decorated with its own chandelier, overlooking the restaurant's pool decorated with ethereal silver orbs. Open only for dinner.

Delmonico Steakhouse
At the Venetian, 3355 Las Vegas Blvd S, 89109 **Tel** *(702) 414-3737*
$$$$ **Map** *3 C3*

Highly acclaimed celebrity chef Emeril Lagasse adds a Creole touch to the steaks, chops, and seafood. House specialties include the bone-in rib-eye steak, Delmonico chicken carved tableside, double-cut pork chops, and baked jumbo Gulf shrimp. An elegant restaurant with high ceilings. Open from 11:30am onwards; closed 2–5pm.

Fin
At the Mirage, 3400 Las Vegas Blvd S, 89109 **Tel** *(702) 791-7111*
$$$$ **Map** *3 C3*

Authentic Chinese cuisine is served in a contemporary setting. Signature dishes include wok-fried beef tenderloin. The decor is dominated by gold and jade color themes, and floating translucent spheres hanging from the ceiling provide privacy between tables. Open only for dinner. Closed on Tuesday and Wednesday.

Okada
At Wynn Las Vegas, 3131 Las Vegas Blvd S, 89109 **Tel** *(702) 770-7800*
$$$$ **Map** *3 C2*

A top-end Japanese restaurant with three sections: a sushi bar, the main restaurant, and a *teppanyaki* room with tables based around *robatayaki* grills. Outside, a huge waterfall cascades into a koi pond on which the chef's table for eight people is set on a "floating" pagoda. Dress is smart casual. Dinner is served nightly.

Switch
At Encore, 3131 Las Vegas Blvd S, 89109 **Tel** *(702) 248-3463*
$$$$ **Map** *3 C2*

A French-style steakhouse offering organic and natural products. The restaurant is named after the walls that go up and down every 20 minutes to reveal different scenes and decor – a show in itself. Their steaks comes from grass- and corn-fed natural beef that is wet-aged for 55 days. Opens at 5:30pm.

Kokomo's
At the Mirage, 3400 Las Vegas Blvd S, 89109 **Tel** *(702) 791-7111*
$$$$$ **Map** *3 C3*

Diners at this eatery feel as if they are in a tropical rainforest surrounded by cascading waterfalls and lush plants. Specialties include seafood, beef, and pork dishes. The fish taco with pineapple sauce is delicious, as is the chocolate raspberry mousse. Open only for dinner.

TAO Asian Bistro
At the Venetian, 3355 Las Vegas Blvd S, 89109 **Tel** *(702) 388-8338*
$$$$$ **Map** *3 C3*

The creators of New York's TAO Asian Bistro have brought their renowned hotspot and celebrity hangout to Las Vegas. The massive TAO features sin city's hippest nightclub, coolest ultra-lounge, largest banquet facility and hottest restaurant. The Asian cuisine has Chinese, Japanese and Thai influences. Open only for dinner.

The Steak House
At Circus Circus, 2880 Las Vegas Blvd S, 89109 **Tel** *(702) 794-3767*
$$$$$ **Map** *3 C2*

The steaks served here are large, thick, and juicy. Mesquite broiled New York, sirloin, porterhouse, and filet mignon are some of the most popular choices with diners. Guests can watch steaks being prepared in an open-hearth charcoal broiler. Open only for dinner.

Top of the World
At the Stratosphere, 2000 Las Vegas Blvd S, 89104 **Tel** *(702) 380-7711*
$$$$$ **Map** *4 D1*

Panoramic views can be enjoyed from this restaurant located 833 ft (255 m) above the Strip. The revolving dining room offers a mixed menu that includes Colorado rack of lamb, Chateaubriand, and the mouthwatering chocolate Stratosphere dessert. Casual attire for lunch and business casual for dinner. Open from 11am onwards.

Key to Price Guide *see p124* **Key to Symbols** *see back cover flap*

DOWNTOWN & FREMONT STREET

Bay City Diner ⑤
At the Golden Gate, 1 Fremont St, 89101 **Tel** *(702) 385-1906* **Map** *2 D3*

Located in the oldest hotel in town, this café-style diner and coffee shop serves bargain-priced breakfasts, porterhouse steaks, and chicken specialties around the clock. Guests can take a window booth and watch the passing parade of downtown visitors. Open 7–2am.

Dona Maria Tamales ⑤
910 Las Vegas Blvd S, 89101 **Tel** *(702) 382-6538* **Map** *2 D4*

This Mexican restaurant is very popular among the residents and tourists alike. The eatery is famous for its *tamales* – red, green, cheese, or a sweet pineapple-and-raisin dessert one. At Christmas, customers have to order *tamales* a week in advance. Other great choices are the *flautas* and *taquitos*. Opens at 8am.

El Sombrero Café ⑤⑤
807 Main St, 89101 **Tel** *(702) 382-9234* **Map** *2 D3*

Although the decor at this modest restaurant resembles the Tijuana jail in Mexico, it is actually one of the better Mexican eateries in town, and one of the oldest. Popular dishes include *menudo*, chili Colorado, shrimp on tomatoes, and diced beef with red chili sauce. Lunch daily, dinner on Fri and Sat. Closed on Sunday.

Pasta Pirate ⑤⑤
At the California, 12 Ogden Ave, 89101 **Tel** *(702) 385-1222* **Map** *2 D3*

The dining room is designed to resemble a dockside fish factory with tin walls and open ventilator ducts. The house specials are steamed clams, Australian sea bass, and snow crabs. Guests can also watch the chefs prepare meals through a glass window. Open only for dinner and closed on Tuesday.

Triple 7 Brew Pub ⑤⑤
At Main Street Station, 200 N Main St, 89101 **Tel** *(702) 387-1896* **Map** *2 D3*

This is a fun place with a 1930s warehouse motif. Because of the microbrewery, the menu leans toward party food. Favorite choices here are the Philly steak and cheese pizza, *chile verde*, pork *tostadas*, black bean chili, burgers, and salads. Also features a sushi bar and a wide assortment of cigars and liquors. Open 11am onwards.

Chicago Joe's ⑤⑤⑤
820 S Fourth St, 89101 **Tel** *(702) 382-5637* **Map** *2 D4*

A favorite among locals for three decades, the restaurant is in an old converted Hollywood Spanish home. A piano bar adjoins the cozy dining room. Specialties include snails and pasta, lobster, veal, eggplant Parmesan, cheese ravioli, clams, and meatball sandwiches. Closed Sunday and Monday. Open only for dinner on Saturday.

Lombardi's Italian Kitchen ⑤⑤⑤
At the Plaza Hotel and Casino, 1 Main St, 89109 **Tel** *(702) 382-5637* **Map** *2 D3*

On the second floor of the North Tower of the Plaza, Lombardi's Italian Kitchen offers a quiet, calm atmosphere. Serving Italian cuisine, including traditional pasta dishes such as rigatoni, pasta primavera, and spaghetti, as well as a variety of pizzas, and typical desserts like tiramisu.

Tinoco's Kitchen ⑤⑤⑤
18 E Fremont St, 89101 **Tel** *(702) 380-5735* **Map** *2 D3*

The walls are covered with colorful paintings at this restaurant, which opened in 2009. Even the tables are shaped liked artists' palettes. This family owned and run restaurant offers a menu of Italian-style cuisine with an emphasis on seafood, which includes seared Ahi tuna. Open daily from 7am–10pm.

Binion's Ranch Steakhouse ⑤⑤⑤⑤
At Binion's, 128 Fremont St, 89101 **Tel** *(702) 382-1600* **Map** *2 D3*

Brocade booths, oil paintings, and wooden paneling underscore the restaurant's Old West theme. This famous Vegas eatery offers a dramatic view of the city as well as huge portions of prime rib, lamb chops, filet, porterhouse, and New York steak. Also has a range of seafood and chicken dishes. Open only for dinner.

Flame Steakhouse ⑤⑤⑤⑤
At the El Cortez, 600 Fremont St, 89101 **Tel** *(702) 385-5200* **Map** *2 E3*

Ambient lighting, white linen tablecloths, and live piano music provide a welcoming and comfortable atmosphere in this classic steakhouse which also offers seafood. Traditional steaks include New York, Porterhouse, and prime rib, while the seafood menu offers Alaskan king crab and lobster tail.

Hugo's Cellar ⑤⑤⑤⑤
At the Four Queens, 202 Fremont St, 89101 **Tel** *(702) 385-4011* **Map** *2 D3*

This basement restaurant has a romantic atmosphere, due to the privacy of the dining booths, and the rose given to every female guest on arrival. Entrées include prime rib, veal, lamb, duck, chicken, and seafood. The chocolate-dipped fruits are a specialty. Open only for dinner. Reservations suggested.

Lillie's Noodle House
☒ $$$$

At the Golden Nugget, 129 Fremont St, 89101 **Tel** *(702) 385-7111*   **Map** *2 D3*

This lavish and stylish dining room has draped booths, Venetian-glass chandeliers, and domed ceiling. Serves Asian specialties. House favorites include beef with oyster sauce, seafood tofu soup, shark's fin soup, *moo goo gai pan* and crab with black bean sauce. Open only for dinner.

Rosemary's Restaurant
☒ ▶ ☒ $$$$

8125 West Sahara Ave, 89117 **Tel** *(702) 869-2251*   **Map** *3 A1*

Both tourists and locals come here for affordable gourmet dining. It has been voted the best gourmet restaurant in the local newspaper poll every year since its opening in 1999. The cuisine is French-inspired with an American regional twist. Business or dressy casual. Open only for dinner except for the first Friday of each month.

Second Street Grill
☒ $$$$

At the Fremont, 200 Fremont St, 89101 **Tel** *(702) 385-6277*   **Map** *2 D3*

The menu is a blend of Continental specialties and, because of the Hawaiian clientele, plenty of Pacific Rim dishes. The former includes veal medallions, crab cakes, and asparagus bisque, while Asian dishes would include bamboo steamed snapper and veal chops with soy-ginger sauce. Open only for dinner. Closed on Tuesday and Wednesday.

Triple George Grill
♫ ☒ $$$$$

201 N 3rd St, 89101 **Tel** *(702) 384-2761*   **Map** *2 D3*

Reminiscent of a 1950s San Francisco diner with black and white floor tiles, this is one of the most popular restaurants in downtown Las Vegas. The menu is based on American-style seafood, with an excellent range of fresh fish dishes. There are also old favorites such as chicken pot pie. Closed for lunch Saturday and dinner Monday.

Vic & Anthony's Steakhouse
☒ ☒ $$$$$

At the Golden Nugget, 129 Fremont St, 89101 **Tel** *(702) 385-7111/(800) 634-3403*   **Map** *2 D3*

Vic & Anthony's steakhouse features the finest selection of mouth-watering prime steaks, lobster, fresh seafood, an extensive wine selection, and impeccable service in an intimate, luxurious atmosphere. The menu features Beluga caviar, maple-glazed quail, ribeye steak, and lamb chops. Open only for dinner.

FARTHER AFIELD

BOULDER CITY Evan's Old Town Grille
☒ $$

1129 Arizona St, Boulder City, NV, 89005 **Tel** *(702) 294-0100*

One of the best places for fine dining when visiting Boulder City. Serves hearty, traditional American fare. The house specialties include appetizing prime ribs, chops, and steaks. Also serves a range of chicken dishes. Open for lunch and dinner. Open only for dinner on Saturday. Closed on Sunday and Monday.

BOULDER CITY Milo's Best Cellars
▶ ☒ $$

538 Nevada Hwy, Boulder City, NV, 89005 **Tel** *(702) 293-9540*

A sidewalk café, wine bar and retail liquor store all rolled into one, Milo's serves a variety of gourmet sandwiches, antipasti and cheese platters, as well as hundreds of wines and over 50 types of beer. Ask for a table outside to take in the sights of the main drag of Boulder City. Open 11am daily.

HENDERSON Marssa
$$$$$

At Loews Lake Las Vegas, 101 Montelago Blvd, Henderson, NV, 89011 **Tel** *(702) 567-6000*

Marssa offers sweeping lake and mountain views surpassed only by its creative menu, which includes the freshest of sushi and a wide selection of tantalizing appetizers and entrées. The wine and sake list is also comprehensive. No artificial trans-fats are used in any of this restaurant's dishes. Open only for dinner. Closed Sunday and Monday.

LAS VEGAS Sourdough Café
▶ $

At Arizona Charlie's, 740 S Decatur Blvd, Las Vegas, NV, 89107 **Tel** *(702) 258-5200*

This hyperactive coffee shop is famous for its Western attitude and affordable prices. Dinner favorites include mouthwatering prime rib, porterhouse steak, and pork dishes. Also offers a wide variety of delicious seafood and chicken specialties, burgers, sandwiches, salads, and much more. Open 24 hours daily.

LAS VEGAS Café Siena
▶ $$

At the Suncoast, 9090 Alta Dr, Las Vegas, NV, 89128 **Tel** *(702) 636-7111*

This cleverly designed dining room adjoins the hotel's casino but still provides diners privacy. Breakfast, lunch, and dinner plus a late-night menu features traditional American favorites, including a variety of sandwiches, as well as a range of Chinese dishes. Open 7am–11pm daily.

LAS VEGAS Memphis Championship Barbecue
☒ $$

2250 E Warm Springs Rd, Las Vegas, NV, 89123 **Tel** *(702) 260-6909*

Superb barbecue from culinary award-winning chef Mike Mills. The meat is slow cooked in a special oven smoked with apple wood. Baby back ribs, chicken, pork shoulder, hot links, and barbecued beef are favored. Also offers great side orders and a special "seasoning dust" can be purchased. Open daily from 11am.

Key to Price Guide *see p124* **Key to Symbols** *see back cover flap*

LAS VEGAS Cabo Cantina 🍸 $$$

At Santa Fe Station, 4949 N Rancho Rd, Las Vegas, NV, 89130 **Tel** *(702) 658-4900*

This festive cantina serves an array of traditional and nouveau Mexican specialties. Diners have the luxury of creating their own entrée by choosing to mix and match menu items. Also offers seafood. A unique blend of margaritas, tequila-based cocktails, and other drinks are also available. Open only for dinner.

MOUNT CHARLESTON A Cut Above 🍸 $$$

At Mount Charleston Hotel, 2 Kyle Canyon Rd, Mount Charleston, NV, 89124 **Tel** *(702) 872-5500*

A lodge-style chalet with open rafters, a fieldstone fireplace, tree trunk pillars, and great views of the surrounding mountains. Steaks, seafood, and chicken dishes include grilled filet mignon and baked salmon. For brunch, choose from an extensive list of American classics, including pancakes and eggs benedict.

BEYOND LAS VEGAS

BRYCE CANYON Bryce Canyon Dining Room $$$$

At Bryce Canyon Lodge, Bryce Canyon National Park, UT, 84717 **Tel** *(435) 834-8760*

This charming restaurant offers breathtaking views of the surrounding scenic landscape and is one of the area's finest spots for dining. The rustic decor creates a romantic atmosphere and makes its a popular destination for honeymooners. A wide range of delectable Continental specialties are available. Closed from November 1–March 31.

CEDAR CITY Market Grill $$

2290 W Highway 56, Cedar City, UT, 84720 **Tel** *(435) 586-9325*

This unique eatery is a popular destination among families and has a rural ambience. Serves hearty fare such as rib-eye steaks and cowboy-sized breakfasts at affordable prices. The service is friendly. The restaurant is located at the livestock yards in Cedar City and also features a livestock auction.

CEDAR CITY Rusty's Ranch House $$

2275 E Hwy 14, Cedar City, UT, 84721 **Tel** *(435) 586-3839*

Ribs, chicken, pastas, and seafood dishes are served at this restaurant located amid a beautiful canyon setting. Diners can take in the spectacular view while enjoying specialties such as barbecued baby back ribs that have been slow-roasted for almost 18 hours. Open only for dinner. Reservations are recommended. Closed on Sunday.

DEATH VALLEY Inn Dining Room 🍸 $$$$

At Furnace Creek Inn, 1 Main St, Death Valley, CA, 92328 **Tel** *(760) 786-2345*

Set in a remote area, this popular restaurant offers magnificent views of the surrounding mountains. Ideal for those looking for an intimate and quiet dining experience. Features an interesting blend of Southwestern, Continental, and Pacific Rim cuisines. Also provides a range of cocktails and fine wines. Closed mid-May–mid-Oct.

DEATH VALLEY Wrangler Steakhouse 🍸 $$$$

At Furnace Creek Ranch, 1 Main St, Death Valley, CA, 92328 **Tel** *(760) 786-2345*

This classic steakhouse features a Southwestern ambience. Specializes in prime ribs, chops, chicken, seafood, and a wide variety of steaks. There is also a well-stocked salad bar and a selection of fine wines and cocktails. Open only for dinner. The restaurant does not accept advance reservations.

GRAND CANYON Bright Angel Restaurant 🍸 $$$

At Bright Angel Lodge, Grand Canyon South Rim, AZ, 86023 **Tel** *(928) 638-2631*

This bustling café and restaurant serves light meals and salads, as well as complete dinners. The atmosphere is comfortable and soothing, which makes it a popular eating destination among residents and the local population alike. Reservations are not accepted so guests might have to line up.

GRAND CANYON El Tovar Hotel 🍸 $$$$$

At El Tovar Hotel, Grand Canyon South Rim, AZ, 86023 **Tel** *(928) 638-2631*

The spacious dining room offers panoramic views of the surrounding scenery. The decor is one of understated elegance. The servings are generous. House specialties include *hoisin* barbeque sea scallops and Native American blue corn *tamales*. Reservations for dinner are essential.

RHYOLITE Stage Coach Inn 🍸 $$$$

At the Stage Coach Inn and Casino, Hwy 95, Beatty, NV, 89003 **Tel** *(775) 553-2419*

This frontier-style dining room reflects a strong Wild-West ambience. Serves traditional American cuisine. House favorites include a wide variety of steaks, chicken, fish, burgers, meat loaf, and prime ribs. The service is friendly, and the restaurant does not require reservations.

ST. GEORGE Painted Pony Restaurant $$$$

2 West St. George Blvd, Suite 2, St. George, UT, 84770 **Tel** *(435) 634-1700*

The decor of this culinary oasis is clean and modern with colorful Southwestern art, wooden tables and chairs, fresh flowers, and, in the evening, a delightfully romantic atmosphere with subdued lighting and patio dining. The cuisine is inventive and intriguing contemporary American.

SHOPPING IN LAS VEGAS

In recent years Las Vegas has consolidated its reputation as a shopper's paradise. Fun and tacky souvenirs are available in small stores along the Strip, whereas jewelry and designer clothes can be found everywhere, from hotel shops to malls. Given the city's hot climate, indoor shopping malls are the norm. All the major resorts have their own covered parades of shops, and some, such as Caesars Palace's Forum Shops, are as flamboyant as the hotels themselves. Several malls in Las

Souvenir from Circus Circus

Vegas, such as the Strip's Fashion Show Mall, house upscale department stores such as Saks Fifth Avenue and Neiman Marcus. For bargains in adult and children's clothes and shoes, as well as a range of household items, there are three outlet shopping malls, Las Vegas Outlet Center, Fashion Outlets of Las Vegas (south of the Strip), and Las Vegas Premium Outlets (near Downtown). Shopping centrally can be expensive, and for everyday items ordinary malls used by the locals are a short drive away.

The Esplanade at Wynn Las Vegas (see p60–61) on North Strip

SHOPPING HOURS

Most stores and malls are open seven days a week. Typical business hours are from 9am to 6pm, Monday to Saturday, and 10am to 5pm on Sunday. The closing time for shops located in a mall or promenade usually extends to 9pm, and some stores in hotel shopping arcades open until midnight. Many gas stations, supermarkets, and convenience stores stay open 24/7.

SALES

The Christmas shopping season, which runs from Thanksgiving to January 1, offers some great bargains in the form of promotional deals and discounts. The week after Christmas is probably the best time to buy anything. During this period, several retail outlets reduce prices to move

merchandize or make way for the next season's products. Check the local newspapers for advertisements announcing these sales.

TAXES

Sales tax in Clark County is 8.1 percent and is added to the purchase price of all goods, except groceries and prescription drugs, at the time of sale. Sales tax is not refundable to overseas visitors. In addition, international travelers may be required to pay import duties and taxes on their purchases once they reach home.

HOW TO PAY

Most stores accept credit cards including Visa, MasterCard, Discover, and American Express, as well as bank debit cards. Traveler's checks are also acceptable

but usually require some form of identification, such as a passport or driver's license. Two-party checks, personal checks drawn on foreign banks, and foreign currency are rarely accepted. Cash is always the best way to pay for small purchases.

RIGHTS AND RETURNS

Be sure you understand the shop's return policy before making an important purchase. The key to obtaining any refund is in the proof of purchase, so keep all sales receipts. It is also important to retain all packaging – original boxes, instructions, and the owner's manuals.

Each store has its own return-and-exchange policy. Most retailers usually give a cash refund or an in-shop credit, assuming the item being returned has not been altered or damaged. If the purchased item is defective, the store will refund its cost, unless it was sold "as is." Many stores have a time limit within which it will refund your money, typically up to 30 days after the purchase. Goods bought on sale are often not returnable.

Modernist interior of Fashion Show Mall (see p57)

The sprawling outlet of Saks Fifth Avenue, Fashion Show Mall *(see p57)*

SHIPPING PACKAGES

Most stores will ship goods worldwide, usually for a fee. Perhaps the best way to send packages is via an international courier such as Federal Express or DHL. Keep copies of shipping forms and airway bills, specially the tracking numbers, which are instrumental in finding lost packages.

DEPARTMENT STORES

Las Vegas has an excellent mix of department stores, most of them clustered in the shopping malls *(see pp136–7)*. These large retail stores offer a wide variety of merchandize from toys to small appliances, and from apparel to cosmetics.

Sears, **JCPenney**, and **Kohl's** are the least expensive. They all offer complete lines of men's, women's, and children's apparel and shoes, plus jewelry, accessories, and recreational equipment.

Mid-priced department stores include **Dillard's** and **Macy's** which feature an expansive line of clothing, including designer labels such as Calvin Klein and Tommy Hilfiger.

At the highest end of the department store chains are **Neiman Marcus**, **Saks Fifth Avenue**, and **Nordstrom**, all of which are located at the Fashion Show Mall. In addition to the finest designer label clothing, Neiman and Saks also offer creative, though pricey, home products, gifts, and specialty items. Nordstrom, known for its fashion apparel and shoes, also has an eclectic collection of jewelry.

SHOPPING FARTHER AFIELD

Good shopping options are also available outside Las Vegas. About 10 miles (16 km) east into the adjacent city of Henderson *(see p82)* is the **Galleria at Sunset**. Fountains, pools, and indoor trees make for a pleasant shopping experience. The mall has about 110 stores that include the usual mix of men's and women's clothing, as well as a variety of gift boutiques.

PARKING

Most shopping malls and large department stores offer valet parking as well as free parking in their parking lots. The only area of town that has parking meters is downtown near Fremont Street. However, the parking garages there usually offer free parking with validation.

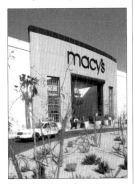

Entrance to Macy's department store, Las Vegas

Shopping Malls and Hotel Shops

Shopping malls in Las Vegas are a quintessential feature of the city, and have achieved the status of must-see attractions in their own right. Apart from the shopping boom that the city is currently experiencing, the major sources of all the excitement are the resorts that have joined the shopping bandwagon with their themed malls. Exclusive, elegant, and expensive, these retail destinations not only offer a wide array of products, but are also an entertaining and enjoyable way to explore the city. Although shopping on the Strip is a costly proposition, it is also undeniably an experience worth savoring.

Cloud-shaped canopy, Fashion Show Mall

FASHION SHOW MALL

Located right across the street from Treasure Island – TI *(see p56)*, the Fashion Show Mall *(see p57)* is the jewel of the city's shopping malls, and features more than 250 shops on several enclosed levels. The mall covers an area of over 2 million sq ft (185,806 sq m), and is home to six major department stores – Saks Fifth Avenue, Nordstrom, Bloomingdale's Home, Macy's, Dillard's, and Neiman Marcus – as well as a range of upscale specialty and designer shops such as Cache, Abercrombie & Fitch, Guess, and Aldo, to name a few.

In additon, the mall hosts an excellent selection of commercial art galleries, including the Centaur Art Galleries that showcase masterpieces by world-renowned artists such as Salvador Dali and Pablo

Picasso along with the works of contemporary artists such as Steve Kaufman and LeRoy Neiman. Stores such as Body Shop and Victoria's Secret cater to the beauty conscious, while GameStop and Future Tronics offer high-tech toys and electronic gizmos to gadget-lovers.

BOULEVARD MALL

The city's oldest shopping mall, Boulevard has 140 stores, an elaborate food court, and a variety of services that cater to customers' needs. Among them are a foreign currency exchange center, valet parking, a taxi stand, and a notary, fax, and copy service. The mall is anchored by three mid-priced department stores – Sears, JCPenney, and Macy's. Most of the men's and women's

clothing stores are geared toward younger, mid-scale buyers. The Boulevard also has a vast array of shoe stores, jewelers, luggage shops, booksellers, pet stores, travel agencies, electronics outlets, hair salons, and various other retailers for nearly every product and service imaginable.

FORUM SHOPS AT CAESARS

Much more than just another glitzy shopping mall – Forum Shops *(see p50)* is a major tourist attraction designed along the lines of an ancient Roman street. The mall, which has been expanded three times, has talking statues, dancing fountains, a *trompe l'oeil* sky that simulates the change from dawn to dusk, the amazing Fall of Atlantis fountain show, which depicts the Atlantis myth and takes place every hour on the hour, and 160 specialty shops and restaurants. Among the stores worth visiting are Tourneau Time Dome (the world's largest watch store). For ultra-chic women's wear, head for Dolce & Gabbana, Marc Jacobs, and Harry Winston.

The Forum also has many gourmet chocolate and gelato shops, as well as a wide choice of restaurants and eateries, including a franchise for renowned LA chef Wolfgang Puck's Spago and Miami-famed Joe's Seafood, Prime Steak and Stone Crab.

Roman statues and a painted sky at Forum Shops, Caesars Palace

Shops along the charming streets of Venice, Grand Canal Shoppes

GRAND CANAL SHOPPES AT THE VENETIAN

Of all the hotel shopping malls, the Grand Canal Shoppes is the most visually arresting with its Venetian streetscapes, piazza-style promenades, daylight ceiling, and a quarter-mile reproduction of Venice's Grand Canal, complete with a fleet of gondolas, singing gondoliers, waterside cafés, and bridges. The massive complex also features a replica of St. Mark's Square, and seems to be in a constant state of festivity asartisans, glassblowers, mask-makers, portrait painters, and street vendors crowd the walkways. The Shoppes house about 70 stores, boutiques, galleries, and restaurants. Notable shops include Mikimoto, for exquisite cultured pearls, and Movado, for handcrafted and elegant Swiss watches.

Crazy Shirts Forever, Miracle Mile

MIRACLE MILE AT PLANET HOLLYWOOD RESORT & CASINO

Desert Passage, the Aladdin's North African-style complex of bazaars and restaurants has been replaced by a modern, streamlined shopping and entertainment mall more in tune with the ethos of the hotel's new owners, Planet Hollywood Resort & Casino. Stores at the Miracle Mile center *(see p46)* include Ben Sherman, Urban Outfitters, Quiksilver, and Benetton.

WYNN ESPLANADE

At one of the city's most luxurious resorts *(see pp60–61)*, this exclusive shopping promenade houses in excess of two dozen designer boutiques and jewelry stores in an exquisite retail space. Famous names include Dior, Graff, Louis Vuitton, and Manolo Blahnik. Personal shoppers are available for guests.

VIA BELLAGIO

Another exclusive group of shops is found at the Bellagio hotel. Fashion and jewelry collections are on display from acclaimed designers such as Giorgio Armani, Prada, Chanel, Tiffany & Co., Gucci, and Hermès.
The elegant setting is bathed in filtered sunlight from an ornate glass ceiling.

OTHER HOTEL SHOPS

In addition to the larger shopping promenades, such as Forum Shops at Caesars and Grand Canal Shoppes, some hotels offer smaller clusters of stores. The **Masquerade Village Shops** at the Rio invite visitors to stroll down replicas of 200-year-old Tuscan streets and browse among its two-dozen retail stores. Among the more interesting outlets are Fortune Cookie for Asian gifts, and Timepieces who offer a selection of high-end watches and accessories.

DIRECTORY

THE MALLS

Boulevard Mall
3528 S Maryland Pkwy.
Map 4 E3. *Open 10am–9pm Mon–Sat; 11am–6pm Sun.*
Tel (702) 732-8949.

Fashion Show Mall
3200 Las Vegas Blvd S.
Map 3 C2. *Open 10am–9pm Mon–Sat; 11am–7pm Sun.*
Tel (702) 369-0704.

HOTEL SHOPPING

Forum Shops at Caesars
Open 10am–11pm Sun–Thu; 10am–midnight Fri–Sat.
Tel (702) 893-4800.

Grand Canal Shoppes
Open 10am–11pm Sun–Thu; 10am–midnight Fri–Sat.
Tel (702) 414-4525.

Le Boulevard
Open 10am–11pm Sun–Thu; 10am–midnight Fri–Sat.
Tel (702) 946-7000.

Masquerade Village Shop
Open 11am–times vary, daily.
Tel (702) 252-7777.

Miracle Mile
Open 10am–11pm Sun–Thu; 10am–midnight Fri–Sat.
Tel (702) 866-0710.

Tower Shops
Open 10am–11pm Sun–Thu; 10am–midnight Fri–Sat.
Tel (702) 380-7777.

Via Bellagio
Open 10am–midnight daily.
Tel (702) 693-7111.

Wynn Esplanade
Open 10am–11pm Sun–Thu; 10am–midnight Fri–Sat.
Tel (702) 770-7000.

Le Boulevard at the Paris hotel is a Francophile's joy and is home to authentic-style Parisian stores selling French goods including children's clothes, cheese, and chocolate.
The **Tower Shops** at the Stratosphere is located one flight up the escalator that leads to the 1,200-ft (366-m) high tower. The 50-plus shops are arranged along a setting inspired by the street scenes of Paris, Hong Kong, and New York.

Factory Outlets and Bargain Shopping Centers

Although Las Vegas is considered to be an expensive destination for shopping, bargain hunters can usually find a range of high-end products at affordable prices in the off-the-Strip outlet malls. Las Vegas Premium Outlets is the largest, and is near Downtown just off I-15. South of the Strip is the Las Vegas Outlet Center and in Primm, on the California border, is Fashion Outlets of Las Vegas. All three are home to a wide variety of stores, including several designer outlets, with claims of savings of 20 to 70 percent below "regular" retail prices. Shoppers can also find great deals at any of the city's pawn shops and stand-alone discount stores, as well as at its massive flea market and swap meet.

Entrance to the massive Las Vegas Outlet Center

LAS VEGAS OUTLET CENTER

Located a few miles south of the Strip, the Las Vegas Outlet Center has more than 130 stores. In addition to the many shops, the mall has a carousel for kids and two food courts. Nearly half the outlet stores, including Jockey, Van Heusen, and Levi's sell men's, women's, and children's clothing, and there are more than 10 jewelry and accessory shops. The complex also has a wide selection of stores for toys, sportswear, home furnishings, beauty products, and shoes – all offering discounts that can sometimes even go up to 75 percent.

Electronics enthusiasts should head to Bose for a selection of turbo-powered speaker systems. One of the most interesting stops here is Flashback. This small shop is crammed with vintage collectibles and replicas, including juke boxes and neon signs.

FASHION OUTLETS OF LAS VEGAS

It's hard to imagine driving to the California border to try on shoes, but Las Vegans are not shy of the 35-minute trip.

The 100-plus outlet stores are a bargain basement for the frugal who nevertheless have an eye for the fineries in life. The impressive list of shops includes designer stores and famous brands such as Gap, Old Navy, Polo Ralph Lauren, Nine West, Kate Spade, Williams-Sonoma Marketplace, St. John Company Store, Tommy Hilfiger, Burberry's, Versace Company Store, Nautica, Guess, Bally, Banana Republic, Coach, and Last Call by Neiman Marcus, to name a few.

Tranquil fountains and live musicians create a soothing and relaxing atmosphere. The mall has also been known to attract many pregnant and nursing celebrities shopping for maternity clothes.

The Gamezone arcade serves a dual purpose as it not only entertains bored kids, but also keeps them occupied for hours while their parents shop.

LAS VEGAS PREMIUM OUTLETS

The largest outlet center, Las Vegas Premium Outlets, is only five minutes from the Strip and Downtown. Situated in a pleasant outdoor setting, it has 150 designer and name-brand stores. Some of the names found here include Dolce & Gabbana, Lacoste, M Missoni, Michael Kors, Ferragamo, and Tommy Hilfiger. There are also unusual stores not often found in an outlet mall, such as True Religion, Ed Hardy, Zoo York and Ann Taylor.

With so much to choose from, to make it easier many shops are grouped by style and demographic.

Designer shops line the walkways of Fashion Outlets of Las Vegas

DISCOUNT STORES

The nation's major discount stores are well represented in Las Vegas. **Kmart, Target**, and **Wal-Mart** sell virtually anything and everything that can be used at home, work, or school. From clothing and appliances to hardware and cleaning supplies, and from jewelry and computers to DVD players, these stores have it all, usually at prices 10 to 45 percent lower than other stores. Las Vegas also has two chains of membership discount stores – **Costco** and **Sam's Club**. The membership cost is about $50 a year, but the prices of goods – including grocery, bakery, and meat products – are significantly less than traditional stores. Note that products in these membership stores are often bundled. For instance, a bottle of ketchup might cost less, but you will have to buy three of them to get the savings.

Colorful exterior of Fantastic Indoor Swap Meet, Las Vegas

PAWN SHOPS

There are plenty of pawn shops in Vegas, perhaps the result of so many casinos catering to gamblers who frequently turn in their jewelry,

Pawn shop

watches, cameras, and other valuable items for quick cash. A sharp eye for bargains can often find an inexpensively-priced VCR, guitar, or a computer among other things. The most well-stocked pawn shops can usually be found downtown, typically on the streets just off Fremont Street. These shops often have a nice mix of diamonds, silverware, watches, tools, and musical instruments. You are also likely to find electronic equipment such as amplifiers, TVs, VCRs, camcorders, and other products. Some even have 24-hour windows for late-night transactions.

The largest operation in town is a chain of pawn shops called **Super Pawn**.

These have the usual range of goods, though the stores are usually brighter and not as cramped as some of the downtown pawn shops.

SWAP MEETS

One of the best places for bargains are swap meets, which are the American equivalent of the European flea markets. **Fantastic Indoor Swap Meet** is the biggest meet in Las Vegas and is held from Friday to Sunday every week. The gigantic indoor mall has about 600 vendors who sell everything, including clothing, electronic equipment, vintage kitchen appliances, tire chains, home-baked bread, power tools, and other knick-knacks. Although there's little to no "trading" taking place, the prices are the lowest.

DIRECTORY

Specialty Shops

Beyond traditional shopping venues, Las Vegas holds
its own on more eclectic shopping options as well. As
one might expect, the city has an extensive selection of
stores selling gambling supplies and memorabilia,
including books and computer systems for learning
casino games. An antiques guild, made up of a small
cluster of shops, offers a variety of treasures that range
from Victorian jewelry to German clocks, while outlets
in the Chinatown Plaza shopping district specialize in
Chinese, Korean, and Japanese art, crafts, and curios.
Las Vegas also has several stores that sell Southwestern
and Native American collectibles and souvenirs.

Shelves packed with gambling supplies, Gamblers General Store

GAMBLING GEAR

A shopping paradise for both
gamblers and memorabilia
hunters, **Gamblers General
Store** houses one of the most
comprehensive collections of
gambling supplies in the city.
These include full-size crap,
blackjack, and roulette tables,
folding poker tables, playing
cards, dice sets, coin changers,
and much more. The store
also stocks every type of gambling paraphernalia imaginable, including hundreds of
books and videos on gam-
bling, customized poker
chips, croupier sticks, green-
felt layouts for every type of
casino game, and even dice-
inlaid toilet seats. A modest
collection of vintage slot
machines is also available.

For the serious enthusiasts
and collectors a visit to **Spinetti's Home Gaming Supplies**
is essential. Here they offer a
comprehensive range of
home gambling supplies and
specialize in customized
poker chips and collectible
gaming chips, cards, and dice
from casinos that are currently
open as well as from estab-

lishments that are now part of
Las Vegas history. Spinetti's
has the world's largest selection of chips with thousands
to choose from. Any purchase
can be packed and shipped
worldwide within 24 hours.

The **Gambler's Book Shop**
has an enormous collection of
books on racing, poker, blackjack, casino games, gin rummy,
slot machines, and jai alai to
name a few. The store also
offers related magazines, special workbooks for tracking
teams and recording outcomes,
and an admirable selection of
archival material. There's even
a section of books on com-
pulsive gambling and the
ways to combat and over-
come the addiction.

ANTIQUES

Las Vegas's biggest selection
of antiques is available at
Antique Square, a complex
made up of a dozen assorted
shops. The owners of the
square, **Nicolas & Osvaldo**,
have several rooms lined with
cabinets to show off their collection of antiques. A mix of
periods, styles, and tastes are

reflected in the crystal, china,
decorative teacups, clocks,
chandeliers, and sterling silver
tea sets, spoons, coasters, salt
and pepper shakers, and more.

Antonio Nicholas Antiques
has an unending selection of
swords, knives, and daggers,
as well as many exquisite jade
and ivory pieces, while **Sugarplums etc.** is a treasure chest
of collectibles, and stocks fancy
crystal and china, porcelain
figurines, silverware, and perfume bottles. The shop is also
home to a perfume and scent-
bottle society with an international membership of 12,000.

Another charming shop,
Silver Horse, offers a large
collection of clocks, including
a genuine Calumet wall clock,
German-made and Tiffany
grandfather clocks, mantel
clocks, and black-iron clocks
from the 1930s. The store
also features a functioning,
one-chair barber shop.

GIFTS AND SOUVENIRS

Shopping for souvenirs and
gifts is a major activity in Las
Vegas. The **Funk House** has a
great range of 1950s, 1960s,
and 1970s modern antiques,
such as glassware, lamps,
ceramics, jewelry, toys, and
quirky items like an old Coca-
Cola vending machine and a
vintage airplane pedal car.

Those looking for ethnic
curios should head for
West of Santa Fe (see p141),
which is billed as "one of the
world's premier sources of
Native American crafted
goods." These crafts blend
contemporary flair with
traditional techniques.

The interior of The Attic, strewn with
clothing from the 1940s to 1970s

A must for those who like all things mystical is the **Psychic Eye Book Shop**. As well as a good selection of books on the subject, this shops sells everything from tarot cards, oils, meditation aids, candles, cauldrons, and more. Also available are on-site psychic consultations, although readings can be conducted over the telephone, too.

The Attic features two floors of men's and women's clothes, shoes, and accessories from the 1940s to the 1970s, such as a white go-go dress with daisies and a 1960s bandstand tuxedo with satin piping.

Bonanza Gift Shop claims to be the world's largest gift shop with products that range from a cheap pair of slot machine earings to luxury sets of poker chips.

ELECTRONICS OUTLETS

With more than two dozen outlets in the Las Vegas area, **Radio Shack** provides cell phones, tape recorders, communications gear, TV and cable equipment, computer accessories, and much more. High-definition TVs and home theaters, DVDs, and CD players are

Oriental cuisine and merchandize at Chinatown Plaza

the specialty of stores such as **Circuit City** and **Best Buy**. The prices at these shops are usually quite competitive.

ARTS AND CRAFTS

West of Santa Fe in the Forum Shops at Caesars Palace carries a variety of quality Southwestern goods, including jewelry, clothing, Native American arts and crafts, pottery, and Old West collectibles. Many of the items are made by well-known Indian artisans. A variety of Kachina dolls representing the spirit world are stocked, several of which are in the $390 to $1,500 price range.

For a selection of Asian

Sign of Bonanza Gift Shop

goods, consider **Chinatown Plaza**. Built in the mid-1990s, this is the city's first shopping center, which was designed specifically for Asian tenants. Merchants here offer jade, gold, and ivory jewelry, exotic herbs and medicines, handcrafted furniture, and Chinese literature, music, and arts. There's also a market for live seafood, including fish and crab, fresh vegetables, and an excellent assortment of condiments, spices, and sauces.

Antiquities International is a fabulous source of antiques and collectibles. The store is centrally located on The Strip among the Forum Shops at Caesars Palace. The place to pick up a Las Vegan keepsake such as a neon sign or an autographed guitar.

DIRECTORY

GAMBLING GEAR

Gambler's Book Shop
1550 E Tropicana. **Map** 3 C4. **Tel** (702) 382-7555.

Gamblers General Store
800 S Main St. **Map** 2 D4. **Tel** (702) 382-9903.

Spinetti's
810 S Commerce St. **Map** 4 D1. **Tel** (702) 362-8767.

ANTIQUES

Antique Square
2014-2026 E Charleston Blvd. **Map** 2 E4.

Antonio Nicholas
Antique Square.
Tel (702) 385-7772.

Nicolas & Osvaldo
Antique Square.
Tel (702) 386-0238.

Silver Horse Antiques
1651 E Charleston Blvd.
Map 2 E4.
Tel (702) 385-2700.

Sugarplums
Antique Square.
Tel (702) 385-6059.

GIFTS AND SOUVENIRS

Bonanza Gift Shop
2440 Las Vegas Blvd S.
Map 4 D1.
Tel (702) 385-7359.

Funk House
1228 S Casino Center

Blvd. **Map** 2 D5.
Tel (702) 678-6278.

Psychic Eye Book Shop
6848 W Charleston Blvd.
Map 1 A4.
Tel (702) 255-4477.

The Attic
1018 S Main St.
Map 2 D4.
Tel (702) 388-4088.

Turquoise Chief
1616 Las Vegas Blvd S.
Map 2 D5.
Tel (702) 383-6069.

ELECTRONICS OUTLETS

Best Buy
www.bestbuy.com

Circuit City
www.circuitcity.com

Radio Shack
www.radioshack.com

ARTS & CRAFTS

Antiquities International
Forum Shops at Caesars,
3570 Las Vegas Blvd S.
Map 3 C3.
Tel (702) 792-2274.

Chinatown Plaza
4255 Spring Mountain Rd.
Map 3 A2.
Tel (702) 221-8448.

West of Santa Fe
Forum Shops, 3570 Las Vegas Blvd S. **Map** 3 C3.
Tel (702) 737-1933

ENTERTAINMENT IN LAS VEGAS

Las Vegas makes a good claim to be the entertainment capital of the world. From free spectaculars such as the *Sirens of TI* show at Treasure Island – TI to lavishly produced theatrical acts, there is a full range of nightlife available. Sinatra and Elvis may be gone but headliners still appear regularly in the city's showrooms, offering a chance to see a star in a surprisingly intimate setting. Most of the

Promotional poster for Bally's *Jubilee!*

major venues can be found in hotels along the Strip and downtown, ranging from small lounges to 1,000-seater showrooms. While visitors can still enjoy the kitsch appeal of a Vegas burlesque show with its scantily clad showgirls, high-quality productions featuring the latest in lighting and special effects are a big draw. Comedy and magic are also widely available, often for free or the price of a cocktail.

INFORMATION

There is no shortage of information on the entertainment scene in Las Vegas. A variety of free publications list all the major productions as well as the latest big acts in town. Magazines and free newspapers such as *Las Vegas Magazine, What's On*, and *Las Vegas Weekly* can usually be picked up at all the major hotels. Even Las Vegas taxis carry free guides to the city, with information on shows and attractions.

The **Las Vegas Convention and Visitors Authority** provides up-to-date showguides, and their website has current listings and reviews on the city's ongoing and upcoming shows and events.

What's On magazine

BUYING TICKETS

The easiest way to book tickets to the major shows or visiting headliners is to call the venue or hotel directly on their toll-free number. Prices can vary, and range from $30 to $200 per ticket. The ticket may also include drinks, a free program, tips, and even dinner. Check in advance if there is preassigned seating, because if there isn't, you can improve your chances of getting a good seat by tipping the maître d'.

Reservations should always be made in advance, but the length of time varies greatly according to the show's popularity. To see the Cirque du Soleil's *(see p144)* stunning *Mystère* at Treasure Island you can book up to 90

Cirque du Soleil act, *Mystère* at Treasure Island – TI *(see pp56-7)*

days in advance, while space for most other shows can be reserved up to 14 days ahead. It is also possible to get tickets on the night of the performance by lining up at the box office an hour or so before showtime. This is especially true at times when there are no major conventions in town and it is not a public holiday. Weekdays are usually a better bet than weekends, although most shows have one or two days off during the week.

For sports events, such as world championship boxing, or the big rock and pop concerts, frequently held at the impressive 16,800-seater MGM Grand Garden, tickets can also be purchased through **Travelocity on Location, Ticketmaster**, and other agency outlets.

Discounts for children and senior citizens may be available from the box office. Free tickets may be offered to the hotel casino's big winners.

Blue Man Group at the Venetian

Beautifully costumed showgirls at the *Jubilee!* show, Bally's *(see p47)*

DISCOUNT TICKETS

The first place to look is in the visitor magazines provided in most hotel rooms. Discount tickets or two-for-one coupons are available for many mid-priced shows, but rarely for top-flight productions. You can also find coupons for discounts in "fun books," which are distributed by casinos and tourist centers along the Strip.

Slot club members receive player rewards that can be discounts on shows, dining, and other events. Regular casino gamblers can ask a host or supervisor to track their play, and by gambling long enough can qualify for discounts or complimentary passes for shows and meals.

The half-price ticket outlet **Tix4Tonight** has one kiosk in the Hawaiian Marketplace, two more on the Strip and one downtown. **Half Price**

Shows sells half price tickets up to four days in advance. **GoldstarEvents** sell discounted tickets through the Internet. Many shows offer discounts to Nevada residents.

FREE EVENTS

In addition to the numerous ticketed events, Las Vegas offers several free performances and shows as well.

Some of the outdoor events include the amazing special effects of the *Sirens of TI* show, the massive erupting volcano at Mirage, the beautifully choreographed dancing fountains at Bellagio, and the singing gondoliers as they pole their gondolas along the Grand Canal at Venetian.

Indoor attractions include the MGM Grand Lion Habitat and an interesting tour of M&Ms World, which also showcases a 3-D movie.

DIRECTORY

Americans with Disabilities Act (ADA)
www.clarkcountylegal.com

Las Vegas Convention and Visitors Authority
3150 Paradise Rd. **Map** 4 D4.
Tel (702) 892-0711.
www.visitlasvegas.com

GoldstarEvents
www.GoldstarEvents.com/events

Halfprice Shows
www.halfpriceshows.com

Ticketmaster
www.ticketmaster.com

Tix4Tonight
www.tix4tonight.com

Travelocity on Location
Tel (702) 597-5970.

FACILITIES FOR DISABLED VISITORS

Las Vegas is perhaps the world's most accessible city for people with disabilities. Most showrooms, theaters, and concert halls are equipped with ramps for wheelchairs and usually provide special access elevators and entrances as well. Some cultural events hire sign language interpreters for the hearing impaired. Entertainment venues in hotels also offer special facilities for the disabled. For any particular needs, contact the hotels' **Americans with Disabilities Act** – ADA – coordinator. Every major hotel has one. For further information see p177.

The battle rages on in the dramatic *Sirens of TI* show at Treasure Island – TI *(see pp56–7)*

Casino Shows

There has never been anything subtle about Las Vegas's casino shows. Since their opening day, each resort has tried to create and provide its customers with the most creative and imaginative entertainment possible. Today, much of the city's nightlife revolves around these casinos and their lavish stage productions, topless revues, celebrity concerts, and comedy clubs. On any given night, visitors can choose from nearly 70 different shows, ranging from star-studded spectaculars such as Barry Manilow's *Music and Passion* at the Las Vegas Hilton, awesome extravaganzas such as *Mystère* and *Zumanity* by Cirque du Soleil, spell-binding magic shows by Lance Burton at Monte Carlo, hilarious comedy acts, and musical tributes to some of the greatest singers of all time.

Performers dressed in creative and colorful costumes, *Mystère*

CIRQUE DU SOLEIL SHOWS

This acclaimed French Canadian production company has virtually taken over Las Vegas with five shows currently playing.

KÀ at MGM Grand is one of the most expensive live shows in town and uses a perfect blend of signature Cirque music, fantastic acrobatics, overall aesthetics, and the language of cinema to narrate a mesmerizing story.

The longest-running Cirque show in Las Vegas is **Mystère** at Treasure Island – TI. Like other Cirque productions, *Mystère* is an enchanting circus act with a mystical thread running through it. It takes audiences on a metaphorical journey that starts at the beginning of time, symbolized by a powerful opening of Japanese taiko drums supposedly sent

from the heavens, and features a riveting mix of music, dance, and stunning athleticism.

It's hard to imagine Cirque du Soleil out-doing itself, but its production of **"O"** at the Bellagio comes close. This spectacular show features swimmers, trapeze artists, and contortionists who navigate an unbelievable stage that transforms from the Arctic Ocean to an African watering hole almost instantaneously. The use of water – as a character and not a theatrical prop – gives fluidity to a show that is like a parade of haunting images with a slightly Fellini-esque quality, and has the feel of climbing inside a painting by surrealist Salvador Dali. Another popular Cirque production is **Zumanity** at New York-New York. The show raised eyebrows when it debuted in 2004 because of its sexual overtones – traditional

Cirque aesthetics are sexually charged to create a European-style cabaret theater, often more crude than bawdy. Still, the host-in-drag Joey Arias and the male and female performers who indulge in comic relief produce some memorable moments.

The latest Cirque show, **LOVE**, is at the Mirage and features Beatles' music, acrobats, and dancers.

MUSICALS AND STAGE SHOWS

Traditional musical variety shows are still popular in Las Vegas, even in the face of the more modern Cirque du Soleil productions. **Jersey Boys** at the Palazzo *(see p56)* is the Las Vegas production of this Broadway smash hit, which won the 2006 Tony Award for Best Musical. The show is a celebration of the music of the sensational 1960s pop group the Four Seasons and the lives of its members, Frankie Valli, Tommy DeVito, Nick Massi, and Bob Gaudio and their rise to stardom. There are electrifying performances of all their greatest hits, such as "Sherry," "Big Girls Don't Cry," "Can't Take My Eyes Off You," "Dawn," "My Eyes Adored You," and many more. The show is staged in the purpose-built Jersey Boys Theatre, which is bedecked with authentic memorabilia of the period on loan from the Rock and Roll Hall of Fame.

Performers in Cirque du Soleil's "O"

Magnificent headdress and costume of a showgirl in *Jubilee!*, **Bally's**

A long-running show, **Jubilee!** at Bally's *(see p47)* is a spectacular musical extravaganza with a huge cast of showgirls. The show's dazzling stage effects range from Samson destroying the Temple of the Philistines to the sinking of the *Titanic* and a World War I aerial dogfight. The 16-minute opening number, based on Broadway composer Jerry Herman's *Hundreds of Girls*, sets the pace with several dancers and singers in beaded costumes and feathered headdresses.

At Wynn Las Vegas *(see p60–61)*, **Le Rêve** is an abstract aquatic masterpiece featuring fabulous costumes, amazing gymnastics, and comedy. It is one of the most popular shows on the Strip and is staged in a magnificent domed aqua theater-in-the-round, so all the seats have great views and no one is more than 40 feet (12 m) from the action. The show's central feature is a circular pond containing nearly a million gallons (4 million liters) of water. The 85 members of the cast perform aerial acrobatics, acts of artistic athleticism, and provocative choreography.

REVUES

Presented on a smaller scale, the revues on the Las Vegas Strip are no less entertaining than the larger musical extravaganzas. The **American Superstars**, which debuted at the Stratosphere in 1996,

continues to enthrall the audience with amazing musical impersonations of stars such as Michael Jackson, Carrie Underwood, Elvis, Tim McGraw, and Britney Spears. Backed by a live band, the singers are less concerned about mimicking their superstar alter egos than they are with delivering stirring performances.

Although some may find it too overly-sexual for their tastes, **Peepshow** at Planet Hollywood *(see p46)* offers a sophisticated and entertaining revue. It stars Holly Madison, from TV reality shows *The Girls Next Door* and *Dancing with the Stars*, and the Broadway veteran Shoshana Bean. Peepshow is a sexy revue based on nursery rhymes with a naughty twist. It is a mix of humor, a contemporary soundtrack, and typical Las Vegas glamor, incorporating modern burlesque-style dancing and tantalizing striptease performed by a cast of gorgeous dancers.

Ignite, at the Greek Isles Hotel and Casino, is a stunning and dramatic fire and illusion show featuring fire performer Antonio Restivo. The cast perform fire stunts, illusions, and dancing. It is described as a fire fantasy in the world of pyrotechnics.

Sculpture for the *Crazy Girls* **show**

ADULT ENTERTAINMENT

A few casinos in Las Vegas host topless shows, which are tastefully done and appropriate for mixed audiences. The longest running topless revue is **Crazy Girls** that has been playing at the Riviera since 1987. The show features eight showgirls who dance to canned music and act out silly skits on a small stage. Excellent solo numbers, rendered by an accomplished singer and an outrageous male comic MC, keep the show from lapsing into banality.

The most artistic of the adult shows is **MGM Grand's Crazy Horse Paris**. The show is an import from the Crazy Horse cabaret show in Paris and stars actual French dancers. Special lighting and stage effects create dramatic visual impressions and enhance the natural beauty of the dancers.

Opened in 2004, **Bite**, at the Stratosphere Casino Hotel, is a show not for the faint-hearted. An erotic vampire adventure with a simple story line of sin, sex, and seduction, it features an array of nimble, topless dancers, the Erotic Angels of Rock, swinging their stuff to a selection of classic rock songs from the 1970s to the 1990s. Members of the audience are chosen to join in with the fun.

Two characters from the spectacular *Le Rêve*, **Wynn Las Vegas**

Glittering sign of the Lance Burton Theater at Monte Carlo

VARIETY SHOWS

Though magicians have become commonplace in Las Vegas, **Lance Burton** at Monte Carlo remains the city's premier illusionist. Presented in an entertaining blend of intimate cabaret and high-powered Vegas extravaganza, the show consists of about 15 illusions, some of them quite majestic in size. These include his levitating act and the disappearing Corvette stunt. Lance is backed on stage by a group of dancers and comic juggler Michael Goudeau.

Penn and Teller at the Rio offer a different style of magic, one that uses intelligent, often dark humor, to punctuate their illusions.

Impersonators and impressionists have always had a spot on the Las Vegas stage. **Gordie Brown** performs at the Golden Nugget. His dead-on impressions capture the known quirks of popular entertainers. At the Monte Carlo is **Frank Caliendo** and his show, which mixes impressions, comedy, live music, video sketches, and more.

Legends in Concert at Harrah's features singing impersonations of stars such as Elton John, Rod Stewart, Elvis Presley, and Janet Jackson, to name a few. This is an energetic, live show that often draws the audience into the spotlight.

The **Tribute to Frank, Sammy, Joey & Dean** plays at the Plaza. The show has a laid-back, fun atmosphere, much like the original Rat Pack generated years ago at the Sands.

Comedians have also entered Las Vegas's main rooms with shows of their own. Some of the comics who have risen to headliner status include **Rita Rudner** at Harrah's, and **George Wallace** at Flamingo.

Stand-up comics and comedy clubs are also doing roaring business in the city. The country's best comedians, along with up-and-coming talent, appear nightly at Las Vegas's top comedy clubs – **The Improv** at Harrah's, **Comedy Stop** at Sahara, and **Riviera Comedy Club** at the Riviera.

Clint Holmes show at Harrah's

Blue Man Group is a popular show at The Venetian, which promotes a party atmosphere. It is unique, funny, and wildly innovative, as three bald blue men take the audience on a multi-sensory journey, featuring theater, percussion, vaudeville and music.

Boarding advertising a variety show at New York-New York

HEADLINER SHOWS

Most headline entertainers are content to play Vegas for a weekend or two, but a handful have been able to establish an entire production around their unique talents. Barry Manilow stars in a full-blown spectacular, **Manilow: Music and Passion**, at the Las Vegas Hilton. The show features all the hi-tech effects of modern music combined with the classic appeal of Las Vegas veterans, such as Frank Sinatra, Elvis Presley, Sammy Davis, and Dean Martin who were so adored by their Vegas audiences. In tribute to Manilow is the biggest hand-painted mural in the city, which illuminates from the Hilton's south-facing main tower.

BROADWAY SHOWS

Broadway shows always face mixed reactions in Las Vegas, evidenced by the limited runs of shows like *Chicago*, *Rent*, and *Notre Dame de Paris*. Yet, a few will catch the fancy of audiences.

Phantom – The Las Vegas Spectacular, at the Venetian, is an all-new staging of the world's most recognized theater masterpiece by Sir Andrew Lloyd Webber. **Lion King**, at Mandalay Bay Resort and Casino, is the Disney Theatrical Group's first long term foray into Vegas. It is virtually identical to the hugely successful Broadway production and unshortened; a rare thing for Vegas.

Reminiscent of the floor shows of the past is **Tony 'n' Tina's Wedding** at the Planet Hollywood Resort & Casino, a rare dinner show that tells the story of two Italian families in New York who clash over their children's wedding. A charming aspect of the show is when cast members, who never break character, circulate the room and mingle with guests. Even though the show has been off-Broadway and touring the country since 1985, it has been a hit in Las Vegas since its debut in 2002.

DIRECTORY

CIRQUE DU SOLEIL SHOWS

KÀ
MGM Grand.
Map 3 C4.
7pm and 9:30pm Tue–Sat.
Tel *(702) 891-7777.*

Love
The Mirage.
Map 3 B3.
7pm and 9:30pm Thu–Mon.
Tel *(702) 792-7777.*

Mystère
Treasure Island – TI.
Map 3 C2.
7pm and 9:30pm Sat–Wed.
Tel *(702) 894-7722.*

"O"
Bellagio.
Map 3 C3.
7.30pm and 10:30pm Wed–Sun.
Tel *(702) 693-7722.*

Zumanity
New York-New York.
Map 3 C4.
7:30pm and 10:30pm Tue–Wed, Fri–Sun.
Tel *(702) 740-6815.*

MUSICALS & STAGE SHOWS

Jubilee!
Bally's.
Map 3 C3.
7:30pm and 10:30pm Sat–Thu. Guests below 18 will not be admitted.
Tel *(702) 967-4567.*

Le Rêve
Wynn Las Vegas.
Map 3 C2.
7pm and 9:30pm Thu–Mon.
Tel *(888) 320-7100.*

REVUES

American Superstars
Stratosphere.
Map 4 D1.
6:30pm and 8:30pm Wed, Fri, & Sat; 7pm Sun–Tue.
Tel *(702) 380-7711.*

Ignite
Greek Isle's Hotel.
Map 4 D2.
8pm Tue, 10:30pm Wed–Sat.
Tel *(702) 877-FIRE.*

ADULT ENTERTAINMENT

Bite
Stratosphere.
Map 4 D1.
10:30pm Fri–Wed. Guests below 18 will not be admitted.
Tel *(702) 380-7711.*

Crazy Girls
Riviera.
Map 3 C2.
9:30pm Wed–Mon. Guests below 18 will not be admitted.
Tel *(702) 794-9433.*

MGM Grand's Crazy Horse Paris
MGM Grand.
Map 3 C4.
8pm and 10:30pm Wed–Mon. Guests below 18 will not be admitted.
Tel *(702) 891-7777.*

Peepshow
Planet Hollywood Resort & Casino.
Map 3 C4.
9pm Mon–Thu and Sun, 8pm and 10:30pm Fri and Sat. **Tel** *(702) 785-5000.*

VARIETY SHOWS

Blue Man Group
Venetian.
Map 3 C3.
7pm and 10pm daily.
Tel *(800) 258-3626.*

Comedy Stop
Sahara.
Map 4 D4.
9pm daily. **Tel** *(702) 737-2111.*

Frank Caliendo
Monte Carlo.
Map 3 C4.
9:30pm Mon, Tue, Fri, Sat. **Tel** *(702) 730-7160.*

George Wallace
Flamingo Las Vegas.
Map 3 C3.
10pm Tue–Sat.
Tel *(702) 733-3333.*

Gordie Brown
Golden Nugget.
Map 2 D3.
7:30pm Tue–Sat.
Tel *(866) 946-5336.*

The Improv
Harrah's.
Map 3 C3.
8:30pm and 10:30pm Tue–Sun.
Tel *(702) 369-5111.*

Lance Burton
Monte Carlo.
Map 3 C4.
7pm Tue–Sat.
Tel *(702) 730-7160.*

Legends in Concert
Harrah's.
Map 3 C3.
7:30pm and 10pm Fri & Sat; 7:30pm Mon–Thu. **Tel** *(702) 369-5222.*

Magic's A Drag
Planet Hollywood Resort & Casino. **Map** 3 C4.
7pm Mon–Sat. **Tel** *(702) 836-0836.*

Penn and Teller
Rio. **Map** 3 B3.
9pm Sat–Wed.
Tel *(702) 777-7776.*

Rita Rudner
Harrah's.
Map 3 C3.
8:30pm Mon, Wed, Sat.
Tel *(702) 369-5222.*

Riviera Comedy Club
Riviera.
Map 3 C2.
8:30pm and 10:30pm daily.
Tel *(702) 794-9433.*

Tribute to Frank, Sammy, Joey & Dean
The Plaza.
Map 2 D3.
7:30pm Mon–Sat.
Tel *(702) 386-2110.*

HEADLINER SHOWS

Bette Midler
Caesars Palace.
Map 3 B3.
7:30pm Tue–Wed, Fri–Sat.
Tel *(877) 723-8836.*

Barry Manilow
Las Vegas Hilton.
Map 4 D2.
8pm Wed–Sat.
Tel *(702) 732-5755.*

BROADWAY SHOWS

Jersey Boys
Palazzo
Map 3 C3.
7pm Thu, Fri, Sun and Mon, 6:30pm and 9:30pm Tue and Sat.
Tel *(702) 414-9000.*

The Lion King
Mandalay Bay
Map 3 C5.
8pm Mon–Thu, 4pm and 8pm Sat–Sun.
Tel *(702) 632-7777.*

Phantom Las Vegas
Venetian.
Map 3 C3.
7pm and 9:30pm Mon and Sat, 7pm Tue–Fri.
Tel *(702) 414-9000.*

Tony 'n' Tina's Wedding
Planet Hollywood Resort & Casino.
Map 3 B3.
7pm Mon–Sat.
Tel *(702) 785-5555.*

Music and Performing Arts Venues

Las Vegas's music venues have always been famous for their atmosphere, grandeur, and quality. Some of the most impressive concert halls and auditoriums can be found in the mega resorts located both on and off the Strip. Built on a majestic scale, these venues provide the perfect backdrop for performances by superstars such as Lionel Richie, Dolly Parton, Alanis Morissette, Tony Bennett, and Wayne Newton, to name a few.

Las Vegas also has a thriving theater, classical music, and dance community. The University of Nevada, Las Vegas's performing arts centers regularly host shows by the Nevada Ballet Theater, the Las Vegas Philharmonic, and several acclaimed classical artists.

Wind and Fire, the 7,000-seat theater has also showcased Broadway shows such as *Chicago* and *Rent*.

The most lavish concert hall in Las Vegas is the **Colosseum** at Caesars Palace. The auditorium's rich architecture is reminiscent of a European opera house, and it periodically hosts concerts.

Some of the Colosseum's regular headliners are singer Elton John and comedian Jerry Seinfeld.

House of Blues Mandalay Bay

Another terrific venue is the **House of Blues** *(see p151)* at Mandalay Bay. The nightclub books the best blues, jazz, and rock performers, who perform on a small floor surrounded by a tabled seating area and a balcony with theater seats. Among the top-notch stars who have played here are Bob Dylan, Taylor Dane, Etta James, Al Green, the Go-Gos, and Seal.

Popular rock 'n' roll venue, Joint, Hard Rock Hotel

POPULAR AND ROCK MUSIC CONCERTS

Arguably the best place to experience a rock concert is the **Joint** at the Hard Rock Hotel. The 4,000-seat hall has great acoustics and features table, balcony, and theater seating, as well as plenty of space for standing guests too. The most notable rock stars play here, including Alanis Morrisette and the Rolling Stones. A close second is the Pearl Concert Theater at The Palms, a 2,500-seat venue that attracts big names such as Gwen Stefani.

The **Garden Arena** at MGM Grand has the city's largest auditorium and can seat up to 17,000 people. Only the most renowned headliners are called to perform at the Arena. In the past, this list has included Eric Clapton and Rod Stewart.

Another spacious venue is the **Theatre for the Performing Arts** at Planet Hollywood Resort & Casino. In addition to hosting mainstream performers and groups such as Styx, Lionel Richie, and Earth,

Most of the hotels in Las Vegas have at least one showroom, though all are pretty much the same as each other. **The Pearl Showroom** is located at the Palms Casino Resort. This large showroom offers great views from all of its seats anywhere in the venue and there are three different seating arrangements. The stage can also be altered to suit a

Grand interior of the Colosseum concert auditorium, Caesars Palace

An actor in a production at UNLV's Performing Arts Center

performer's needs. Beyond the resorts, there is only one concert venue of note. The **Thomas & Mack Center** on the University of Nevada, Las Vegas (UNLV) campus, which also occasionally hosts music concerts and programs.

THEATER

Las Vegas has a flourishing theater arts community who stage their productions either on the UNLV campus, in public library auditoriums, or at schools throughout the city. UNLV's Performing Arts Center features the **Judy Bayley Theater**, a 500-seat theater that frequently

presents events such as the Best of the New York Stage Series that features prominent jazz, cabaret, and Broadway artists such as Kristin Chenoweth, Dianne Reeves, and Ramsey Lewis. Also on the UNLV campus, **Black Box Theater** is an intimate, 175-seat center used for theatrical events staged by university groups and departments.

There are numerous amateur theater groups in Las Vegas that hold classes and conduct workshops, as well as produce several theatrical plays each year.

The **Las Vegas Little Theater** presents a range of contemporary dramas, while the **Rainbow Company** features family-oriented productions from a company of 40 members between the ages of ten and 18. Recent classics have included *Cheaper by the Dozen*, *One to Grow On* and *A Year with Frog and Toad*.

Community centers that often host productions by local theatrical groups include the **Reed Whipple Cultural Center** located next to the downtown library, the **Clark County Library Theater** on Flamingo Road, the **Clark**

Clark County Amphitheater emblem

County **Amphitheater**, the **Summerlin Library Performing Arts Center**, and the **Charleston Heights Arts Center**.

CLASSICAL MUSIC AND BALLET

The primary site for operas, symphonies, and ballet productions in Las Vegas is the **Artemus Ham Concert Hall** on the UNLV campus. It is also the home of the Las Vegas Philharmonic orchestra and frequently presents shows by various touring companies. The 2,000-seat theater has a 500-seat balcony, class A stage, and movable orchestra towers. The university's highly celebrated annual cultural event, Charles Vanda Master Series, takes place here and features some of the biggest names in classical music and dance. Artists such as Leontyne Price and Itshak Perlman have visited Las Vegas as part of the series, as have groups such as the Vienna Chamber Orchestra and Moscow Grigorovich Ballet. Local performing arts groups such as the Las Vegas Civic Ballet and the Nevada Ballet Theater also stage shows here.

DIRECTORY

Nightclubs, Lounges, & Bars

No city in the world has more to offer in the form of after-dark excitement than Las Vegas. From hip hotel nightclubs to punk discos and from flashy bars to retro dance clubs – it's all here, basking in neon, blinking until dawn. For decades the city's nightlife revolved around the hotel casinos, but the nightclub scene is no longer the exclusive province of the gaming resorts. As the city has grown, so has the number of nightclubs, sports bars, cowboy saloons, and other after-dark haunts. Among the plethora of new nightlife, Las Vegas has spawned a new genre of pub, the ultra lounge. These upscale bars are often chic, exclusive, and on top of everyone's "A" list.

Packed dance floor at Studio 54, MGM Grand

HOTEL NIGHTCLUBS

Tryst *(see p61)* at Wynn Las Vegas is a popular hot spot for the nocturnal set, featuring an open-air dance floor and 90-ft (28-m) high waterfall.

Moon, an exclusive penthouse nightclub atop The Palms, offers sweeping views of the Strip – and the stars above. The club's floor is crafted from glass tiles that change color. Floor-to-ceiling windows are flanked by glass bead curtains featuring moving projections. The main feature, however, is located overhead – a massive retractable roof.

Pure at Caesars Palace is a three-level mega-club owned by, among others, Andre Agassi, Steffi Graf, and Céline Dion. It attracts some of the Strip's most stylish crowds with its VIP service. Opulent, oversized beds ring the main

TRYST
the nightclub at wynn

Wynn Las Vegas'
popular nightclub

dance floor, while a huge outdoor terrace provides great views.

A magnet for visiting celebrities, **Studio 54** in MGM Grand is a spectacular two-level nightclub with four bars, five dance floors, and two VIP lounges. While it preserves its roots in disco, Studio 54 is a cutting-edge club that serves up the hottest mix of hip-hop, top 40, and deep house music. Another club that has caught the attention of the Hollywood crowd is **The Bank** at Bellagio. Located above the casino floor, The Bank manages to retain its stylish elegance while churning out an electrifying mix of techno and hip-hop music. For a slightly more mature clubbing experience, **Drai's** at Bill's Gamblin' Hall and Saloon has rooms that flow into one another through French doors and twisting hallways. On the club's two dance floors the party goes on well after sunrise.

Body English at Hard Rock Hotel & Casino is one of the most fashionable and stylish nightclubs in town, with mirrored walls, Baccarat crystal chandeliers, and minimalist black walls. The crowded dance floor is located below a mezzanine level that is lined with leather booths. The club also has a VIP seating area.

STAND-ALONE NIGHTCLUBS

Las Vegas is home to a couple of highly popular, non-resort nightclubs with a number of different rooms to dance away the night in. Located at Town Square, **Blue Martini** is a restaurant, bar and nightclub, all rolled neatly into one elegant package. It's the place in town to sip a martini and watch one of the live bands that perform nightly.

Located next to the Fremont Street Experience, is **Downtown Cocktail Room**, a sophisticated and swanky gathering place. The cleverly disguised door is marked only by a tiny Downtown sign and the speakeasy atmosphere is part of the appeal. There are DJs every night.

ULTRA LOUNGES

Most of the ultra lounges in the city have a private club atmosphere with plush furnishings and frequent live entertainment. One of the most exclusive is the **ghostbar** at the Palms. Located on the hotel's 55th floor, the bar offers stunning views of the Strip. Also at the Palms, situated at the top of the Fantasy Tower, is the iconic **Playboy Club**, the first to open in more than 25 years.

Waterfalls, giant Buddha statues, and an artificial sandy

Neon lighting and futuristic
setting at ghostbar, Palms Hotel

Sports fans watch the screens at Bally's lounge sports book

beach are the major features of Asian-themed club **TAO** at The Venetian *(see p20–21)*. On Saturday nights the beach is transformed into an exotic nightspot, complete with a light show and floating Chinese lanterns in the pool. Enjoy magnificent views from the terrace.

Blush at Wynn Las Vegas is an elegant place to enjoy music, a cocktail and conversation. It has a lit, onyx dance floor and 300 crème lantern ceiling sculptures that change color so enhancing the vibe and atmosphere of the club.

One of the best spots to enjoy live music is the **House of Blues** at Mandalay Bay. Its intimate setting of Southern folk art and decor is complimented by the jazz and blues musicians who play here. For something a little different, head to **Minus 5 Ice Lounge**. Vodka is the drink of choice here and comes served in ice glasses. Mocktails are also available, and there are ice sculptures.

SPORTS BARS

Virtually all the casinos in Las Vegas that have a substantial sports book also have a bar either in or adjacent to the book. Most of these bars have wide-screen TV monitors to view the sporting action. Among the best are at Mirage, Bellagio, Caesars Palace, Bally's, Gold Coast, and Las Vegas Hilton. Perhaps the quintessential sports bar is the **ESPN Zone** *(see p124)* at New York-New York that has a constant stream of sports shows running on the TVs. They also have a screening room that contains 12 leather reclining chairs with speakers in the headrests.

Las Vegas has dozens of non-casino sports bars as well, such as **Kerry's Sports Pub**, which shows all the college and NFL football games during the season.

WESTERN SALOONS

For a real taste of the Wild West, head for any of the many country-western saloons and bars that Las Vegas has to offer. With its great live bands, **Stoney's Rockin' Country** is the hotspot for country aficionados. Another local favorite is **Dylan's Dance Hall**, decorated with cow skulls and branding irons, while the hottest Wild West bar is the **Silver Saddle Saloon** that has a huge dance floor and live music each night.

DIRECTORY

HOTEL NIGHTCLUBS

Body English
Hard Rock Hotel & Casino.
Map 4 D4.
Tel *(702) 693-4000.*

Drai's
Bill's Gamblin' Hall &
Saloon. **Map** 3 C3. **Tel**
(702) 737-0555.

The Bank
Bellagio. **Map** 3 C3.
Tel *(702) 693-8300.*

Moon
Palms Casino Resort.
Map 3 A3.
Tel *(702) 942-7777.*

Pure
Caesars Palace. **Map** 3
C3. **Tel** *(702) 731-7873.*

Studio 54
MGM Grand. **Map** 3 C4.
Tel *(702) 891-7254.*

Tryst
Wynn Las Vegas. **Map** 3
C2. **Tel** *(702) 770-3375.*

STAND-ALONE NIGHTCLUBS

Blue Martini
Town Square, 6593
Las Vegas Blvd S.
Map 4 D2.
Tel *(702) 949-2583.*

**Downtown Cocktail
Room**
111 Las Vegas Blvd S.
Map 2 D3.
Tel *(702) 300-6268.*

ULTRA LOUNGES

Blush
Wynn Las Vegas.
Map 3 C2.
Tel *(702) 770-3633.*

ghostbar
Palms Hotel & Casino.
Map 3 A3.
Tel *(702) 942-7777.*

House of Blues
Mandalay Bay.
Map 3 C5.
Tel *(702) 632-7777.*

Minus 5 Ice Lounge
Mandalay Bay.
Map 3 C5.
Tel *(702) 632-7714.*

TAO
The Venetian.
Map 3 C3.
Tel *(702) 388-8588.*

SPORTS BARS

ESPN Zone
New York-New York.
Map 3 C4.
Tel *(702) 740-6969.*

Kerry's Sports Pub
3520 N Rancho Dr.
Map 1 A1.
Tel *(702) 645-8844.*

WESTERN SALOONS

Dylan's Dance Hall
4660 Boulder Hwy.
Tel *(702) 451-4006.*

**Silver Saddle
Saloon**
2501 E Charleston Blvd.
Tel *(702) 474-2900.*

**Stoney's Rockin'
Country**
9151 Las Vegas Blvd S.
Map 3 C3.
Tel *(702) 435-2855.*

Gay and Lesbian Venues

With a vibrant and ever-flourishing gay community, Las Vegas has much to offer its gay visitors in the way of entertainment and recreation. The city's Gay Quarter – though not on the scale of LA's West Hollywood or San Francisco's Castro district – is mainly concentrated along Harmon Avenue, Paradise Road, and the Naples Drive areas. It consists of a cluster of businesses, as well as several bars, nightclubs, and restaurants – all conveniently located at just a stone's throw from each other. Another popular area among the local gay population is Commercial Center, a past-its-prime shopping center at the corner of Sahara Avenue and Maryland Parkway. In addition, Las Vegas's Gay and Lesbian Community Center sponsors frequent social events and is a venue for various gay group meetings.

Colorful interior of the famous gay hangout, Freezone

INFORMATION SOURCES

Las Vegas is home to more than 75 organizations representing the interests of the city's gay population. Publications such as **Q Vegas**, a monthly magazine serving the gay and lesbian community, does an excellent job of providing information about local bars, restaurants, workshops, local politics, support groups, professional services, events, and more. Copies of the magazine are available in all gay bars, bookstores, and coffee shops, and online at QVegas.com. Various websites, including Gayvegas.com and GayNVegas.com also provide extensive information. These sites offer advice on lodging, nightlife, and restaurants in Las Vegas.

The main support group in Las Vegas is the **Gay and Lesbian Community Center**, which frequently sponsors social events, and is a gathering place for various gay and lesbian groups. It also provides free and confidential HIV tests. The **Lambda Business and Professional Association** is also a support and development group for gays.

GAY QUARTER

One of the best places to get local news and information on gay-related events and happenings is the city's well-stocked bookshop, **Get Booked**. Located in the heart of the Gay Quarter, this small shop features a vast collection of gay, lesbian, and feminist print material. These include journals, magazines, flyers,

and a newsletter. There is a wide selection of gay and lesbian videos too, and patrons can also purchase Billy, the world's first out-and-proud gay doll. On weekends, the shop offers free psychic readings as well.

Next door to the bookstore, is **The Buffalo**, a Levi's and leather bar where groups of locals relax and shoot pool in an informal atmosphere.

Just around the corner of Naples Drive is the entrance to **Freezone**, one of Las Vegas's most popular gay bars. Tuesdays is Ladies Night at this club, while Thursday is Boyz Night. On Fridays and Saturdays, Freezone stages the *Queens of Las Vegas* show at 10pm. This exciting dance party usually lasts till the small hours of the morning.

The wildest and hottest action, however, takes place at **Gipsy**, which is located near the Hard Rock Hotel & Casino. This is reputed to be the city's premier gay disco and also its most famous dance club. While some of the Strip nightclubs have strict dress codes and hard-to-get-past bouncers guarding their entrances, Gipsy is known for its easy-going and casual ambience, and will admit

Neon sign of the popular dance club, Gipsy

anyone and everyone. Reminiscent of the discotheques of the 1970s, Gipsy is fun, boisterous, and utterly free of pretension.

Decorated in a rustic style, **FunHog Ranch** attracts a good crowd with its festive atmosphere and central location.

Get Booked, a comprehensive bookstore for gays

Female impersonator Cashetta

Whilst fetish and leather wear is strongly encouraged, it is not compulsory. The staff at FunHog are renowned for their friendly service.

COMMERCIAL CENTER

The center has four good bars, each with its own unique ambience. **Spotlight Lounge**, which has become very popular with locals since it opened in 1998, offers everything from casino games to free beer nights. Known as probably the friendliest gay bar in town, Spotlight Lounge welcomes everyone regardless of their backgrounds.

There's a different kind of hospitality at the **Badlands Saloon**, a neighborhood country-western bar, which is also the original home of the Nevada Gay Rodeo Association. On the last weekend of each month, the association hosts a fund-raising beer night and line dancing event.

Located in a nondescript strip mall setting is one of the hottest spots for the transsexual crowd. Open 24 hours, **Las Vegas Lounge** offers a comfortable environment for a night of fun. Remarkably, in a town where cover charges are abundant, visitors here enter for free. Guests are invited to participate in an amateur drag competition, which is held on Monday at midnight. A professional drag

lip-syncing contest is held on Wednesday nights. "The Big Show" takes place every Friday and Saturday night with live music and singing by transgender performers.

THE STRIP

The "alternative" nightclub, **Krave**, was the first of its kind to open on the Strip. Situated on Harmon Avenue inside the Miracle Mile shopping center at Planet Hollywood Resort & Casino (see p46), the club features weekend dancing to DJ Jeffrey Sanker, and a variety of week-night themed parties. It has one of the largest dance floors on the Strip.

The uniquely entertaining show *Magic's A Drag*, which is performed at Krave, stars the magnificently larger-than-life female impersonator Cashetta (Scott Weston). The Queen of Magic is one of the few female impersonator magicians in the world. Cashetta amazes her audience with mind-boggling illusions, mentalism, cards that appear and disappear in surprising places, and a gypsy rope illusion similar to one performed by the great Harry Houdini. An important and distinctive feature of the show is the involvement of the audience. Cashetta invites members of the audience to join her on stage to assist in the performance, and even gets them dressed in drag and teaches them how to perform one of the illusions. This creates a great party atmosphere rather than just a typical show format and will appeal to all kinds of audience over the age of 21.

Slightly to the west of the Strip is **Charlie's Las Vegas**, a country and western nightclub. Charlie's hosts fundraisers and has a daily happy hour from 7–9pm. Theme nights are a regular and popular feature on the social calendar, ranging from bingo to rodeo, and even Men of Charlie's contests.

A unique road sign, Las Vegas

> GAY →
> LESBIAN →
> ← TRANSGENDER
> BISEXUAL →
> ← HETEROSEXUAL
> ← TRANSVESTITE

DIRECTORY

INFORMATION SOURCES

Gay and Lesbian Community Center
953 E Sahara Ave. **Map** 4 E1.
Tel (702) 733-9800.

Lambda Business and Professional Association
953 E Sahara Ave. **Map** 4 E1.
Tel (702) 593-2875.
www.lambdalv.com

Q Vegas
2408 Pardee Place. **Map** 2 E5.
Tel (702) 650-0636.
www.qvegas.com

GAY QUARTER

The Buffalo
4640 Paradise Rd. **Map** 4 D4.
Tel (702) 733-8355.

Free Zone
610 E Naples Dr. **Map** 4 D4.
Tel (702) 794-2300.

FunHog Ranch
495 E Twain Ave.
Map 3 A3.
Tel (702) 791-7001.

Get Booked
4640 Paradise Rd. **Map** 4 D4.
Tel (702) 737-7780.

Gipsy
4605 Paradise Rd. **Map** 4 D4.
Tel (702) 731-1919.

COMMERCIAL CENTER

Badlands Saloon
953 E Sahara Ave. **Map** 4 E1.
Tel (702) 792-9262.

Las Vegas Lounge
900 E Karen Ave. **Map** 4 E1.
Tel (702) 737-9350.

Spotlight Lounge
957 E Sahara Ave. **Map** 4 E1.
Tel (702) 696-0202.

THE STRIP

Charlie's Las Vegas
5012 S Arville St 4. **Map** 3 A2.
Tel (702) 876-1844.

Krave
3663 Las Vegas Blvd S.
Map 3 C4.
Tel (702) 836-0830.

OUTDOOR ACTIVITIES AND SPORTS

Beyond the lure of the Las Vegas casinos and malls lies some of the country's most magnificent wilderness waiting to be explored by hikers and rock climbers, anglers, bird-watchers, skiers, and snowboarders. From the pine-fringed creeks of Red Rock Canyon and the alpine forestry of Mount Charleston to the blue-green grandeur of Lake Mead, enthusiasts will find a never-ending source of outdoor adventures.

Actor Kevin Dillon at the Royal Links Golf Club

Besides these outlying areas, many of which lie within an hour's drive from Las Vegas, the city's resorts and clubs offer a wide range of facilities for activities such as tennis, basketball, cycling, rollerblading, swimming, and jogging, to name a few. Add to this Las Vegas's internationally-renowned, superbly designed golf courses and you have a recreational menu more diverse than any of the city's legendary buffets.

HOTEL RECREATION AND HEALTH CLUBS

Most of the resorts in Las Vegas present a variety of sports-related opportunities to their visitors. These include tennis, racquetball, basketball, and volleyball courts, as well as swimming pools and jogging tracks. Those who prefer running on grass can opt for the local parks or the athletic fields at University of Nevada, Las Vegas (UNLV). Some hotels, such as Las Vegas Hilton, offer scenic, meandering paths – ideal for cyclists and roller skaters.

Las Vegas also hosts numerous health clubs. One of the city's premier fitness centers is the **Las Vegas Athletic Club**. It contains all the usual gym equipment, along with virtual-reality exercise machines.

HIKING AND ROCK CLIMBING

One of the best destinations for hiking and rock climbing is Red Rock Canyon *(see p80)* – just a 20-minute drive from Las Vegas. Guides and area maps are available at the canyon's visitor center. Most of the hikes are 2–3 mile (3–5 km) long hikes over moderate terrain. One of the most popular hiking trails is at Pine Creek Canyon, where you can trek past the sweet-smelling pinion pines to a meadow with the ruins of a historic homestead. Visitors can also take a close look at the area's geological history on the Keystone Thrust trail, a moderate 3-mile (5-km) walk to the older gray dolomite on top of the younger red-and-buff sandstone. The sheer rock faces of the mountains entice many climbers as well. Contact **Jackson Hole Mountain Guides** for information on guided climbs. Another favorite location is Mount Charleston *(see p81)*, which is a 45-minute drive from Las Vegas.

The hiking trails here vary from easy, half-hour walks to two-day treks. Most of the trailheads are accessible by car and have water and restroom facilities. One of the trails leads to Deer Creek Road (State Route 158), which is a short distance from the Desert View Scenic Outlook – a point that offers a breathtaking panorama of the valley and dry lakebeds below. The 1–2 hour hike to the top of Cathedral Rock, which provides spectacular views of Kyle Canyon is also worth a visit. Check with the **Mount Charleston Ranger Station** for directions and maps before starting. Most of the trails are open throughout the year, but some are closed during winter and early spring. Be sure to follow the marked trails, especially at higher elevations. The vertical cliffs can be dangerous and have claimed lives.

WATER SPORTS

The scenic shoreline of Lake Mead *(see p82)* is one of the most sought-after destinations for water sports, sailing, water-skiing, and white-water rafting. The 11-mile (18-km) stretch of Colorado River from Hoover Dam to Willow Beach is open year-round to rafts, canoes, and kayaks, but the best times for canoeing, kayaking, and rafting are spring and fall. A permit from the **US Bureau of Reclamation** is required for river rafting. Further information can be obtained

Sheer sandstone cliffs at Red Rock Canyon

from the visitor center at Lake Mead. Those who do not have their own equipment can rent boats and related supplies at the **Las Vegas Boat Harbor** and several other shops lining the marinas on the lake.

A fisherman on the shores of Lake Mead Recreational Area

FISHING

It is open season on fishing all through the year at Lake Mead, where anglers will find an abundance of catfish, trout, bluegill, crappie, and striped bass. Anglers consider the Overton arm of Lake Mead (see p82) an ideal location for striped bass. Also worth trying are Calico Basin, the Meadows, Stewart's Point, and Meat Hole.

Fishing is excellent along the Colorado River, south of Hoover Dam, and extending to Laughlin and Bullhead City as well. The cold water below Davis Dam, near Laughlin, is also a good spot, while the area above the dam on Lake Mohave is noted for its bass and rainbow trout.

A fishing license is required by all anglers 12 years of age and older. Non-resident fishermen can purchase a year-long license, but at almost double the cost of a resident fishing license, which requires a minimum six months residency. Fishermen can also purchase a one-day fishing permit. Baits, tackles, fishing lines, and other goods, as well as licenses can be obtained from marinas and equipment stores such as **Las Vegas Bass Pro Shops** and **Big 5 Sporting Goods**.

BIRD-WATCHING

Although many southern Nevada wilderness areas are suitable for bird-watching, the grounds of **Corn Creek Field Station** at the Desert National Wildlife Range are some of the most frequented.

The natural springs of Corn Creek have formed upper and lower ponds that are connected by a gurgling brook. This small, rugged oasis boasts an astonishing selection of bird life. The fruited mulberry trees attract pine crossbills, tanagers, grosbeaks, and orioles. Other species, such as Wilson's warblers, western bluebirds, flycatchers, and Cooper's hawks, can also be seen. The bird life at this sanctuary is so diverse that the Audubon Society, a wildlife conservation organization, has included it as part of its Adopt a Refuge program.

WINTER SPORTS

The snow-laden slopes of Mount Charleston are a sought-after locale for a wide array of winter sports. These include skiing, snowboarding, and snowmobiling. Visitors can also enjoy magnificent cross-country skiing at Lee Canyon, Scout Canyon, Bristlecone Trail, and Mack's Canyon. Most of the resorts at Mount Charleston run snow-making equipment from November through April, depending on the weather conditions. There are also plenty of equipment rental outlets although resort packages usually include skis, lift passes, and lessons as well.

DIRECTORY

HEALTH CLUBS

Las Vegas Athletic Club
2655 S Maryland Pkwy. **Map** 4 E1.
Tel (702) 822-5822.

HIKING AND ROCK CLIMBING

Jackson Hole Mountain Guides
8221 W Charleston, Suite 106.
Tel (702) 254-0885.
www.jhmg.com

Mount Charleston Ranger Station
Tel (702) 515-5400.

WATER SPORTS

Las Vegas Boat Harbor
Hemenway Harbor, Lake Mead.
Tel (702) 293-1191.
www.lasvegasboatharbor.com

US Bureau of Reclamation
PO Box 61470, Boulder City.
Tel (702) 293-8000.
www.usbr.gov

FISHING

Big 5 Sporting Goods
2797 S Maryland Pkwy. **Map** 4 E1.
Tel (702) 734-6664

Las Vegas Bass Pro Shops
Silverton Hotel, 8200 Dean Martin Drive. *Tel (702) 730-5200*

BIRD-WATCHING

Corn Creek Field Station
Desert National Wildlife Refuge, Hwy 95, 8 miles W of Kyle Canyon Rd.
Tel (1-702) 879-6110

Skiers and tourists at a snow-covered resort on Mount Charleston

Golf

Las Vegas's year-round warm weather makes it a golfer's paradise, which attracts both amateurs and professionals. Within easy driving distance of the Strip resorts are more than 35 beautifully designed golf courses, many internationally acclaimed, some positioned in the midst of spectacular scenery. Although almost a third of these are private, the city has many public courses as well. There are essentially two types of courses in Las Vegas – the standard 18-hole courses found in most communities, and the desert golf course or "target" course, in which only tee boxes, fairways, and greens are maintained and the surrounding natural desert landscape is left intact.

The fairway at Las Vegas National Golf Club

GENERAL INFORMATION

A large number of golf courses in Las Vegas are private, so players will need to be acquainted with a club member in order to book a tee time. It might be better to plan ahead and get a decent tee time at one of the city's public tracks. Most courses accept reservations up to seven days in advance. The winter and spring months are the busiest seasons for golf so try and make bookings as much in advance as possible. Visitors can rent golf clubs from pro shops at the golf course or at selected stores in town such as the **Callaway Golf Center** or the **Las Vegas Golf and Tennis**. The dress code on the course is casual, though most require collared shirts and no cut-off jeans. Soft spikes are a must.

Many courses will charge at least $100 a round, and most clubs expect a cart to be used, which is an additional cost. However, there are a few layouts where a round can be played for less than $50. You may also find some real bargains during the hot summer months of June, July, and August when prices are at their lowest. Some hotels offer golf packages to their guests. Check with the booking office or concierge upon arrival.

LAS VEGAS COURSES

The city's municipal golf course, **Angel Park**, offers players the chance to enjoy the challenge and beauty of two Arnold Palmer-designed 18-hole courses, known as the Palm and the Mountain. The park's Cloud Nine course offers 12 holes and a par-3 layout with replica holes from the world's most famous par 3s.

If you were wondering what "target" courses are like, visit the **Badlands Golf Club**. The scenic 27-hole course is built around picturesque desert arroyos. This target course was designed by Johnny Miller and is not for the faint of heart as it demands immense accuracy over its 7,000-yard (6,400-m), par 72 layout.

Just steps away from the Mandalay Bay and Four Seasons hotels, the **Bali Hai Golf Club** features thick stands of palm trees, big water hazards, tropical plants, and flowers, all set in a South Seas design.

The **Las Vegas National Golf Club** was established in 1961. This par-72 course has a classic layout with mature trees, grass fairways, and deep greens. It was also the scene of champion Tiger Woods' first PGA (Professional Golf Association) victory in 1996. Bargain hunters can get a great round of golf for under $100

The expansive, beautifully-maintained grounds at Angel Park Golf Club

Greens at Legacy Golf Club, overlooking Nevada's desert landscape

at **Desert Rose Golf Club**, a public course with narrow fairways and Bermuda turf.

The exclusive **Royal Links Golf Club** was designed to simulate play on some of the finest courses on the British Open rotation. Tee times here are somewhat pricy, with rates typically around $200.

The enormous 18-hole par-70 **Wynn Las Vegas Golf Course and Country Club** is set right on the Strip. It is exclusively for the use of guests at the luxury resort.

FARTHER AFIELD COURSES

Designed by golf course architect, Jay Morrish, **Painted Desert** is the former site of the Nevada Open and is consistently rated as one of the best-maintained public courses in Nevada. The course is set within a natural desert habitat with challenging greens and roughs, and there are also several lakes that come into play. The desert areas provide a beautiful setting not found in many courses. The clubhouse provides an impressive range of facilities, which includes a restaurant and a well stocked golf shop.

Rated among the best 100 courses in the US, the 7,200-yard (6,580-m), par-72 **Legacy Golf Club** course in Henderson features wall-to-wall turf, two lakes, rolling terrain, and plenty of trees. A notable highlight is the Devil's Triangle, where a canyon creek runs

through the 11th, 12th, and 13th holes, spoiling many fine tee shots. Players who master the triple header walk away calling it "Amen Corner."

The **Black Mountain Golf Course** in Henderson is a good course for beginners, but still has plenty of sand bunkers and two lakes to keep your iron game honest. Established in 1959, the course is peppered with cacti and Joshua trees. The green fees here are usually under $100.

The **Shadow Creek Golf Club** is located in North Las Vegas and is the only course in Southern Nevada to have earned a place in *Golf* magazine's survey of the world's top 100 courses. The layout at Shadow Creek was designed by world-renowned golf course architect Tom Fazio and hotelier Steve Wynn. The woodland-style course is private, but guests staying at any of the MGM Mirage properties – MGM Grand, Mirage, Bellagio, and Treasure Island – are allowed to play here on weekdays.

Tiger Woods, championship golfer

MAJOR TOURNAMENTS

The Justin Timberlake Shriners Hospitals for Children Open *(see p32)* continues a long history of professional golf in Las Vegas. The tournament was the first in the history of the PGA Tour to offer a $1 million purse and the first non-major to

offer a $5 million purse. The 72-hole event is played over three days and features amateurs along with tour professionals.

DIRECTORY

Angel Park
100 S Rampart Blvd.
Tel (702) 254-4653.
www.angelpark.com

Badlands Golf Club
9119 Alta Dr.
Tel (702) 363-0754.

Bali Hai Golf Club
5160 Las Vegas Blvd. S.
Map 3 C5. *Tel (702) 450-8000.*

Black Mountain Golf Course
500 Greenway Rd, Henderson.
Tel (702) 565-7933.

Callaway Golf Center
6730 Las Vegas Blvd. S.
Tel (702) 896-4100.

Desert Rose Golf Club
5483 Clubhouse Dr.
Tel (702) 431-4653.

Las Vegas Golf and Tennis
4211 Paradise Rd.
Map 4 D3. *Tel (702) 892-9999.*
www.lvgolf.com

Las Vegas National Golf Club
1911 E Desert Inn Rd.
Map 4 F2. *Tel (702) 734-1796.*
www.lasvegasnational.com

Legacy Golf Club
130 Par Excellence Dr.
Tel (702) 897-2187.
www.thelegacygc.com

Painted Desert
5555 Painted Mirage Way, 8129.
Tel (702) 655-2570.
www.painteddesertgc.com

Royal Links Golf Club
5955 E Vegas Valley Dr.
Tel (702) 450-8000.

Shadow Creek Golf Club
3 Shadow Creek Dr, N Las Vegas.
Tel (702) 399-6495.

Wynn Las Vegas Golf Course and Country Club
3131 Las Vegas Blvd S.
Map 3 C2.
Tel (702) 770-7000.
www.wynnlasvegas.com

GAMBLING IN LAS VEGAS

Despite its growing fame as an all-round adult amusement park, Las Vegas remains famous for its casinos. More than 30 million visitors come to the city every year and, on average, each spends about $80 gambling every day. Do not come expecting to make your fortune; with a combined annual income of $10 billion, the casinos appear to have the advantage.

The secret pleasure of gambling is the lure of the unknown – you never know what the next card will be. Casinos know this and aim to keep you playing

Cards displaying the hearts suit

for as long as possible. Free drinks are available for gamblers, but it is not a good idea to gamble without a clear head. Before you start, decide on an amount that you can afford to lose and be sure to stick to it. For a first-timer, the casino can seem daunting, but, with a basic understanding of the rules, most of the games are relatively simple *(see pp160–65)*. Some hotels have gaming guides on their in-house TV channels and Las Vegas's visitor center supplies printed guides. Several large casinos give free lessons at the tables.

Row upon row of slot machines on the gaming floor of New York-New York casino *(see p43)*

GENERAL INFORMATION

You need to be at least 21 years old to gamble in Las Vegas, so be sure to carry some ID at all times if you look young. Children are not welcome on the casino floor at any time. If you hit a substantial slot jackpot, the casino will ask for two forms of identification, usually a driver's license and Social Security card. This is in keeping with certain IRS regulations regarding jackpots of $1,200 or more. Nonresident winners are subject to a withholding tax of 30 percent to be deducted from the jackpot winnings before payment.

All Las Vegas casinos deal in the same basic commodity – a chance to beat the odds. As the casino enjoys a statistical advantage in every game, the longer you expose yourself to it, the greater your chance of losing. The house advantage is the result of a combination of things – the odds or percentages inherent in the game, rules tailored to favor the casino, payoffs at less than actual odds, or predetermined payoffs like those in slot machines. The casino's edge may be small, as in baccarat, blackjack, and sports betting, or enor-

mous, as in keno and the wheel of fortune, but it still generates billions of dollars a year in gambling profits. In rare instances it can be highly profitable for the gambler too.

Tipping is common in a casino, but is not a requirement. It can be to your advantage to tip when you first sit down at the table, as it is a good idea to get the dealer on your side. It is casino etiquette to tip the dealer if you are winning at the tables. Slot winners usually tip the change person about 5 to 10 percent of their winnings.

Poker chips

Guests placing bets on the roulette table at a casino in Las Vegas

ANATOMY OF A CASINO

Every casino has a main cashier, also known as the main cage by the staff. This is where players can establish credit, cash checks, purchase coins or tokens for play in slot machines, and redeem their chips, coins, and tokens for cash. The cage, however, will not sell you chips, which you must purchase from the dealers when you "buy in" – the amount of cash you use to enter a game – at the various tables. In addition to the main cage, most casinos have other satellite cashiers. Slot machines usually take only paper money or vouchers bought from the cashier.

Casino player's card

TIPS

• *Always play within your means. That is, only gamble with money you can afford to lose.*

• *Gambling is meant to be an enjoyable form of entertainment. Hence head for the tables where players are talking and laughing. Chances are, a row of glum faces means that you are in for an equally dull time.*

• *Dealers can prevent inexperienced gamblers from making silly mistakes and will usually explain the finer points and intricacies of the game if asked.*

• *Slots is one of the easiest games and a lot of fun too. But take the time to understand what you are betting and what it takes to win. This philosophy should extend to all the other games as well.*

Nearly every casino has a slot club, which awards its members various types of freebies for a required amount of play. Ordinarily, slot club members accumulate points while playing, and then redeem their points for free meals, room discounts, merchandise, and any other benefits that might be on offer. There is no charge for joining a slot club and you can get more information about it at the slot promotions or redemption booth located in the casino.

You can also expect to find automated teller machines (ATMs) placed at several points in most casinos. But you will rarely, if ever, find any clocks in the casino. The hotel executives want their customers to play as long as possible, so clocks are never part of the decor. The same is true for windows. You will not get the chance to see a sunset through a glass window as the casinos want time to stand still during the entire gambling experience.

GAMBLING ETIQUETTE

Much of the etiquette in the casino stems from common courtesy. However, there are some guidelines that should be kept in mind. If you are browsing among table games – blackjack, Caribbean Stud, and poker – note that the chairs are for players, not observers. If you want to watch a game, you will have to stand in the back or to the side of the players. This is not so true in other areas of the casino, such as the slot floor, keno lounge, or sports book. Here, sitting is okay, although slot players may request you to either play or leave if no machine is free.

Most disputes arise at the slot machines. Players often leave to get a drink, wash their hands, or buy cigarettes, and find someone else at "their" machine when they come back. Always ask a change person or floor supervisor to baby-sit your machine while you are away. They are usually happy to do it.

CASINOS OFFERING GAMING LESSONS

Boulder Station
Classes Thu–Tue. Poker: 2pm.

Circus Circus
Mon–Fri. Blackjack: 10:30am, Roulette: 11:30am & Craps: 12:30am.

Excalibur
Mon–Fri. Craps and blackjack: noon.

Flamingo
Daily. Dice: 11am.

Gold Coast
Daily. Craps: 11:30am.

Golden Nugget
Daily. Roulette: 11:30am; Blackjack: noon; Craps: 11am.

Luxor
Tue, Fri, and Sat. Craps, roulette, and blackjack: 11am.

Monte Carlo
Daily. Poker: 11am.

Palms Casino Resort
Mon–Fri. Poker: noon.

Planet Hollywood Resort & Casino
Mon–Fri. Blackjack: 11:30am; Daily. Texas Hold 'Em: 8am

Sahara
Mon–Thu. Blackjack: noon; Craps: upon request.

Treasure Island – TI
Upon request.

Tropicana
Upon request.

Since everything in the casino is recorded by the "eye in the sky" security system, do not hesitate to take your dispute to a higher authority – the casino manager. The tape will tell the tale and resolve the issue.

Craps

Often the most fun game on the floor, a sense of camaraderie develops in craps because players are betting either with or against the "shooter" (whoever has the dice) on what the next number rolled will be.

Craps dice

The aim of the shooter's first roll, or "coming out," is to make 7 or 11 in any combination (say 3/4, 5/6) to win. A roll of 2, 3, or 12 is craps; everyone loses and the shooter rolls the dice again. If a total of 4, 5, 6, 8, 9, or 10 is rolled, this becomes the "point" number, and the shooter must roll this number again before rolling a 7 to win. Craps etiquette says that you place your money on the table rather than handing it to the dealer; wooden holders around the table will keep your chips. Always roll with one hand; the dice must hit the end of the table. All betting and laying down of chips must be completed before the next roll.

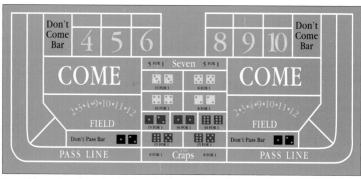

Craps table seen from above, showing the various boxes and areas for the many bets

BETS

Craps can seem confusing as there appears to be a lot going on at any one time; this is largely due to the wide variety of bets it is possible to lay. If you are a beginner, the following bets are the best ones to lay.

Laying bets during a craps game

The Pass Line Bet

In this, you are basically betting that the shooter will roll a 7/11 on the first roll in order for you to win. The odds at this point are even, so if you do win you get the same amount you laid down. If a point number is rolled, the shooter has to throw the same number before he rolls another 7. Since there are more ways to roll a 7 than any point number, it pays to take the odds once the shooter has a point, which means placing an additional bet behind your pass line bet. This will pay you the true house odds if the shooter rolls his point. The odds change according to the number, so check with the dealer first.

The Don't Pass Bet

This is the opposite of a pass line bet. The aim here is for the shooter to lose by throwing a 2 or 3 on the first roll, or by rolling a losing 7, which happens before he makes his point number.

The Come Bet

This is an optional bet you can make during the game, when your money comes to the next number that rolls. For example, if the point is 6 you make a come bet, and the shooter rolls an 8. Your come bet "comes" to the 8, and now you have two numbers in play. You can also take odds on a come bet.

The Place Bet

Another way of getting additional numbers is by making a place bet. In this case, you simply pick the number you want and make a place bet on that number. The advantage of place bets is that you pick the number yourself and you can remove your bet at any time. The disadvantage is that the casino charges you from 50 cents to $1 for each $5 bet you place.

SLOT MACHINES

Slots of every kind dominate Las Vegas casinos. The simple one-armed bandit, where pulling a handle spun the reels and a win resulted from a row of cherries or some

other icon, has been largely superseded by computerized push-button machines offering a confusing variety of plays. There are basically two kinds of slots; flat-top machines and progressive machines. A

One-armed bandit slot

flat-top machine has a range of fixed payouts depending on different arrangements of winning symbols. There will usually be a choice of stakes, and if you hit a winning display you will win less if you play a low stake than if you play the limits.

On progressive slots, you give up smaller jackpots in exchange for winning a progressive jackpot. To be eligible for the progressive jackpot, the maximum number of coins allowed must always be played. The payout on these machines increases as you play, and the rising jackpot figure is

SLOT MACHINE TIPS

• *Always play the machine limit because if you win, you will receive the maximum amount.*

• *Wins on both types of machine allow you to receive coins back or else they rack up credits, which you can use for subsequent bets. Monitoring your display of credits will help keep track of how much you are spending. If your original stake was 10 quarters and you win 30, using credits allows you to decide to walk away when the credit display is down to 20, leaving you 10 quarters up.*

• *Join a slot club. Most casinos have clubs that offer a range of incentives to get you to play with them; which range from cash back to various discounts. Members are also issued an electronic-strip plastic loyalty card.*

Slot machines lined along the casino floor at Excalibur hotel

displayed above each machine. The biggest payout is currently from the Megabucks slots, which operate all across Nevada. A waitress at the Desert Inn won almost $35 million on a machine there in January 2000.

The majority of slot machines in larger casinos now take only vouchers or paper money (though some older machines, primarily found in the older casinos downtown, are coin-operated). A player inserts $1, $5, $10, $20 or $100 bills, or vouchers for money he/she has won on other machines into the receptor of a machine.

Slot machine at Caesars Palace

When play stops, the machine issues a paper voucher for the amount of money that has been won, or not spent.

BINGO

A very popular game with the locals is bingo. In fact, generally the city's bingo halls are located in off-the-Strip casinos, such as Gold Coast. Plaza is the only casino located downtown that has a bingo hall.

Bingo is a very simple game. Players purchase their cards and mark off numbers as they are being called. Numbers are usually marked with a dauber, but some casinos also offer electronic bingo tabulators that allow players to control dozens of cards at one time.

Bingo is a relatively inexpensive game. Sessions often cost just a few dollars and players can play at practically any time of day. Typically, casinos offer a series of sessions, of one or two hours duration, that begin at 9am and run on until 11pm. New cards must be purchased for each session.

Winnings can be huge. Casinos such as Sam's Town, Fiesta, and Station Casinos have instituted progressive jackpots, often reaching six figures. These jackpots are usually placed on a cover-all game. That is, all the numbers must be covered within a certain number of balls. Most of the cover-alls start with around 46 to 48 numbers, and the casino adds one number per week until someone hits it.

Crowded bingo room at the Gold Coast casino

BLACKJACK

This card game is one of the most popular games on the floor; casino blackjack tables offer minimum bet games from $2 to $500. The game is played against the dealer and whoever gets closest to a total card value of 21 without going over is the winner. Cards are worth their numerical value, with all the picture cards worth 10 and an ace worth 1 or 11. Hands that have aces are called "soft" hands and the ones without aces are known as "hard" hands.

Generally, the dealer will deal from a "shoe" – a box containing up to six decks of cards. Each player receives two cards face up. The dealer also gets two cards – one face up and one face down. Players must not touch the cards and should use hand signals to indicate if they wish to "hit," scratch the

Dealing cards to players at the blackjack table, Monte Carlo

Ideal cards for blackjack

table with their forefinger to receive another card or "stand," wave a flat hand over their cards. Players can also "double down," double their bet or "split," a hand that has two cards of the same value can be separated into two hands, each with individual bets. Once each player has decided to stand or hit the 21 limit, the dealer turns over his second card and plays his hand, hitting 16 or less and standing with 17 or more. This is an essential part of blackjack's "basic strategy." The assumption here is that the dealer's second card will be a 10 and that the next card in the shoe will also be a 10. This is because there are more tens in the deck than any other card – there are 96 tens in six decks.

BIG SIX OR WHEEL OF FORTUNE

One of the oldest games of chance, the Wheel of Fortune, also known as Big Six, is easier to play than the more intensive table games.

The ornate wooden wheel is 6 ft (1.8 m) in diameter with a pointer attached to it, and is divided into nine sections. Each of these sections is further divided into six pockets. This gives the wheel a total of 54 pockets, each holding a symbol you can bet on.

Out of these, 52 contain symbols of US currency bills of $1, $2, $5, $10, and $20 denominations and the two remaining symbols are of a joker and the casino's logo. The wheel's symbols are reproduced on a table layout. The players choose any of these symbols and place their bet on it. A dealer spins the wheel. When it stops, the number that the pointer is aimed at wins. The payoff is a multiple of the currency amount the player bet on. For instance, a $1 bet on a $2 symbol wins $2, a $5 bet on a $10 symbol wins $50, and so on. Bets placed on the casino logo and joker, usually pay at 40 to 1 – so a winning bet of, say, $2 on any of these symbols wins a payoff of $80.

BASIC BLACKJACK STRATEGY

Blackjack's basic winning strategy, based on computer-generated studies, is given below. It tells the player when to hit, stand, double down, or split pairs, depending on the dealer's up card. Using basic strategy is permitted in casinos, and many dealers even advise gamblers on how to play.

1. Hit or Stand: With a hard hand – no aces – against the dealer's 7 or higher, the player should hit until he/she reaches at least 17. With a hard hand against the dealer's 4, 5, or 6, stand on a 12 or higher; if against the dealer's 2 or 3, hit a 12. With a soft hand, hit all totals of 17 or lower. Against the dealer's 9 or 10, hit a soft 18.

2. Doubling Down: Double down on any 11, no matter what the dealer shows. Double down on 10 when the dealer shows anything except a 10 – dealer's "10" includes picture cards. Double down on 9 when the dealer shows 2, 3, 4, 5, or 6. Double down on a soft 17 (ace + 6) if the dealer shows 2, 3, 4, 5, or 6. Double down on a soft 18 (ace + 7) if the dealer shows a 3, 4, 5, or 6. Double down on a soft 13, 14, 15, or 16 against the dealer's 4, 5, or 6.

3. Splitting Pairs: Always split aces and 8-8. Never split 5-5 or 10-10. Split 4-4 against the dealer's 5 or 6. Split 9-9 against the dealer's 2, 3, 4, 5, 6, 8, or 9. Split 7-7 against the dealer's 2, 3, 4, 5, 6, or 7. Split 6-6 against the dealer's 2, 3, 4, 5, or 6. Split 2-2 and 3-3 against dealer's 2, 3, 4, 5, 6, or 7.

A winning hand on a blackjack table

Poker

Over the last few years, the popularity of poker has skyrocketed in Las Vegas, largely due to events such as the World Poker Tour, Las Vegas's World Series of Poker, and numerous other celebrity tournaments.

Unlike blackjack and Caribbean Stud poker, "live" poker is not played against the casino but against other players. The casino simply provides the dealer and charges a rental for the seat at the table, which is actually a percentage taken out of every pot – this is called

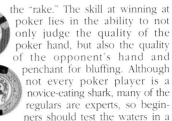

Casino poker chips

the "rake." The skill at winning at poker lies in the ability to not only judge the quality of the poker hand, but also the quality of the opponent's hand and penchant for bluffing. Although not every poker player is a novice-eating shark, many of the regulars are experts, so beginners should test the waters in a low-stakes game or take a few lessons before taking on the pros. Even after lessons, it might be a good idea to watch a game for a while to understand the method of play.

There are basically two poker games played in Las Vegas – seven card stud and Texas Hold 'em. In recent years, Texas Hold 'em has become more popular, perhaps because it is usually the championship game in most tournaments.

SEVEN-CARD STUD

Most beginners start with this game. The dealer gives each player two cards face down and then one card face up. The player with the lowest card showing makes the first bet. Other players can either match the bet, increase it, or withdraw. Another card is dealt face up, and the player with the highest hand showing starts this round of betting. This is repeated until four cards have been dealt face up. Finally the seventh card is dealt to those who have remained in the game, and the final round of betting begins. During this "showdown," players may "raise" a bet up to three times. When the last bet is "called," the dealer asks for a showing of hands and the highest hand wins.

TEXAS HOLD 'EM

This game is very similar to seven-card stud except only two of the seven cards are dealt to each player; the other five are dealt face up and used collectively by all

Essential ingredients of a poker game

An excellent poker hand

the players. The dealer gives each player two cards face down. The player next to the dealer starts the betting and the other players have to match the bet or withdraw.

The dealer discards, or "burns," the top card from the deck, then deals three cards face up in the center of the table – this deal is called the "flop." A round of betting occurs again. The dealer burns another card and adds a fourth face-up card, known as the "turn" card, to the center. Once again, a round of betting takes place. Finally, a fifth face-up card, called the "river" card, is dealt to the center. A final round of betting occurs, along with a showdown and revealing of hands. Once again, the highest hand wins.

Strategy

Texas Hold 'em's strategy is based on your first two cards. Most pros, agree that if you do not have any of the combinations below, drop out.

1. A pair of aces or a pair of kings: Hold and bet from the first round.

2. A pair of queens or jacks: Hold and cover all bets until the fourth up card is dealt. If the value of your hand has not increased, drop out.

3. Two high-value cards – ace, king, or queen: Hold and cover all bets until fourth up card is dealt. If your hand has not improved, drop out.

4. Two high-value cards of the same suit: Hold until the fourth up card. If your hand has not improved, drop out.

5. A small pair – 10s or less: Hold until the fourth up card. If the value of your hand has not increased, drop out.

POKER HANDS

Several versions of poker are played in Las Vegas casinos. You should know the hierarchy of poker hands to play any of these. From the lowest to the highest, the hands are as follows: Pair, two cards of the same value; Two Pair, two separate pairs; Three-of-a-Kind, three cards of the same value; Straight, five cards of any suit in sequence; Flush, any five cards of the same suit; Full House, three cards of the same value and a pair; Four-of-a-Kind, four cards of the same value; Straight Flush, any five-card sequence of the same suit; and finally Royal Flush, ace, king, queen, jack, and ten of the same suit.

CARIBBEAN STUD POKER

A type of five-card stud poker played on a table with a layout like a blackjack table, where the aim is to beat the dealer. There is a progressive jackpot where winnings increase according to a player's hand. Players win all or part of a progressive jackpot with a Royal Flush, Straight Flush, Four-of-a-Kind, Full House, or Flush.

PAI GOW POKER

Combining the Chinese game of Pai Gow with American poker, this game has a joker card that is used as an ace or to complete a straight or flush. Players have to make the best two-card and five-card hand to beat the banker's two hands.

LET IT RIDE POKER

In this game, players do not compete against the dealer or each other. They try to get a good hand by combining three cards dealt to them with the dealer's two "community" cards that are revealed during play. Players can remove up to two-thirds of their bet during play if chances for a win seem grim.

VIDEO POKER

No other casino game has gained the popularity that video poker has enjoyed over the past few years. It is the game of choice for locals, those who live and work in Las Vegas, and generates up to 75 percent of the revenue in some casinos. There are several reasons for video poker's popularity. The first is that people can play at their own pace, without pressure from dealers, croupiers, or other players. Secondly, there is an element of skill in video poker. Decisions must be made which, unlike slot machines, will determine whether and how much you can win. And, most importantly, there is the chance of hitting the jackpot.

The basic video poker game is five-card draw poker, in which the machine "deals" five cards to the player. The player can then decide to "hold," keep those cards or "draw," replace some or all the cards. The winnings are based on the value of the poker hand.

Initially, the game started as jacks or better poker, in which the minimum payback was based on a pair of jacks or

Poker chips

A dealt hand on a video poker machine, Las Vegas

better – a pair of queens, kings, or aces, and the bottom row is dealt face up. The player Today, there are many variations of video poker, including deuces wild poker, joker wild poker, and bonus poker, to name a few.

In 1998, inventor Ernie Moody pioneered a multi-hand concept called Triple Play Draw Poker. This new game allows the player to play three hands at once by dealing three rows of five cards. The first two rows are dealt face down, and the bottom row is dealt face up. The player then chooses the cards they want to hold from the bottom hand, and those cards automatically appear in the corresponding spaces in the top two hands. After hitting the "draw" button, the player gets three different draws from three different decks. So players who hold three-of-a-kind from the bottom deck, have three different chances to get Four-of-a-Kind.

Adding to the game's popularity is the fact that when dealt a big hand like a Royal Flush, players receive three times as much as they did on the older, single-hand video poker games. Many players say that after playing Triple Play, they can never go back to playing regular video poker. Triple Play poker has since given birth to Five Play, Ten Play, Fifty Play, and Hundred Play Poker, in which players can play 100 hands at a time.

Although it might be inconceivable to play such a large number of hands at once, the game's manufacturer has made it easier by offering the game in small denominations – 1 cent and 2 cents per hand.

Pai Gow Poker dealer laying out the table at Palace Station casino

THREE-CARD POKER

This card game debuted in 2002 and by 2004 had more placements than Let it Ride and Caribbean Stud combined. Virtually every casino in North America and the United Kingdom offers Three Card Poker.

In this game, players compete against the dealer and against a bonus paytable. The bonus bet, called Pair Plus, is the key to the game's popularity. It is so strong that several other games have borrowed it – 3-5-7 Poker, Pai Gow Mania, and Boston 5.

Players win the Pair Plus bet if their three-card poker hand contains a pair or better. Payouts increase for hands like flushes, straights, and three-of-a-kinds. The top hand, a straight flush, pays 40-1. And unlike bonus bets in five-card games, Pair Plus winners are easy to get.

The game against the dealer is simple. Players ante – a poker stake that goes into the pot – and receive their cards. They may fold or make an additional bet equal to their ante. The dealer then reveals his hand. If he qualifies – has a queen-high or better – the dealer pays the winners who have higher cards than him and takes the bet of the losers. If the dealer doesn't qualify, players win their ante as well as the secondary bet money.

ROULETTE

Roulette is quite a simple game but with a great variety of bets. A ball is spun on a wheel containing numbers 1 to 36 divided equally between red and black, plus a single and a double zero, colored green. Each player's chips are a different color so they can be easily identified on the table. The aim is to guess the number that will come up on the spin of the wheel. Bets are placed on the table that has a grid marked out with the numbers and a choice of betting options.

Croupier setting up roulette in a private gaming room

The highest payout odds are 35 to 1 for a straight bet on one number such as 10 black. You can also make a "split bet" on two numbers that pays 17 to 1 if either number comes up.

Roulette wheel

The most popular bets are the outside bets that are placed in the boxes outside the numbered grid. These only pay even money, but allow you to cover more numbers such as Odd or Even, Red or Black, First 18 Numbers or Second 18 Numbers. You can also make a Column Bet covering 12 numbers, which pays 2 to 1.

BACCARAT

A variation of *chemin de fer*, baccarat is played at a leisurely pace with eight decks of cards, the deal rotating from player to player. The object of the game is to guess which hand will be closest to 9: the player's or the banker's. You can bet on either hand.

Two cards in each hand of baccarat

KENO

One of the easiest games to play, keno is a close relative of bingo. Out of the 80 numbers on a keno ticket, players may choose up to 20. A range of bets is possible and winning depends on your chosen numbers coming up. The prize depends on the amount of numbers matched.

A game of keno in progress at Circus Circus *(see pp64-5)*

RACE AND SPORTS BOOK

Giant video screens adorn these areas of the casino, where you can bet on almost any sport, such as car racing and boxing tournaments. The race book is for betting on thoroughbred horse racing and features live coverage from racetracks across the US. The sports book covers the main sporting events taking place all over the country, as well as the major championships staged in Las Vegas itself. Sports fans can watch the progress of their team on the nearby TVs.

WEDDINGS IN LAS VEGAS

Sign of Cupid's
Wedding Chapel

Apart from its fame as one of the most popular entertainment destinations in the country, Las Vegas is also widely acclaimed as the wedding capital of the world. Each year, more than 110,000 couples, including several celebrities, such as Elvis Presley and Britney Spears, tie the knot here, which is about one-fifth of all the marriages that take place in the nation. The city has dozens of stand-alone chapels (see pp28–9), many of which are converted Victorian homes decorated with bells and cherubs. Most of the resorts also have at least one chapel. Weddings in Las Vegas can range from simple civil affairs and exotic themed events to full-blown, lavish extravaganzas. While some chapels hire an Elvis impersonator to croon a few tunes to the newlyweds, others offer romantic hot-air balloon rides over the city or the Grand Canyon. Those in a hurry can even get married at a 24-hour drive-through chapel. In addition to the quick, easy, and relatively inexpensive ceremonies, couples getting married here find it a great place to spend their honeymoon as well.

A couple waiting for a marriage license, Clark County Courthouse

LEGALITIES

The requirements for a marriage license in Las Vegas are less stringent than those in other parts of the US. No blood tests are needed, nor is it necessary to wait a set period after the license has been issued. The only prerequisite to marriage is that you must be at least 18 years of age. Those aged between 16 and 18 must have parental consent. To obtain a license, both partners must appear at the **Clark County Marriage License Bureau**. Civil ceremonies are performed one block from the courthouse in the office of the **Commissioner of Civil Marriages**. The cost of a license at both these places is $60 and must be obtained at the Marriage Bureau. A civil ceremony costs $50 (cash only and exact change is required). Be prepared to produce your social security number and proof of identity such as a driver's license, certified copy of birth certificate, passport, or military ID. Divorced applicants must know the month, year, city, and state where the final decree was granted, but no papers are necessary. Couples planning to tie the knot on Valentine's Day or New Year's Eve, two of the year's most popular days for weddings, should get their licenses well in advance in order to avoid long queues at the County Clerk's office.

INDOOR SPECTACULARS

Perhaps the most elaborate weddings in Las Vegas take place at **Bellagio** (see pp48–9). The resort's two romantic and elegant chapels have a stained-glass window behind the altar, while ornate lamps, chandeliers of amethyst, and Venetian glass compliment the pastel shades of the furnishings and the flower-decked passages.

Fresh flowers adorning the richly decorated interiors of the wedding chapels at Bellagio

A newly married couple at the elegant chapel at Bellagio

Weddings here are expensive and couples can spend up to $18,000 for a lavish ceremony that includes every service right down to the exquisite flower petals that carpet the aisle. Personalized services are also available for room reservations as well as for the wedding and reception planning.

Couples can also take advantage of any of the hotel's wide variety of wedding packages. One of the most exclusive is the Cosa Bella Wedding Package. This offers spa treatments for the bride and groom, hair and make-up services at the salon, an impressive penthouse suite for two nights, dinner at the five-star Picasso restaurant, and two tickets to Cirque du Soleil's production, *"O"* (see p144).

Couples can also exchange vows at **Planet Hollywood Resort & Casino** (see p46), formerly known as the Aladdin, where Elvis Presley wed Priscilla in 1967. The hotel has two chapels, the larger of which is adorned with arches and columns, soft desert colors, hand-painted murals, and will accommodate up to 60 guests. The smaller chapel is more intimate and can host 12 guests.

At the **MGM Grand** (see p44), couples can tie the knot in the Forever Grand chapel.

The chandeliered halls here offer a stunning backdrop.

Wynn Las Vegas (see pp60–61) has some of the nicest wedding rooms in the city, decorated in warm tones with elegant fabrics and hand-blown glass chandeliers. The Lavender Salon seats 120, the Lilac Salon has room for 65, and Primrose Court is an outdoor venue for 40 guests. Personal consultants help to plan every aspect of the wedding.

Another favorite Las Vegas wedding venue is the Chapel in the Clouds at **Stratosphere** hotel (see p63). Located in the resort's tower, 800 ft (244 m), above the ground, this claims to be the country's highest wedding chapel, and presents a breathtaking view of the city's bright lights.

For a ceremony much more intimate though no less spec-

The Forever Grand chapel at MGM Grand

tacular, **Graceland Wedding Chapel** (see p76) will stage a quiet, romantic ceremony with an Elvis impersonator handling the services. There is a small stone bridge and a New England church building. Inside there are stained-glass windows and off-white pews. A large number of celebrities, including singer Jon Bon Jovi and TV personality Jay Leno, have exchanged vows here. The chapel also offers a range of wedding packages.

OUTDOOR EXTRAVAGANZAS

Although the Southern Nevada desert is far from any seashore, tropical-themed weddings are hugely popular in Las Vegas. These usually take place at resorts that feature lush, landscaped areas, which have been artistically designed to resemble an exotic island. The **Flamingo** (see p51), for instance, hosts weddings in its charming garden gazebo chapel, and offers cascading waterfalls, palm trees, and fresh flowers. Couples can choose from several packages, which often provide wedding coordinators, a leather bound album, a pianist or violinist, champagne and toasting glasses, and a two-night stay in the hotel's lavish Royal Suite.

Caesars Palace's (see p50) Garden of the Gods makes for an impressive pastoral backdrop with its striking terraces, fountains, and waterfalls. And at the **Treasure Island – TI** resort (see p56), couples can marry on the deck of a pirate galleon in the middle of Buccaneer Bay. The ceremony is performed by the ship's "captain" while guests watch from the adjacent patio. A pirate may even swing down from the crow's nest to deliver the rings to the couple.

One of the most beautiful settings for an outdoor wedding is at **JW Marriott Hotel** in Summerlin. The wedding arbor is set among dense trees and offers remarkable views of the Red Rock Canyon. Outdoor wedding packages include white garden chair seating and a reception.

Wedding procession outside Little White Chapel

UNUSUAL WEDDINGS

Most chapels in Las Vegas seek to offer something different and unique in order to separate themselves from the rest of the crowd. For instance, the **Little White Chapel** has a reputation of hosting rather unconventional weddings. For the bride and groom who are either acting on impulse or are in a huge hurry, the chapel offers the world's only Drive-Up Wedding Window, where they can exchange vows without leaving the front seat of their car. The window never closes and an appointment is not necessary. The chapel also offers the "Weddings on Wheels" program, where a minister travels to a location chosen by the couple in order to perform the ceremony.

The Little White Chapel also collaborates with hot-air balloon companies to offer airborne marriages. The balloon hovers above the Las Vegas neon-lit skyline while the knot is tied.

Many chapels in Las Vegas feature a range of themed weddings. The **Viva Las Vegas Wedding Chapel** probably performs more themed marriages than any other – between 15–20 ceremonies each day. One of its most popular weddings is the Blue Hawaii package, which comes complete with a tropical set,

dancing hula girls, theatrical fog, and of course, a singing Elvis. For couples who want something more exotic, there is an Egyptian wedding, where King Tut performs the service, and a Camelot wedding in which Merlin the Magician conjures up the nuptials.

New York-New York *(see p43)* offers couples the chance to reserve one of the most exhilarating wedding experiences on the Strip. The "Weddings on the Coaster" package allows couples the chance to say "I do" on the roller coaster, featuring its 180-degree "heartline" twist-and-dive maneuver and reaching speeds of 67 mph (107 km/h). Package rates begin at $600 with weddings available Sunday through Thursday (10:45am or 11:15pm) and Friday and Saturday (10:15am or 12:15am) – weather permitting. Couples can take the plunge with up to 14 guests and a minister.

A large number of resorts also offer weddings that tie into their theme, if they have one. The **Excalibur** *(see p42)*

Elvis impersonator, Little White chapel

extends its King Arthur's castle theme into the chapel, where couples can dress in medieval outfits. The canals at the **Venetian** *(see pp58–9)* are worked into some wedding ceremonies, which can be performed on a gondola, or on one of the bridges that span the waterways.

Unusual weddings are not confined to the earth-bound. **Papillon Tours** will elevate nuptial vows with its helicopter wedding packages. One package whisks couples via helicopter to the awe-inspiring Grand Canyon, where they are set down on the floor of the canyon, adjacent to the Colorado River. The couple exchanges vows on the riverbank, after which they are flown back to their hotel. Another Papillon package flies the betrothed high above the glittering Strip at night, where they are wed by an airborne minister. Serving as a spectacular backdrop are dramatic views of Paris Las Vegas's Eiffel Tower, Luxor's pyramid, and the fountains at the Bellagio.

WEDDING AND HONEYMOON PACKAGES

One of the reasons so many couples choose Las Vegas for their wedding is that they have a built-in honeymoon destination at their fingertips.

An Egyptian-themed ceremony in progress at the Viva Las Vegas Chapel

A newlywed couple stepping out of a helicopter, Papillon Tours

Virtually all the hotels in the city offer wedding and honeymoon packages. These include a bottle of champagne, optional breakfast in bed, a reception in the banquet hall, tickets to production shows, spa treatments, dinner at one of the hotel's restaurants, and of course, accommodation in a honeymoon or master suite.

The cost of these packages can vary from season to season. For instance, a week-long honeymoon during the annual giant CES (*see p33*) convention, which attracts thousands of delegates, may cost two to four times more than it might during the preceeding or following week. As far as accommodations are concerned, the general rule is that the farther you are located from the Strip, the less expensive are the rooms. However, since there are exceptions to this rule, it would be a good idea to check the hotels websites or your travel agent for any special deals.

Sign at Viva Las Vegas Wedding Chapel

WEDDING DETAILS

The hotel wedding chapels usually have a planner on staff who will make all the arrangements, including the photographer, florist, pianist, limousine service, harpist, albums, boutonnieres and bouquets, refreshments, and so forth. Couples can also hire professional services, such as **Las Vegas Weddings and Rooms** and **Moments to Cherish**, to handle all the details. These companies will typically find a chapel or any other venue that meets the couple's needs, arrange for the ceremony, make bookings for the honeymoon, and provide the flowers, wedding cake, photographer (both still and video), limousine, music, champagne, fresh flowers, balloons, and last but not least, a garter for the bride. In fact, these services will arrange almost anything you want. One of the most well-known wedding planners in the city are **Las Vegas Weddings**, who have been arranging weddings and honeymoons since 1973.

GAY AND LESBIAN WEDDINGS

Even though Las Vegas has a thriving gay and lesbian community, Nevada is somewhat conservative politically. A few years ago, the state approved a constitutional amendment banning same-sex marriages. Hence, it is not believed that any of the chapels in Las Vegas will perform a same-sex marriage, even if it is only a symbolic commitment ceremony.

DIRECTORY

LEGALITIES

Clark County Marriage License Bureau
201 Clark Ave.
Map 2 D4.
Open *8am–midnight daily*
Tel *(702) 671-0600.*
www.co.clark.nv.us

Commissioner of Civil Marriages
309 South Third St.
Map 2 D5.
Open *8am–10pm daily.*
Tel *(702) 671-0600.*

WEDDINGS SITES

JW Marriott Hotel
221 N Rampart Blvd.
Tel *(702) 869-7777.*
www.marriott.com

Little White Chapel
1301 Las Vegas Blvd S.
Map 2 D5.
Tel *(702) 382-5943.*
www.littlewhitechapel.com

Papillon Tours
3900 Paradise Rd.
Map 4 D3.
Tel *(702) 736-7243; (888) 635-7272.* **www**.papillon.com

Viva Las Vegas Wedding Chapel
1205 Las Vegas Blvd S.
Map 2 D5. **Tel** *(702) 384-0771/ (800) 574-4450.* **www**.vivalasvegasweddings.com

WEDDING DETAILS

Las Vegas Weddings and Rooms
2770 S Maryland Pkwy.
Map 4 E1.
Tel *(800) 322-8697.*
Tel *(702) 737-6800.*
www.lasvegasweddings.com

Las Vegas Weddings
www.las-vegas-weddings.co.uk

Moments to Cherish
PO Box 42802.
Tel *(702) 452-5160.*
www.momentstocherish.com

CHILDREN IN LAS VEGAS

Las Vegas hosts a variety of attractions for children. Most hotels and resorts feature activities that cater to the younger generation. From the thrill rides at Stratosphere and Circus Circus's Adventuredome to the *Tournament of Kings* show at Excalibur and the massive Shark Reef aquarium at Mandalay Bay, there is plenty to satisfy a child's neverending quest for adventure and fun. Some resorts even offer day care facilities for

A merry-go-round ride at Adventuredome

young children while their parents are busy. The city also has several non-hotel attractions, including a zoological park, a huge arcade at GameWorks, a chocolate factory, and the famous Lied Discovery Children's Museum, which showcases interactive exhibits tailored to spark a child's imagination. Las Vegas has numerous outdoor activities for kids of all ages too, such as miniature golf, skateboarding, swimming, and biking.

TRAVELING WITH CHILDREN

There are a few general guidelines that are helpful when traveling with children. Book your accommodations well in advance, and ensure the hotel or motel has the extra crib or cot you require. The more expensive resorts provide baby-sitting services and children's clubs offering supervised activities. Remember to carry everything you might need – diapers, food, toys, and extra clothes for kids and parents alike. A first aid kit is always a good idea. The glare of the desert sun can be harmful to young eyes so carry sunglasses and hats.

SOURCES OF INFORMATION

For updates and special promotions on upcoming activities around the city, the *Las Vegas Family* magazine is a good source of information. This free monthly publication carries a month-to-month calendar of no-cost or lowcost child-oriented events. The magazine can be picked up at any local library and at most supermarkets.

CHILDREN'S DISCOUNTS

The long-established custom of allowing children to stay for free in their parents' hotel room is no longer taken for granted. While some hotels still allow young children to share the room at no extra cost, many others require an added charge, usually no more than $10 or $12 per person. Be sure to check with the resort and booking agent in advance. Most restaurants also provide reasonably priced children's menus, although do not expect to find any at the more exclusive dining rooms. Many museums,

shows, and special events offer discounted rates or free admission to children of a certain age and below. Check with the establishment you plan to visit since this varies from place to place. Children also receive reduced fares on the city's public transportation systems.

DAY CARE AND BABY-SITTING SERVICES

Several hotels in the city will provide or arrange for licensed baby-sitting services. Sitters are typically available 24 hours a day and will come to the hotel room, often equipped with toys, games, books, and videos to entertain your children. It is a good idea to make reservations for the sitters in advance.

Some hotels also maintain day care centers for the children of guests as well as those of their casino personnel and other staff. These centers generally require a written consent form from the parents, and cater mostly to children who are pre-school aged and past the diaper stage.

Moreover, **Station Casinos** and **Coast Casinos** – two of Las Vegas's most prominent gaming corporations – also operate child care centers in select hotels. These are available to toddlers and children up to 12 years of age, and require that the parent must remain on the property while the child is in the center, up to a maximum of five hours.

Tournament of Kings **show at Excalibur**

Day care workers looking after children

Boulder Station, for instance, features the **Kids Quest** center that tends to children 6 weeks–12 years old. The center is open to all tourists, not just hotel guests, and offers many forms of entertainment such as movies, arts and crafts, jungle gym, Nintendo games, table tennis, board games, a pre-school room, and more.

Parents can also contact independent baby-sitting services such as **Shamrock Sitters** and **Around the Clock Child Care**, which provides professional sitters trained in administering CPR or mouth-to-mouth resuscitation, if required.

CITY TABOOS

It is important to remember that Las Vegas is, first and foremost, an adult playground. Games of chance beckon everywhere – from the slots at the corner convenience store to the baccarat rooms at the mega resorts. Although the gambling halls attempt to keep restaurants, shops, and other general attractions separate from the adult games, the trip sometimes invariably requires a walk through parts of the casino. Visitors younger than 21 cannot tarry, so the stroll must be brisk. Parents are not permitted to wager or place bets at any of the tables while youngsters are in tow.

Most of Las Vegas's production shows are geared toward adult audiences. In general, the earlier of the day's two shows will be less racier than the late edition, when many of the showgirls become "uncovered." Shows such as *Jubilee!* at Bally's fall into this category. Many clubs offer adults-only entertainment and feature topless waitresses as well as strip shows and contests. Children below the age of 18 are not allowed anywhere near these areas.

The drinking age in Nevada is 21, so anyone who looks under the age may be asked for some form of identification when purchasing alcohol. In addition, Las Vegas has a 10pm curfew, so minors – those younger than 18 – must be off the street by that time or be accompanied by either a parent or a legal guardian.

HOTEL ATTRACTIONS

One of the most exciting destinations in Las Vegas is **Shark Reef** *(see p41)* at Mandalay Bay. This enormous aquarium houses a wide selection of marine life including sharks, komodo dragons, reptiles, and various species of tropical fish. Kids especially enjoy the petting section where they can touch eels, jellyfish, stingrays, and small sharks.

The **Adventuredome** *(see pp64–5)* at Circus Circus is another popular children's attraction in Las Vegas. This indoor amusement park has an extensive array of rides and games designed to keep kids entertained for hours. They can ride the Canyon Blaster, a looping, corkscrewing roller coaster or get wet on a water flume ride called Rim Runner. Also available are laser tag, bumper cars, and carnival midway games.

Visitors gaze at predatory sharks through a transparent glass barrier, Shark Reef, Mandalay Bay

A thrilling spin on Chaos, Adventuredome, Circus Circus

Kids also enjoy the exhilarating ride on Chaos, which spins its passengers at varying speeds. Moreover, the mezzanine above the Circus Circus casino presents circus performances such as trapeze artists and tightrope walkers, and a midway filled with games.

Another hot spot on the Strip is **Excalibur** *(see p42)*, which, below its casino, houses a "fun zone" of carnival games enticing youngsters in games of skill, as well as the incredible Magic Motion Machine, which puts visitors in hydraulically activated seats for a rollicking simulated ride. One of the highlights here is the **Tournament of Kings** show – a wholesome family entertainment where guests can enjoy a meal while watching jousting knights, and exciting sword play. Kids may also be tempted by the SpongeBob SquarePants ride.

Siegfried and Roy's Secret Garden and Dolphin Habitat *(see p56)* at Mirage is one of the city's must-see attractions. This delightful facility, created by the famed conservationists, is home to several lions and threatened white tigers. Designed to resemble the natural habitat of these magnificent big cats, the lush, landscaped environment of the garden provides exceptional viewing

The Trojan Horse at FAO Schwartz

opportunities. The stunning and spacious Dolphin Habitat is where a family of Atlantic bottlenose dolphins can be observed at play.

Older kids can head over to the **SoBe Ice Arena** at Fiesta Rancho Casino Hotel. In keeping with National Hockey League regulations, the ice rink measures a massive 31,000 sq ft (2,880 sq m) and is home to several youth and adult hockey leagues. SoBe offers figure skating and ice hockey facilities, as well as skate rental and private rooms that can be hired for birthday parties. Skate School is held every Tuesday and Saturday and is open to all ages.

If you count white-knuckle adventure as fun, the Strip

The hair-raising Big Shot ride at the Stratosphere Tower

offers many thrill- and rollercoaster rides. A gut-wrenching ride at Stratosphere Tower *(see p63)* is the **Big Shot**, which is located on the observation deck and shoots passengers 160 ft (49 m) up into the air. Riders for this must be at least 48 inches (4ft) tall. Probably the best roller coaster in town is the **The Roller Coaster** at New York-New York *(see p43)*, and the fastest is the appropriately named **Speed – The Ride** *(see p63)* at Sahara.

GAMEWORKS

Situated next to the MGM Grand, GameWorks *(see p44)* is the ultimate arcade complex. This massive facility is the brainchild of movie mogul Steven Spielberg, Sega Enterprises, and Universal Studios. In its basement-like setting are games such as Vertical Reality and GameArc, where teams of players battle each other in mock warfare. Also included is a 75-ft (23-m) high rock-climbing wall, the latest video equipment, and more than 250 arcade games.

MUSEUMS

Art, science and a lot more come alive at the **Lied Discovery Children's Museum** *(see p77)*, located in downtown Las Vegas. This interactive facility showcases more than 100 exhibits and schedules numerous workshops and activities for kids.

One of the most popular stops here is Green Village, where youngsters can try out various jobs, earn a paycheck, use a bank ATM machine, and shop for groceries in a pint-sized store. They can experience life lessons with an environmentally conscious theme. The village also includes the State Capitol, an airport terminal, and a car-care center. Most of the activities are geared to elementary-age children, though preschoolers and teens will find enough to keep them entertained.

The **Las Vegas Natural History Museum** *(see p77)* exhibits sharks, dinosaurs,

Façade of the Lied Discovery Children's Museum

and other creatures. Its Young Scientists' Center showcases hands-on displays, and kids can also pet a 13-ft (4-m) long python and dig for fossils in the museum's workshop.

LAS VEGAS MINI GRAN PRIX

This venue has plenty to do with a games arcade, 90 ft (23 m) Super Fun Slide, and a selection of rides, but the main attractions are its four tracks. These cater to all ages, offering vehicles ranging from Kiddie Karts, for children aged 4, to Gran Prix Cars, for adults with a driver's license.

SOUTHERN NEVADA ZOOLOGICAL PARK

Nevada's only zoo features a collection of animals indigenous to the state, and a few domestic animals that can be seen up close. The zoo *(see pp90–91)* is also home to a family of rare Barbary apes, as well as many other mammals, birds, and reptiles. Kids are sure to love the petting zoo. The botanical displays are also worth a visit.

SPORTS AND OUTDOOR ATTRACTIONS

There are several places in Las Vegas where children can burn off excess energy. Many hotels, including **Gold Coast** *(see p47)*, **Fiesta Rancho**, and **Sam's Town** have bowling alleys, and provide special equipment and prices for kids.

Youngsters who like to roller skate or rollerblade can visit **Crystal Palace**, which operates two skating rinks in the Las Vegas area, or head for one of the many municipal parks in town that offer specific paths for roller skating or skateboarding. These parks feature a host of innovative attractions, such as bicycle courses, skateboard paths, water playgrounds, and more.

The city's most popular park is **Sunset Park**, which has joggers' paths, volleyball and tennis courts, a place to fly kites and sail boats, swimming pool, some of the best picnic spots in town, and a massive lake with ducks and fish.

The **Freedom Park** offers facilities for traditional games such as horseshoe pits and shuffleboard courts, as well as modern resources that include a skating park. The **Wetlands Park** is spread over an expansive area, a portion of which is designated as a Nature Preserve. This wildlife habitat has beautiful trails, viewing ponds, and a visitors' center.

Swimming is possibly the best way to beat the summer heat. Practically every hotel in Las Vegas has a swimming pool, though these are usually open only to hotel guests.

Parents can also take their children on trips to wilderness areas close to the city such as Mt. Charleston and Lake Mead.

DIRECTORY

Around the Clock Child Care
2692 Red Rock St, Suite 102.
Tel (702) 365-1040.
www.
aroundtheclockchildcare.net

Coast Casinos
www.coastcasinos.com

Crystal Palace
4680 Boulder Hwy.
Tel (702) 458-7107.
3901 N Rancho Dr.
Tel (702) 645-4892.
www.skatevegas.com

Fiesta Rancho
2400 N Rancho Dr.
Tel (702) 631-7000.

Freedom Park
800 N Mojave Rd.

Kids Quest
4111 Boulder Hwy,
Boulder Station Hotel.
Tel (702) 432-7777.

Las Vegas Mini Gran Prix
1401 North Rainbow Blvd.
Tel (702) 259-7000.
www.lvmgp.com

Sam's Town
5111 Boulder Hwy.
Tel (702) 456-7777.
www.samstownlv.com

Shamrock Sitters
Tel (702) 218-2221.

Southern Nevada Zoological Park
1775 N Rancho Rd.
Map 1 A2.
Tel (702) 647-4685
www.lasvegaszoo.org

Station Casinos
www.stationcasinos.com

Sunset Park
2601 E Sunset Rd, E Ave.

Wetlands Park
7050 Wetlands Park Lane at E Tropicana Ave.

Volleyball game at Sunset Park

SURVIVAL
GUIDE

PRACTICAL INFORMATION

As one of the world's most popular playgrounds, Las Vegas attracts millions of visitors each year. Lavish resorts and casinos, spectacular shows, and the frantic pursuit of around-the-clock entertainment, 365 days a year, are just some of the amusements that tourists never seem to tire of. The city's surrounding wilderness, harsh and cruel in some places but always fascinating and beautiful, also offers a choice of pleasures, including a wide variety of outdoor activities such as swimming, hiking, waterskiing,

A four-wheel drive for rent

horseback riding, snowboarding, fishing, parasailing, camping, and white-water rafting. With so much to choose from, it is a good idea to do some advance planning. The information on the following pages contains useful tips on personal security and health *(see pp178–9)*, and helps answer any queries related to banking *(see pp180–81)* and communications *(see pp182–3)*. There is also information on traveling in and outside the city by both public transportation and car *(see pp186–9)*.

Poster warning readers of the dangers of strong sun

WHEN TO GO

Las Vegas is a highly popular year-round destination. The most comfortable time to visit the city is during spring and fall, when the days are sunny without being overly hot. The summer months are extremely warm with an average July temperature of 105°F (40°C). Winter is unpredictable; some days are warm enough to wear shorts, while others are cold and windy with nighttime temperatures that can dip below freezing. It has even been known to snow in Las Vegas on rare occasions.

For most of the year, visitors can pack light and casual clothes, as shorts and T-shirts or tops are usually the norm. Some restaurants, however, require casual-style jackets or coats, but neckties are not always a requisite. Most people dress up when going to production shows or special events. Warm clothing – an extra sweater or lined jacket – is required during the winter.

Remember to carry comfortable and lightweight shoes if you intend to do a lot of exploring on foot. Also, since the sun shines more than 300 days a year, be sure to pack a swimsuit, hat, sunscreen, and lip balm. Las Vegas is also host to some of the country's biggest conventions. Avoid planning your trip at this time as room rates are high and traffic is heavy.

ENTRY REQUIREMENTS

Citizens from Australia, New Zealand, the UK, and many other European countries can visit the US without a visa if staying 90 days or less. However, visitors must apply for entry clearance via the Electronic System for Authorization. Applications should be made at least 72 hours before

travel and a passport that is valid for at least six months after the trip is required. When Canadians enter the US overland, they are required to show a photo ID, such as a citizenship card, or a passport when arriving by air. Beware that entry requirements are prone to change and visitors should always check with the nearest US embassy.

Visitors from countries who do need a visa must apply to a US consulate or embassy. Any visitor wishing to extend their stay beyond the 90-day limit should contact the nearest US Immigration and Naturalization Service (INS) well in advance of the date stamped on their visa waiver form or visa.

TOURIST INFORMATION

Several agencies and tourist centers offer free information and maps to hotels and Strip sights. The **Las Vegas Convention and Visitors Authority** *(see p142)* provides

Exterior of the Las Vegas Convention Center, Las Vegas

◁ Heavy traffic along the Strip at night

Angel Park Golf Club *(see p156)*, one of the many golf courses in Las Vegas

excellent information packs, and also has a website offering additional information on different aspects of your trip. The **Las Vegas Chamber of Commerce** is also a good source for brochures and maps, as well as a variety of visitor publications that often include discount coupons. The **Nevada Commission on Nevada** provides information on scenic, recreational, and historic sites. In addition, all the national and state parks have their own visitor centers.

OPENING HOURS AND ADMISSION CHARGES

The casinos in Las Vegas are open round the clock, as are many of their restaurants, bars, and gift shops. As far as casinos are concerned, this applies to the holidays as well. Museums and galleries tend to keep regular business hours, though they are usually open weekends and some holidays. Most museums, parks, and other attractions charge an admission fee. The amount can vary and many sights offer discounts to families, children, and ID-carrying students and senior citizens.

SENIOR TRAVELERS

Because of its inexpensive dining and lodging costs and outdoor activities, such as golf, tennis, and water sports, Las Vegas is an ideal destination for older travelers. A wide range of discounts are available to people over the age of 50. The Las Vegas Convention and Visitors Authority is a good source for information on these

concessions. Several organizations proffer discounts as well. The **National Park Service** offers a Senior Pass that reduces the cost of park tours and services. **Elderhostel** arranges educational trips, with economical lodgings and meals, for those over the age of 55, while the **American Association of Retired Persons (AARP)** offers good travel discounts to its members.

TRAVELING WITH CHILDREN

Once strictly a haven for adults, Las Vegas now provides entertainment for the entire family *(see pp170–73)*. Theme hotels such as Circus Circus and Excalibur feature attractions just for kids. Las Vegas also has a zoological park, chocolate factory, children's museum, and miniature golf courses for kids. The age at which a child is eligible for discounts varies from four and under to under 18 years. Some hotels provide babysitting services and children's clubs. Many restaurants offer low-priced children's menus.

Miniature golf at Adventuredome, Circus Circus *(see pp64–5)*

DIRECTORY

Access-Able Travel Source
PO Box 1796, Wheat Ridge, CO 80034.
www.access-able.com

American Association of Retired Persons (AARP)
3200 E Carson St, Lakewood, CA 90712.
Tel (888) 687-2277.
www.aarp.com

Elderhostel
11 Ave de Laffayette, Boston, MA 02111.
Tel (800) 454-5768.
www.elderhostel.org

Electronic System for Authorization
http://.esta.cbp.dhs.gov

Las Vegas Chamber of Commerce
3720 Howard Hughes Pkwy, Las Vegas.
Tel (702) 735-1616.
www.lvchamber.com

Las Vegas Convention and Visitors Authority
3150 Paradise Rd, Las Vegas.
Tel (702) 892-0711.
www.lvcva.com
www.visitlasvegas.com

National Park Service
www.nps.gov

Nevada Commission on Tourism
www.travelnevada.com

Society for Accessible Travel & Hospitality
347 Fifth Ave, Suite 610, New York, NY 10016.
Tel (212) 447-7284.
www.sath.org

TRAVELERS WITH DISABILITIES

All the hotels, restaurants, and other buildings in Las Vegas provide excellent facilities for the disabled *(see p143)*. Road crossings at busy intersections have audio crosswalk signs for the visually impaired. All city buses, shuttles, and the monorail are wheelchair accessible, as are some taxis. The **Access-Able Travel Source** and **Society for Accessible Travel & Hospitality** offer advice to disabled travelers.

Personal Security and Health

Las Vegas is a relatively safe place to visit as long as some general safety precautions are observed. In contrast to large urban centers, the crime rate in town is relatively low, but it is wise to be aware of areas that might not be safe at night. The area around Stratosphere hotel and several blocks on either side of Fremont Street are sections to avoid after dark. When driving in the desert regions outside of Las Vegas, take a reliable map as well as a good compass, and follow the advice of local rangers and visitor information services. These sources provide invaluable guidelines for survival in the wilderness and safety procedures to be followed by those engaging in outdoor activities. Also, heed any flash flood warnings because thunderstorms in the desert can often cause dramatic downpours.

Flash flood warning sign

Metropolitan policeman on duty on the streets of Las Vegas

PERSONAL SAFETY

Like any major city, Las Vegas has a criminal element. Casino visitors are often targets for robbery because it is likely they are carrying large amounts of money. Although the local police department and hotel security place a high priority on keeping tourists safe, it is wise to observe a few basic rules. Never wear expensive jewelry, hold huge sums of cash, or keep your wallet in your back-pocket, as these are the main temptations for pickpockets. It is also advisable to avoid certain parts of the city while you are sightseeing. Downtown is generally safe, but it is not advisable to wander from the well-lit hotel and shopping areas, particularly north of Fremont Street and east of Maryland Parkway. Another district to avoid is the area west of the Strip, from the Sahara hotel north to downtown. The section has been called the "naked city" and is not somewhere you want to explore, especially at night. Otherwise, follow the rules of common sense, keeping your valuables close at all times. While driving, be sure to lock expensive belongings in the trunk, and to park only in well-lit areas.

LOST PROPERTY

It is unlikely that small items of lost or stolen property will be retrieved, but it is necessary to report all such incidents to the police in order to make an insurance claim. Telephone the **Police Non-Emergency Line** to report the loss or theft, and they will issue you with a police report so that you can make a claim with your insurance company. If a credit card is missing, call the credit company's toll-free number immediately. Lost or stolen traveler's checks should also be reported to the issuer. If you have kept a record of the checks' numbers, replacing them should be a painless experience, and new ones are usually issued within 24 hours.

If you lose your passport, contact the nearest embassy or consulate. They will be able to issue a temporary replacement as visitors do not generally need a new full passport if they plan to return directly to their home country. However, if you are traveling on to another destination, you will need a full passport. It is also useful to hold photo-copies of your driver's license and birth certificate, as well as notarized passport photographs if you are considering an extended visit or need additional identification.

TRAVEL INSURANCE

The United States has excellent medical services, but they are very expensive. All visitors to the US are strongly advised to make sure they have comprehensive medical and dental coverage for the duration of their stay.

MEDICAL TREATMENT

For serious emergencies requiring assistance from the medical, police, or fire services call 911. The state organization, **HELP of Southern Nevada**, may offer help in a variety of emergencies. The **University Medical Center of Southern Nevada** (UMC) is the city's primary provider of emergency medical care. UMC is the only hospital in Nevada with Level 1 Trauma and Burn Care centers. The hospital also has a Flight for Life medivac helicopter and operates several quick-care facilities throughout the city for non-emergency medical care. Other hospitals with emergency rooms can be found in the Blue Pages of the telephone directory, but

Police car

Paramedics vehicle

Fire engine

they are often overcrowded. Private hospitals offer more personal treatment and are listed in the Yellow Pages of the telephone book. You may be required to provide evidence of your ability to pay before a doctor will agree to treat you. Hotels will usually call a doctor for you, and nonprescription painkillers and other medicines can be obtained from drugstores that are open 24 hours. Prescription drugs can be dispensed only from a pharmacy. Be sure to carry extra supplies of any prescribed medication you might be taking. Also consider carrying your medical records. No specific vaccinations are required before entering the US.

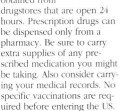

Pharmacy sign

Young couple walking in the desert sun near Las Vegas

OUTDOOR HAZARDS

Due to its location in the Mojave Desert, visitors to Las Vegas can expect extreme temperatures and weather conditions. Sudden summer storms can cause flash floods, specially along the major washes. The **Regional Flood Control District** can answer questions about a specific wash. Visitors may obtain the latest weather information from the ranger stations in the national parks, as well as by listening to the reports on local radio and television channels. If you are planning a hike in wilderness territory, always inform someone where you are going and when you will return.

The dry heat of the region's summers can often be underestimated by visitors, and hikers especially are advised to carry with them at least a gallon (4 liters) of drinking water per person for each day of walking. If you are planning on hiking or indulging in other outdoor activities during the summer, an effective sunscreen and a sunhat should always be worn.

Watch out for venomous creatures such as snakes and scorpions. They mostly hide under rocks and in crevices during the heat of the day. If bitten, you should seek medical help immediately.

DIRECTORY

EMERGENCY SERVICES

All Emergencies
Tel 911 to alert police, fire, or medical services.

HELP of Southern Nevada
Tel (702) 369-4357.

Police Non-Emergency Line
Tel (702) 828-3111.

Regional Flood Control District
Tel (702) 685-0000.

University Medical Center of Southern Nevada
1800 E Charleston Ave.
Tel (702) 383-2000.

LOST PROPERTY

Lost or Stolen Credit Cards (Toll free)
American Express
Tel (800) 528-4800.
Diners Club
Tel (800) 234-6377.
MasterCard (Access)
Tel (800) 627-8372.
VISA
Tel (800) 336-8472.

CONSULATES

The consulates closest to Las Vegas are found in California.

Australian Consulate
Century Plaza Tower, 19th Floor,
2049 Century Park E,
Los Angeles, CA 90067.
Tel (310) 229-4800.

British Consulate
11766 Wilshire Blvd, Suite 1200,
Los Angeles, CA 90025.
Tel (310) 481-0031.

Canadian Consulate
550 S Hope St, 9th Floor,
Los Angeles, CA 90071-2627.
Tel (213) 346-2700.

New Zealand Consulate
2425 Olympic Blvd, Suite 600E,
Santa Monica, CA 90404.
Tel (310) 566-6555.

Banking and Currency

Aside from the risk of gambling away all of their money in the casinos, visitors should encounter no problems with financial transactions in Las Vegas. Foreign travelers can exchange currency at hotel cashiers and major banks. There is an abundance of automated teller machines (ATMs) in the casinos and throughout the city that enable visitors to make cash withdrawals 24 hours a day. Credit cards are a more common form of payment than hard currency, especially at hotels or car rental companies. In fact, most hotels and car agencies will not book a room or car without a credit card.

Automated teller machine (ATM), open 24 hours a day

BANKS AND FOREIGN CURRENCY EXCHANGES

Bank opening times can vary in Las Vegas, but generally they are open between 9 or 10am and 5 or 6pm. Most major banks exchange foreign currency and cash traveler's checks. Always ask if any special fees apply before you make your transaction.

TRAVELER'S CHECKS

Traveler's checks are safer than cash because they can be replaced if lost or stolen. Foreign currency traveler's checks may be cashed at large banks or at major hotels. The McCarran International Airport also offers foreign currency exchanges where traveler's checks can be changed, as do the branches of **American Express** and **Thomas Cook**, which will change them at a slightly higher rate than that offered at a bank. Checks bought in US dollars are accepted as cash in many restaurants, hotels, and stores, and visitors will not be subject to a transaction fee. A passport is required as identification when using traveler's checks.

CREDIT, CHARGE, AND DEBIT CARDS

Credit and charge cards are practically essential when traveling in the US. The cards are accepted as a guarantee when renting a car *(see p189)*, and are used to book tickets for most forms of entertainment. The most widely used cards are VISA, American Express, Master-Card, and Diner's Club.

All credit, charge, and debit cards can be used to draw money from an ATM. These are usually found at banks, bus stations, airports, and convenience stores. Withdrawing cash on a debit card costs less than doing it on a credit or charge card. The

American Express charge cards

most common international systems are Cirrus and Plus. Ask both your own bank and credit card company which ATM system your card can access, and how much you will be charged for transactions of differing amounts. Withdrawals from ATMs may provide a better foreign currency exchange rate than cash transactions.

WIRING MONEY

If you need extra cash, it is possible to have money wired from your bank at home in minutes using an electronic money service. Cash can be wired to major bank branches or to any **Western Union**, **Thomas Cook**, or **American Express Moneygram** outlet.

CURRENCY

American currency, based on the decimal system, has 100 cents to the dollar. Bills are all the same size and color, so check the number before paying. Smaller denominations are preferred in small towns and remote gas stations. Large $500–10,000 bills are no longer printed but are still legal tender, usually found in the hands of collectors. The 25-cent piece is useful for public telephones. Always carry cash for tips, public transportation, and taxis.

Wells Fargo Bank, a prominent bank in Las Vegas

Coins

American coins come in 50-, 25-, 10-, 5- and 1-cent pieces. The new gold-tone $1 coins are now in circulation as are the State quarters, which feature an historical scene on one side. Each value of coin has a popular name: 25-cent pieces are called quarters, 10-cent pieces are called dimes, 5-cent pieces called nickels and 1-cent pieces called pennies.

25-cent coin
(a quarter)

10-cent coin
(a dime)

5-cent coin
(a nickel)

1-cent coin
(a penny)

A one-dollar coin
or 'buck'

Bank Notes (Bills)

Units of currency in the United States are dollars and cents. There are 100 cents to a dollar. Notes come in $1, $5, $10, $20, $50 and $100s. The new $10, $20, and $50 bills are now in circulation; security features include subtle colour hues and improved colour-shifting ink in the lower right hand corner of the face of each note.

DIRECTORY

American Express
Moneygram US only
Tel (800) 543-4080.

Check replacement
Tel (800) 221-7282.

Stolen credit and charge cards
Tel (800) 528-4800.

Diner's Club
Check replacement and stolen credit cards
Tel (800) 234-6377.

Thomas Cook (and MasterCard)
Check replacement and stolen credit cards
Tel (800) 223-9920.

VISA
Check replacement
Tel (800) 227-6811.

Stolen credit cards
Tel (800) 336-8472.

Western Union
Wiring money, US
Tel (800) 325-6000.

Wiring money, UK
Tel 0800 833833.

1-dollar bill ($1)

5-dollar bill ($5)

10-dollar bill ($50)

20-dollar bill ($20)

50-dollar bill ($50)

100-dollar bill ($100)

Media and Communications

US mail stamp

Las Vegas is well-connected to the rest of the world and its communication systems are, usually, both efficient and affordably priced. Telephone, mail, and Internet services are all readily available in Las Vegas, providing fast and efficient services to destinations both local and international. The city also has a large supply of public pay phones, although you often have to hunt for them in a casino. In addition, Las Vegas has two daily newspapers and a plethora of visitor magazines that offer information on ongoing and upcoming events, as well as special discount coupons.

AT&T phonecards, available from local stores and vending machines

TELEPHONES

Pay phones are plentiful in Las Vegas and are easy to use with the instructions clearly marked on each phone. All numbers within a local area have seven digits.

To dial long-distance, add a one and the three-digit area code in front of the seven-digit number. The cost of a local call within the same area code is between 35 to 50 cents for three minutes. Long-distance calls are to any number outside the area code you are in and cost less when dialed

direct and at off-peak times, generally in the evenings and at weekends. Be aware that if you use your hotel telephone to make calls you may find you are charged at a much higher rate.

International numbers are preceded by 011, then the country code, followed by the city code (dropping the initial 0), and the number. International calls can be made from a pay phone, but you may need a stack of change to dial direct and will be interrupted by the operator for more money when

your time runs out. It is easier to buy a phonecard from one of the major telephone companies such as **AT&T**. These can be obtained from hotels, convenience stores, and vending machines for up to $50 worth of calls.

USEFUL DIALING CODES

- To make a direct-dial call outside the local area code, but within the US and Canada, dial **1** then the area code.
- The area code of all telephone numbers in Clark County is **702**; this includes Las Vegas, Mount Charleston, Laughlin, Searchlight, and Mesquite. The area code in the rest of Nevada is **775**.
- For international direct-dial calls, dial **011** and the appropriate country code. Then dial the area code, omitting the first 0, and the local number.
- To make an international call via the operator, dial 01 and then follow the same procedure as detailed above.
- For international operator assistance, dial **01**.
- For local operator assistance, dial **0**.
- For international directory inquiries, dial **00**.
- For local directory inquiries, dial **411**.
- For emergency police, fire, or ambulance services, dial **911**.
- **800**, **877**, and **888** indicate a toll-free number.

USING A COIN-OPERATED PHONE

1 Lift the receiver.

2 Insert the necessary coin or coins. The money drops as soon as you insert it.

3 Press the number.

Coins
Make sure you have the correct coins before you dial.

5 cents

10 cents

25 cents

4 If you wish to cancel a call before it connects, or if the call does not get through, you can retrieve the coin(s) by pressing the coin release lever.

5 If the call is answered and you talk longer than the allotted three minutes, the operator will interrupt and ask you to deposit more coins. Pay phones do not give change.

They usually operate by giving you a series of code numbers to punch into the phone, which accesses your account and tells you how much call time you have left before you dial. There are clear instructions on how to use them on each card. If you have any difficulty getting through, call the operator and request to be connected as a collect call (in which case the recipient will be liable for the cost of the call).

Toll-free calls have 1-800, 877, or 888 numbers, and are widely-used in the US, offering free calls to a range of businesses and services such as hotels and car rental companies. If you call from outside the US, you will hear a message explaining how you will actually be charged for the call, at the usual toll rate.

CELL PHONES, E-MAIL, AND FAX SERVICES

Most of the major service providers are represented in Las Vegas, so virtually any cellular phone will function here. These include Sprint, Nextel, Verizon, T-Mobile, Cingular, and AT&T. It is also possible to rent a cell phone by the day or week from stores such as **Bearcom**. Most hotels provide modem outlets or high-speed Internet access in their rooms so guests can hook up with their personal computers. Las Vegas also has a number of Internet cafés such as **Cyber Stop Internet Café**. Faxes can be sent from most hotels, as well as from the post office.

MAIL SERVICES

Within the US, all mail is first class and generally takes between one and five days to arrive. The correct zip (postal) code usually ensures a swifter delivery.

International mail sent by air takes between five and ten days to arrive, but parcels that are sent at the surface parcel rate may take as long as four to six weeks. There are two

special parcel services run by the federal mail – Priority Mail promises faster delivery than normal first class mail, while the more expensive Express Mail guarantees next-day delivery within the US and up to 72 hours delivery for international packages. Several private international delivery services offer swift, next-day delivery for overseas mail, the best known being **DHL** and **Federal Express**.

Like all major cities, Las Vegas also has a main post office and many local offices. If you have the correct value of postage stamps, both letters and parcels can be mailed in any one of the many mailboxes around town. These are generally dark blue and have the collection times posted on them. It is also possible to buy postage stamps from vending machines, convenience stores, and even some hotels.

US mailbox

NEWSPAPERS, TELEVISION, AND RADIO

The best-selling national newspaper, *USA Today*, is popular in Vegas because many hotels offer it free to their guests. For local news, the *Las Vegas Review-Journal* is invaluable. It includes a weekly supplement on Fridays, *Neon*, with entertainment and museum event listings. Magazines such as *Las Vegas Magazine* and *What's On* contain restaurant profiles, show reviews, and shopping guides, as well as many discount coupons.

DIRECTORY

TELECOMMUNICATIONS

AT&T
Tel (212) 387-5400.

CELL PHONE RENTALS

Bearcom
5905 S. Decatur Blvd, 13.
Tel (702) 740-2800.

INTERNET CAFES

Cyber Stop Internet Café
2200 Las Vegas Blvd S.
Map 3 C2.
Tel (702) 736-4782.

POSTAL SERVICES

DHL
Tel (800) 225-5345.
www.dhl.com

Federal Express
Tel (800) 463-3339.
www.fedex.com

Las Vegas Main Post Office
1001E Sunset Rd.
Tel (800) 275-8777.

Las Vegas has several radio stations, including sports, talk, news, and rock stations. The television market in Las Vegas is similar to most major cities – all the major networks are represented here. Most hotels and motels provide at least the network channels, as well as PBS, CNN, and HBO.

Las Vegas Review-Journal, Neon, and other visitor magazines

TRAVEL INFORMATION

Despite its location in a remote part of Mojave Desert, Las Vegas is easily reached by two major highways, Greyhound buses, and several commercial and charter airlines. It is one of the few Southwestern cities that services non-stop international flights. Moreover, the city's position in southern Nevada puts it at the hub of brief stopover commuter flights from Los Angeles, San Francisco, Phoenix, Denver, Kansas City, and other destinations in the western half of the United States. While getting to Las Vegas is easy, traveling around town can prove to be a challenge. Because of Las Vegas's unprecedented growth, which started in the 1990s and continues with no end in sight, the city's streets have become a maze of traffic, gridlock, and road construction. Helping facilitate traveling around town are a large fleet of frenetic cab drivers, a highly efficient and well-laid out municipal bus system, and several monorails.

United Airlines plane

Las Vegas's McCarran International Airport overlooking the Strip

ARRIVING BY AIR

Located south of the city, McCarran International Airport is one of the busiest airports in the US – millions of passengers fly into Las Vegas each year. In addition to servicing about 35 domestic airlines, McCarran accepts direct flights from international carriers, including **American Airlines**, **British Airways**, **AeroMexico**, **Air Canada**, **Japan Airlines**, **Virgin Atlantic**, **Hawaiian Airlines**, and **Philippine Airlines**.

McCARRAN INTERNATIONAL AIRPORT

The traffic at McCarran International Airport includes more than 800 flights a day, with direct flights to nearly 80 cities in the US, Europe, and Asia. Las Vegas is also one of the few non-West Coast cities to offer direct flights to the Hawaiian Islands. Apart from domestic and foreign airlines, the airport is also served by a helicopter service, two commuter lines, and,

The control tower at McCarran International Airport, Las Vegas

depending on the season, up to 20 charter flights.

Because of the rapid growth in Las Vegas air traffic, the airport has undergone several expansions since the early 1990s. Passengers arriving at this well-designed facility should have no problem locating the baggage claim area, even though it is often a long walk from the gate. This area also has the counters of various car rental companies. The Ground Transportation section is situated just outside baggage claim. This is a focal point for taxis, hotel shuttles, city buses, and courtesy shuttles provided by car rental companies.

For travelers with time to spare, McCarran features many attractions such as a fitness center, slot machines, shopping arcade, an art gallery, and an aviation museum.

INTERNATIONAL ARRIVALS

Travelers using the waiver scheme must register online with the Electronic System for Travel Authorization (ESTA) at http://esta.cbp.dhs.gov well in advance of departure. If you are not a US citizen or resident, you must present your passport and visa, along with completed customs declaration forms to immigration officials before claiming your baggage. Adult nonresidents are permitted to bring in a limited amount of duty free goods. These include 0.2 gallons (1 liter) of alcohol, 200 cigarettes, 50 cigars (but not Cuban), and up to $100 worth of gifts. Cash amounts over $10,000 should be declared, but there is no legal limit on the amount of money brought into the US. In addition to providing a direct

Airport official unloading bags from a tourist flight

shuttle service, many of the major Las Vegas hotels will check guests in at the airport.
Travel requirements constantly change, so check what documentation you need before traveling.

AIR FARES

If you are traveling from outside the US, research the market well in advance of your trip, as the least expensive tickets are usually booked early. This is particularly so during busy seasons, which are between June and September, as well as around Thanksgiving and Christmas.

Although there are several travel websites that offer bargains on last-minute bookings, direct flights to Las Vegas are more likely to be booked in advance through an airline or travel agents. The McCarran Airport website offers a list of all the airlines with flights to Las Vegas, along with their phone numbers and web addresses. Travel agents can provide information on the latest bargains and ticket restrictions as well. They may also offer special deals to those booking rental cars, accommodations, and domestic flights in addition to their international tickets. Fly-drive deals, where the cost of the ticket includes car rental are also a low-priced option, as is booking an APEX (Advanced Purchase Excursion) fare, which must be bought at least seven days in advance.

ARRIVING BY CAR

Las Vegas is connected to the rest of the world by two major highways – Interstate 15 and US Highway 95. Heading southwest, I-15 is the major connector to Southern California and the city of Los Angeles, which is about 270 miles (434 km) from Las Vegas. All the major hotels, McCarran International Airport, and the Las Vegas Convention Center have exits along I-15, which also connects the Strip with the downtown area.
Another way to reach Las Vegas from Southern California is to take Interstate 40 across the desert to Needles, California, then proceed north on US 95 to the Colorado River resort town of Laughlin that is situated about 100 miles (161 km) south of Las Vegas.

GREYHOUND BUS

Though it may not be the fastest mode of travel, a

DIRECTORY

AIRPORTS

McCarran International Airport
5757 Wayne Newton Blvd.
Map 3 D5.
Tel (702) 261-5211.
www.mccarran.com

AIRLINE CARRIERS (US CONTACT NUMBERS)

AeroMexico
Tel (800) 237-6639.

Air Canada
Tel (888) 247-2262.

American Airlines
Tel (800) 433-7300.

British Airways
Tel (800) 247-9297.

Japan Airlines
Tel (800) 525-3663

Hawaiian Airlines
Tel (800) 367-5320

US Airways
Tel (800) 428-4322

Virgin Atlantic
Tel (800) 862-8621.

TRAVEL SITES

www.lastminute.com
www.telme.com

BUSES

Greyhound
www.greyhound.com

Greyhound bus provides a relatively inexpensive and often leisurely way to visit Las Vegas. Buses arrive daily from Los Angeles, Phoenix, Salt Lake City, Denver, Reno, and San Diego.

A typical Greyhound bus

Getting Around Las Vegas

A taxi from Whittlesea Blue Cab company

Most of the visitor districts in Las Vegas are concentrated in three areas – the Strip, downtown, and Convention Center district – so it is not necessary to rent a car unless you plan sightseeing excursions to the outlying areas. The city's transportation, which includes a municipal bus system, monorail, and elevated trams, is an efficient and inexpensive (often free) way to commute among the various resorts and other tourist attractions. Taxis are plentiful and can be found at most casinos and hotels.

Monorail linking various hotels along the Strip

CITIZENS AREA TRANSIT (CAT)

The Las Vegas transit authority, CAT, operates about 51 scheduled bus routes throughout the city. Most of these begin operations at 4:30am and continue running till 1am. Some routes – including services to the airport, along the Convention Center corridor on Paradise Road, and the busy Strip to downtown route – operate 24 hours a day. All buses feature bicycle racks and hydraulic lifts for wheelchair-users. Bus fares are inexpensive – $1.75 each way on all residential routes and $3 on the Strip buses. Seniors above the age of 62 and youngsters between the ages of five and 17 can ride for half-fare, while children less than five years old ride free. A reduced rate ID card is required for these special fares. Frequent riders can purchase a 30-day pass, which is good for unlimited riding.

ELEVATED TRAMS AND MONORAIL

Free elevated trams operate between certain hotels – one links the Excalibur, Luxor, and Mandalay hotels, while another connects the Mirage and Treasure Island resorts.

The Las Vegas Monorail runs mainly on the east side of the Strip along a 3.9 mile (6.3 km) route which extends from the Sahara to the MGM Grand. There are seven stations on the system: the MGM Grand; Bally's/Paris Las Vegas; Flamingo/Caesars Palace; Harrah's/Imperial Palace; Las Vegas Convention Center; Las Vegas Hilton; and the Sahara. It takes 15 minutes to travel the length of the Strip in a safe and comfortable environment. It is the first driverless public monorail system in the world and can reach speeds of up to 50 mph (80 km/h). Single ride tickets cost $5, an all-day pass is $13, and three-day passes for unlimited rides are $28. The monorail's hours of operation are from 7am to 2am Monday to Thursday and from 7am to 3am Friday to Sunday.

WALKING

Walking may well be the best way to travel along the 3-mile (5-km) long Strip and the downtown area. The sidewalks here are wide and the terrain is flat so you will not have to tackle any hilly areas during your outing. Walking also offers you the option of exploring the major sights and shopping areas without worrying about the traffic or spending time searching for a parking place.

BICYCLING

Las Vegas is not a very bike-friendly city. The traffic can be congested and snarly. Though bicycling along the main arteries is not advised, riding through the residential neighborhoods and in outlying areas, such as Red Rock Canyon and Lake Mead, can be very pleasant and scenic. Be sure to wear a safety helmet when cycling. There are various outlets that provide bicycles to rent. The fee usually includes helmets and water bottles.

The Deuce service operates 24 hours a day

Cars lined up at an intersection along the Las Vegas Strip

DRIVING

Vehicles are driven on the right-hand side of the road in the US, except on one-way streets *(see p188)*. If driving in town, be prepared for heavy traffic and fast driving. Avoid heading out during the rush hours, from about 7 to 9am and 4 to 7pm. Congestion on the Strip begins late morning and continues until after midnight, especially on weekends and during large special events.

PARKING

Most of the hotels and casinos on the Strip and in downtown provide free parking in high-rise garages, and almost all hotels offer valet parking services. However, when valet parking is full, preference is usually given to hotel guests over casino visitors.

The city also has many huge parking lots and garages. When parking on the street, be sure to read all the posted signs about parking restrictions to avoid incurring fines or having your vehicle towed away. The fine for parking in a disability-reserved space without a valid placard can range from $100 to $1,000.

TAXIS

Taxis are plentiful in Las Vegas – the city has more than 1,200 of them – but they are usually clustered around the hotels, Convention Center, and airport. It is often difficult to flag one, so call ahead if you need one. The basic rate is $3.30 for the first mile plus 53 cents for each additional 0.2 miles and 48 cents a minute when waiting at a red light. There is no charge for extra riders, but the maximum per cab is five people. On average, a taxi ride from the airport to the Strip costs about $15–20, and $20–25 from the airport to downtown. In heavy traffic, it can cost more than $20 to go from one end of the Strip to the other. All cabs companies in Vegas have handicap accessible vehicles. The city's main operators are **Yellow Checker Star Transportation**, **Whittlesea Blue Cab**, and **Desert Cab**.

LIMOUSINES

Perhaps the ultimate Las Vegas travel experience is the limousine. It is possible to rent a range of these vehicles, including stretch and super-stretch versions that are fitted out with a cocktail bar, stereo, TV, telephone, moon roof, and even a Jacuzzi. The average cost for a limo and driver starts at $40 to $46 an hour, a

stretch limo will cost from $54 to $60, while a superstretch will cost about $80 an hour. There are many limo operators in Las Vegas, including **Bell Trans, Presidential Limousines, Las Vegas Limousines**, and **24-7 Entertainment Limousines**. Several wedding chapels and hotels also offer limo service to their clients and guests.

DIRECTORY

USEFUL NUMBERS

Citizens Area Transit
300 North Casino Center.
Tel (702) 228-7433.
www.rtcsnv.com

Las Vegas Monorail
3960 Howard Hughes Pkwy.
Map 4 D3.
Tel (702) 699-8200.
www.lvmonorail.com

TAXIS

Desert Cab
Tel (702) 386-9102.

Yellow Checker Star Transportation
Tel (702) 873-2000.

Whittlesea Blue Cab
Tel (702) 384-6111.

LIMOUSINE SERVICES

24-7 Entertainment Limousines
4200 W Russell Rd. **Map** 3 A5.
Tel (702) 616-6000.
www.24-7limousines.com

Bell Trans
1900 Industrial Rd. **Map** 1 C5.
Tel (702) 739-7990.
www.bell-trans.com

Las Vegas Limousines
5010 S Valley View Blvd.
Map 3 B4. *Tel (702) 736-1419.*
www.lasvegaslimo.com

Presidential Limousines
2030 Industrial Rd. **Map** 1 C5.
Tel (702) 731-5577.
www.presidentiallimov.com

Stretch limo from NewYork-NewYork

Traveling Outside Las Vegas

Gas pump

Many visitors are surprised to learn of the numerous sights and attractions located just a short distance from the bright lights of Las Vegas. The panoramic wilderness of southern Utah, California, and Arizona surrounds the city and forms a landscape filled with awe-inspiring canyons and parks, such as Grand Canyon and Zion National Park. As public transportation to these destinations is limited, renting a vehicle is often necessary. In any case, the best way to see these picturesque locations is by car since the entire area is served by a network of well-maintained roads, from multi-lane highways to scenic routes.

state and can be altered because of ongoing construction or weather conditions. The highway patrol in Nevada, California, and other states are in charge of enforcing the highway laws and speeding violations are usually accompanied by a strict fine. Also note that drivers can be cited for driving too slowly on the interstates. The most serious offense, however, is driving under the influence of alcohol or other substances. Heavy penalties are exacted from those who violate these laws. Moreover, it is illegal to pass a stationary school bus.

Pay attention to road signs, especially in remote areas where they may issue warnings about local hazards. You can get more information on US driving rules from your car rental agency or the **American Automobile Association** (AAA). For instance, you can turn right on a red light if there is no oncoming traffic, and the first vehicle to reach a four-way Stop sign junction has the right of way. Americans also drive on the right.

Travelers can also obtain maps and travel guides from the AAA and other agencies.

A rental car driving through Red Rock Canyon, near Las Vegas

INTERSTATES AND HIGHWAYS

Driving northeast from Las Vegas along the I-15 leads to the Valley of Fire State Park, the border town of Mesquite, Nevada, and St. George, Utah, about 95 miles (153 km) from Las Vegas. Close to Mesquite are the magnificent national parks of southern Utah, Dixie National Forest, and the quaint town of Cedar Springs, home to the annual Utah Shakespearean Festival, held each year in late summer.

Traveling south on US 95 takes visitors to Lake Mead, Hoover Dam, and Boulder City, about 30 miles (48 km) from Las Vegas. Driving north on US 95 leads to Tonopah, Reno, and Lake Tahoe, about 450 miles (724 km) from Las Vegas, and the Northern California cities of Sacramento, Stockton, and San Francisco.

Many hamlets and towns along this way offer tourists a taste of the Wild West.

For the Grand Canyon, travel east on US 93 till you reach the city of Kingman and then US highways 40 and 64 to the canyon's national park. The South Rim of the canyon, which is easier to access via road than the North Rim, is a five-hour drive from Las Vegas.

RULES OF THE ROAD

The major highways leading into and out of Las Vegas are known as either freeways or interstates. Highway speed limits vary from state to state, but in no instance are speeds in excess of 75 mph (120 km/h) permitted. Cars that pull trailers or campers are restricted to 55 mph (90 km/h). Always be aware of the posted speed limits because they will vary from state to

Speed limit
(in mph)

Rest area
indicated off an
Interstate

Wildlife
warning

Stop at
intersection

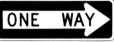

Traffic flows in a single direction

Traffic signs
A range of different traffic signs offer warnings and instructions to drivers, and should be adhered to.

Gas service station on the way to Grand Canyon

GAS AND SERVICE STATIONS

Gas prices are less in US than in Europe, though the cost took a hike in 2005 and 2008. Generally, costs are higher at remote locations than in the heart of the city. Most gas stations are self-service, in which case it is usual to pay before filling up. Service station attendants have become a rarity in the US, so do not expect a gas station to provide maintenance services such as oil, transmission fluid, and the like. Be sure to fill your tank before driving across remote areas.

Backcountry byway sign

BACKCOUNTRY DRIVING

For exploring any of the remote wilderness areas surrounding Las Vegas, it is important to check if a four-wheel-drive vehicle is required. Many of the backcountry areas can be accessed only by "fire roads," which are unpaved or dirt roads. Maintenance agencies, such as the US Forest Service at Mount Charleston and the Bureau of Land Management at Red Rock Canyon, can provide maps and tips for drivers.

There are basic safety points to be observed on any trip of this kind. Plan your route and carry up-to-date maps. If you are traveling between remote locations, let the park warden or caretaker know about your itinerary. Check the road conditions before you start by calling the **Nevada Highway Patrol**, and be aware of seasonal dangers such as flash floods, which can occur with little warning in the southern Nevada desert. Native flora and fauna are protected in most areas and should not be removed or damaged.

Do not drive off-road unless in a specially-designated area, and if you are in an RV, you must stop overnight in designated campgrounds.

RENTAL CARS

Visitors from abroad must have a full driver's license that has been issued for at least a year before the date of travel. International driving licenses are not necessary, but they can be helpful if your license is in a script other than Roman. Although it is legal to rent a car to those over the age of 21, some rental companies charge extra to those under 25. It is also essential to have a credit card to pay the rental deposit as few companies are willing to accept cash deposit. There are many car rental companies in Las Vegas. Most of the major businesses such as **Alamo**, **Avis**, **Enterprise**, and **Hertz**, and some of the lower-priced dealers, such as **Budget** and **Thrifty Auto** have outlets at the airport and at most major hotels as well. Rental rates vary but the average price for an economy car

Hertz car-rental logo

DIRECTORY

USEFUL NUMBERS

American Automobile Association
4100 E Arkansas Dr,
Denver, CO 80222.
Tel (303) 753-8800.
www.aaa.com

Nevada Highway Patrol
Tel (702) 486-4100.

CAR RENTAL AGENCIES

Alamo
Tel (702) 263-8411/(800) 327-9633. www.alamo.com

Avis
Tel (702) 531-1500/(800) 331-1212. www.avis.com

Budget
Tel (702) 736-1212/(888) 724-6212. www.budget.com

Enterprise
Tel (702) 795-8842/(800) 736-8222. www.enterprise.com

Hertz
Tel (702) 262-7700/(800) 654-3131. www.hertz.com

Thrifty Auto Rental
Tel (702) 896-7600/(800) 847-4389. www.thrifty.com

runs in the $41 to $49 a day range. Added to the rental rate are an airport surcharge, sales tax, and license tag fee. For an extra $20 to $23 you can purchase the collision damage waiver, which saves you from being charged for any visible defects on the car. Besides larger, more comfortable vehicles and SUVs, travelers can also opt for a BMW, Mercedes, Ferrari, or even a Rolls Royce. Be prepared to pay handsomely as these cars command a rent of $89–3,500 a day. If you are traveling in summer, air conditioning is a necessity. Most rental cars have automatic transmission. Child seats or cars for disabled drivers must be arranged in advance.

LAS VEGAS STREET FINDER

The map references given in this guide for all sights, hotels, casinos, restaurants, shops, and entertainment venues refer to the Street Finder maps on the following pages. The map below shows the area of Las Vegas covered by the four Street Finder maps, including the sightseeing areas, which are color-coded. The key, set out below, indicates the scale of the maps and shows what other features are marked on them, including post offices, bus stations, monorails, tourist information centers, police stations, and hospitals. An index of the street names can be found on the opposite page.

Glittering lights and a busy cross-section of streets along the Las Vegas Strip

SCALE OF MAPS 1–2

| 0 meters | 800 |
| 0 yards | 800 |

SCALE OF MAPS 3–4

| 0 meters | 800 |
| 0 yards | 800 |

KEY TO STREET FINDER

	Major sight
	Minor sight
	Other building
✈	International airport
	Las Vegas Monorail
	Free monorail
	Bus station
P	Parking
	Tourist information
	Hospital
	Police station
⊠	Post office
⋯	Expressway
	Pedestrian way
	Monorail route

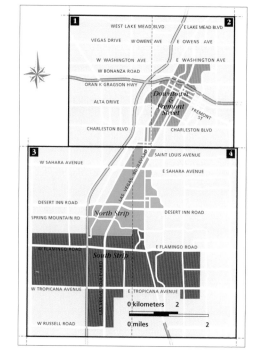

Street Finder Index

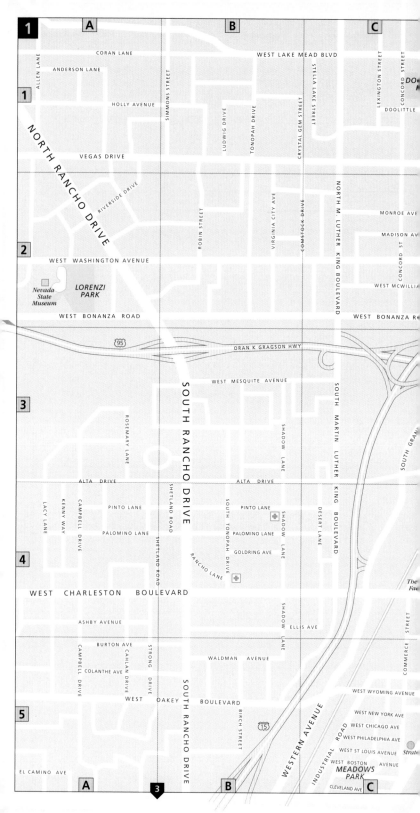

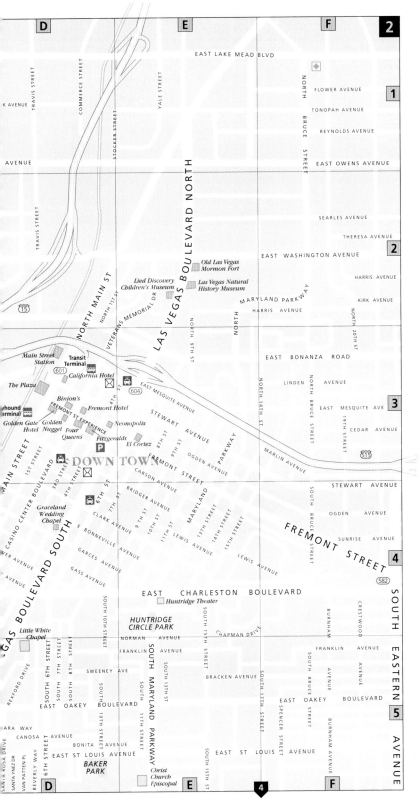

D · E · F · 2

EAST LAKE MEAD BLVD

1

K AVENUE
FLOWER AVENUE
NORTH
TONOPAH AVENUE
BRUCE
REYNOLDS AVENUE
STREET

TRAVIS STREET
COMMERCE STREET
STOCKER STREET
YALE STREET

AVENUE
EAST OWENS AVENUE

SEARLES AVENUE

THERESA AVENUE

2
TRAVIS STREET
LAS VEGAS BOULEVARD NORTH
EAST WASHINGTON AVENUE

HARRIS AVENUE

Old Las Vegas
Mormon Fort
Lied Discovery
Children's Museum
Las Vegas Natural
History Museum
MARYLAND PARKWAY
KIRK AVENUE

NORTH MAIN ST
NORTH 15TH ST
VETERANS MEMORIAL DR
NORTH 9TH ST
NORTH
HARRIS AVENUE
NORTH 20TH ST

15

EAST BONANZA ROAD

LINDEN
NORTH 14TH ST
AVENUE
NORTH BRUCE STREET

Main Street
Station
Transit
Terminal
EAST MESQUITE AVE
19TH STREET

601
California Hotel
604
EAST MESQUITE AVENUE
CEDAR AVENUE

The Plaza
STEWART AVENUE
MARYLAND PARKWAY
MARLIN AVENUE

3
Binion's
hound
rminal
FREMONT ST EXPERIENCE
Fremont Hotel
615

Golden Gate
Hotel
Golden
Nugget
Four
Queens
Neonopolis
STEWART AVENUE

Fitzgeralds
El Cortez
8TH ST
9TH ST
OGDEN AVENUE
SOUTH BRUCE STREET
OGDEN AVENUE

DOWN TOWN
FREMONT STREET
CARSON AVENUE
SUNRISE AVENUE

FREMONT STREET

4
MAIN STREET
1ST STREET
3RD STREET
4TH STREET
6TH ST
Graceland
Wedding
Chapel
BRIDGER AVENUE
CLARK AVENUE
7TH ST
9TH ST
10TH ST
MARYLAND STREET
13TH STREET
14TH STREET
15TH STREET
582

CASINO CENTER BOULEVARD
E BONNEVILLE AVENUE
11TH ST
LEWIS AVENUE
LEWIS AVENUE

ER AVENUE
GARCES AVENUE
GAS STREET

AVENUE
GAS BOULEVARD SOUTH
EAST CHARLESTON BOULEVARD

Huntridge Theater
BURNHAM
CRESTWOOD
SOUTH

HUNTRIDGE
CIRCLE PARK
SOUTH 10TH STREET
CHAPMAN DRIVE
EASTERN

Little White
Chapel
NORMAN AVENUE
SOUTH 15TH STREET
FRANKLIN AVENUE
SOUTH 17TH STREET
AVENUE

5
REXFORD DRIVE
SOUTH 6TH STREET
SOUTH 7TH STREET
SOUTH 8TH STREET
FRANKLIN AVENUE
SWEENEY AVE
SOUTH 13TH ST
BRACKEN AVENUE
SOUTH BRUCE STREET
SPENCER STREET
BURNHAM AVENUE
AVENUE

SOUTH MARYLAND PARKWAY
SOUTH 11TH STREET
EAST OAKEY BOULEVARD
EAST OAKEY BOULEVARD

ARA WAY
CANOSA AVENUE
BONITA AVENUE
EAST ST LOUIS AVENUE

SANTA ROSA DRIVE
SANTA YNEZ DR
VAN PATTEN PL
BEVERLY WAY
6TH STREET
10TH STREET
SOUTH 15TH ST
EAST ST LOUIS AVENUE

BAKER
PARK
Christ
Church
Episcopal

D · E · F

4

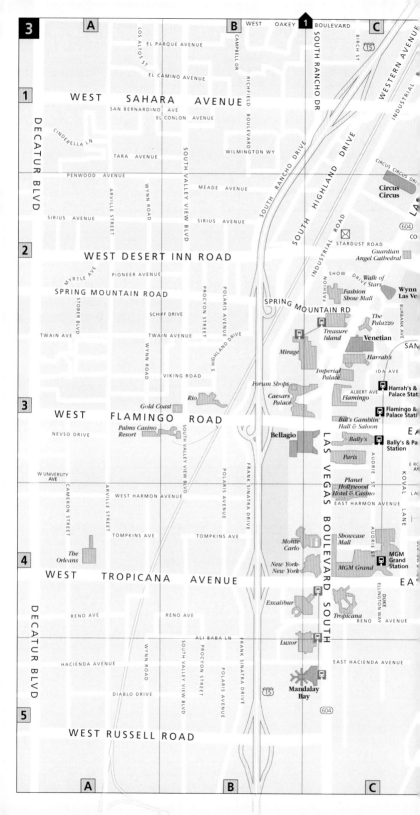

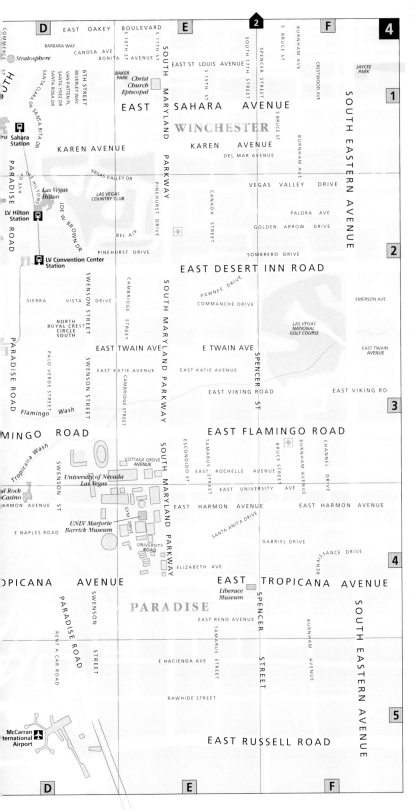

General Index

Acknowledgments

Main Contributors

David Stratton is a freelance writer based in Las Vegas. A former newspaper editor in Las Vegas and Southern California, David has authored several Las Vegas travel guides. His magazine articles about Las Vegas have appeared in the *Los Angeles Times, National Geographic Traveler*, and *Travel Agent* magazine.

Factcheckers

Bob Barnes, Paul Franklin, Rebecca Ingram, Nancy Mikula.

Proofreader

Word-by-Word.

Indexer

Jyoti Dhar.

Additional Illustrations

Jo Cameron.

Additional Photography

Demetrio Carrasco, Andy Crawford, Philip Gatwad, Alan Keohane, Dave King, Tim Mann, Clive Streeter, Scott Suchman, Mathew Ward, Stephen Whitehorn, Linda Whitwam, Francesca Yorke.

DK London

Publisher

Douglas Amrine.

Publishing Manager

Lucinda Cooke.

Managing Art Editor

Kate Poole.

Senior Designer

Tessa Bindloss.

Senior Cartographic Editor

Casper Morris.

Senior DTP Designer

Jason Little.

DK Picture Library

Martin Copeland, Hayley Smith, Romaine Werblow, Gemma Woodward.

Production Controller

Louise Daly.

Design and Editorial Assistance

Emma Anacootee, Bob Barnes, Connie Emerson, Anna Freiberger, Rhiannon Furbear, Vinod Harish, Vicki Ingle, Claire Jones, Laura Jones, Delphine Lawrance, Carly Madden, Sam Merrell, Kate Molan, Catherine Palmi, Collette Sadler, Azeem A. Siddiqui, Susana Smith, Ros Walford.

Special Assistance

Many thanks for the invaluable help of the following individuals and organizations: Debbie Munch at Caesars Entertainment; Madeleine Weekley at Harrah's Entertainment; Las Vegas Convention & Visitors Authority; Las Vegas News Bureau; Alan Feldman at MGM MIRAGE; Nevada Commission on Tourism.

Photography Permissions

Dorling Kindersley would like to thank the following for their assistance and kind permission to photograph at their establishments:

Bill Johnson at Atomic Research Museum (Desert Research Institute); Stacy Solovey, Deanna Pettit and Debbie Munch at Caesars Entertainment Inc.; Antionette Correia at Circus Circus, Las Vegas; Desert Inn; Fashion Show Mall; Nancy Archer at Fremont Hotel & Casino; Lisa Robinson at Fremont Street Experience; Susan Essex at Gold Coast Hotel & Casino; Sylke Neal-Finnegan at Golden Nugget Hotel; Deidra Duffy at Graceland Wedding Chapel; Alissa Kelly at Hard Rock Hotel & Casino, Las Vegas; Karen Cowen at Hoover Dam Bureau of Reclamation; Jeremy Handel at Imperial Palace Hotel & Casino; Las Vegas Natural History Museum; Alexandra Goranseon at Las Vegas Outlet Center; Jamie James at Liberace Museum; Madame Tussaud's, London; Main Street Station; Kimberly Barraclough at Mandalay Resort Group; Teri McGeachy at Marjorie Barrick Museum of Natural History; Christi Braginton at MGM MIRAGE; Brandy Payne at Neonopolis; Greta Brunschwyler at Nevada State Museum; Nicole Favorito at New Frontier Hotel & Casino; Brian Albertson at Palms Hotel & Casino; Red Rock Canyon National Conservation Area; Lisa Sanders and Jim Sea-grave at Stardust Resort & Casino; Lisa Keim at Tropicana Resort & Casino; Martha Sandez at The Venetian, Las Vegas; Ron DeCar at Viva Las Vegas; Jeffrey M. Gloeb and Kimberley Ryan at Wynn Las Vegas.

Dorling Kindersley would also like to thank all the churches, museums, hotels, restaurants, cafés, shops, galleries, national and state parks, and other sights too numerous to mention individually, who aided us with our photography.

Placement Key – t=top; tl=top left; tlc=top left center; tc=top center; trc=top right center; tr=top right; cla=center left above; ca=center above; cra=center right above; cl=center left; c=center; cr=center right; clb=center left below; cb=center below; crb=center right below; bl=bottom left; b=bottom; bc=bottom center; bcl=bottom center left; br=bottom right; d=detail.

Works of art have been reproduced with the permission of the following copyright holders:

Courtesy of THE MUSEUM OF CHURCH HISTORY AND ART: *The Handcart Pioneers* by C.C.A. Christensen © by Intellectual Reserve, Inc. 18t; courtesy of THE DONNA BEAM FINE ART GALLERY "From the Studio of Tony Curtis Exhibition:" 87br.

The publishers are grateful to the following individuals, companies, and picture libraries for their permission to reproduce their photographs:

ALAMY: EuroStyle Graphics 33bl; THE ATTIC: Sophye Wagner 140br.
BLUE MAN GROUP: Ken Howard 142bl.
© CAESARS ENTERTAINMENT, INC.: 14c, 28ca, 39clb, 46br, 50tc, 89br, 110br, 123tl, 143tl, 145tl, 148b, 151tl; CHAPEL OF THE FLOWERS: Adam Shane 29cb; CIRCUS CIRCUS LAS VEGAS: 65tl; © CIRQUE DU SOLEIL INC.: costumes Dominique Lemieux photo Al Seib © 1999 15clb, © 2000 142cra, © 2003 144cl, Tomasz Rossa 144br; CORBIS: 9 (inset), 12cla, 76cra, 92–3, 105tr, 164tr; Tom Bean 94tr, 97br; Patrick Bennett 185cl; Bettmann 19tc, 19br, 20tr, 20cla, 20cl, 20bl, 21tr, 21crb, 21clb, 22tr, 22clb, 22bl, 26cla, 26br, 27bc, 175 (inset), 184tc; D. Boone 163bl; David Butow 171tl; Joseph Sohm, ChromoSohm Inc. 17br; Richard Cummins 63cl, 69cra, 190ca; EPA/ Julian Smith 27tl; Robert Essel 23cb; Chris Farina 26clb, 30cra, 154tc, 157cb; Eye Ubiquito, Laurence Fordyce 32cra; Werner Forman 17bl; Marc Garanger 106cl; Mark E. Gibson 24; Gunter Marx Photography 105bc; Robert Holmes 45tc; Dave G. Houser 83tl; Ann Johansson 33cra, 168br; Dewitt Jones 17ca; Catherine Karnow 49bl; Michael Keller 1 (inset); Richard Klune 41cr; Bob Krist 2–3; Lake County Museum 8–9, 16, 19crb, 19bc, 20–21c; Lester Lefkowitz 83bl; James Marshall 32bl; David Muench 99cra; Douglas Peebles 28bl; PictureNet 73tr; Roger Ressmeyer 69br; SABA David Butow 163cra; Scott T. Smith 95tl; Ron Watts 96cl; Katy Winn 27crb; Michael S. Yamashita 68cb; CRAZY SHIRTS INC.: 46c, 137c.
EL CORTEZ HOTEL & CASINO: Erin O'Boyle 76tl; EXCALIBUR HOTEL & CASINO: 42br, 122tc, 161tr, 170bl. PAUL FRANKLIN: 98br, 101tr.
Courtesy of GET BOOKED: 152br; © GOLD COAST HOTEL & CASINO: 47br, 161br; Courtesy of GOLDEN NUGGET LAS VEGAS: 71tr, 74–5, 111tl; GRACELAND WEDDING CHAPEL: 76bc; THE GRANGER COLLECTION, NEW YORK: 93 (inset).
HARD ROCK HOTEL: 148cl; HARRAH'S ENTERTAINMENT:

14bl; 151bl; HOOVER DAM: 25bc; SEAN HUNTER: 95bc.
LAS VEGAS NEWS BUREAU/LVCVA: 11tr, 21bc, 63tc, 64tl, 97cra, 122cl, 134cl, 135tl, 135bl, 138cl, 138br, 159tl, 166cl, 168tl, 168c, 169tl, 172tl, Bob Brye 54tr; Darrin Bush 15br; Brian Jones 145br; 186br; Glenn Pinkerton 62bc, 153tr; LONELY PLANET IMAGES: Richard Cummins 29tc, 40tl, 40tr; Ray Laskowitz 81tc, 146tl, 152cla, 155br.
© MANDALAY RESORT GROUP: 11br, 38cla; MARY EVANS PICTURE LIBRARY: 35 (inset), 109 (inset); MASTERFILE: DK & Dennie Cody 190tc, Steve Craft 34–5, 174–5; courtesy of MGM MIRAGE: 10br, 25cla, 28cl, 33c, 36, 44bc, 48tl, 48tr, 48bc, 51br, 54ca, 57t, 122br, 143b, 144cl, 150cl, 166b, 167tl, 167bc; MONTE CARLO RESORT & CASINO: 162tr.
OSCAR EINZIG PHOTOGRAPHY: 31b.
PETER NEWARK PICTURES: 18bc; PHOTOLIBRARY.COM: 153cb.
STEVE REYES: 178bl; RIVIERA HOTEL AND CASINO: 55cb, 62tl; REUTERS: Ethan Miller 30bl.
STARCHIP ENTERPRISE: 30tc.
TLC Casinos: 71bc; © TROPICANA RESORT & CASINO: 123br.
UNLV PHOTO SERVICES: Geri Kodey 84, 149tl; UNLV Special Collection 18c.
Courtesy of THE VENETIAN, LAS VEGAS: 52.
WELLS FARGO BANK: 180br; WYNN LAS VEGAS: 150cb; Ferrari of North America 61cr; Robert Miller 60tr; Bill Milne 60b, 61tr.
Front endpaper: All DK images except CORBIS: cl; MGM MIRAGE: br; The Venetian: cr.

Jacket
Front – DK IMAGES: Andy Crawford clb; GETTY IMAGES: Adam Jones main image.
Back – DK IMAGES: Sean Hunter cla; Greg Ward tl, clb; ALAMY IMAGES: Glen Allison bl.
Spine – DK IMAGES: Alan Keohane b; GETTY IMAGES: Adam Jones t.

All other images © Dorling Kindersley. For further information: see www.dkimages.com.

SPECIAL EDITIONS OF DK TRAVEL GUIDES

DK Travel Guides can be purchased in bulk quantities at discounted prices for use in promotions or as premiums. We are also able to offer special editions and personalized jackets, corporate imprints, and excerpts from all of our books, tailored specifically to meet your own needs.

To find out more, please contact:
(in the United States) **SpecialSales@dk.com**
(in the UK) **TravelSpecialSales@uk.dk.com**
(in Canada) DK Special Sales at **general@tourmaline.ca**
(in Australia) **business.development@pearson.com.au**

Las Vegas Transport Map

104-208 WEST WASHINGTON AVENUE

103

104

207

95

402

101-207

207

ORAN K. GRAGSON HWY

207

ALTA DRIVE

207

402

ALT

104

W CHA

206

206

101

102

103

104

WEST OAKEY BOULEVARD

SOUTH DECATUR

WEST OA

204

204

SOUTH VALLEY VIEW

BOULEVARD

TENAYA WAY

SOUTH RAINBOW BLVD

SOUTH TORREY PINES DRIVE

SOUTH JONES BOULEVARD

WEST SAHARA AVENUE

213

104-213

101

102

103-213

BOULEVARD

213

WEST DESERT INN

203

203

SPRING MOUNTAIN ROAD

WEST FLAMINGO ROAD

202

202

201

101

102

103

104

WEST HARMON AVENUE

KEY

202 CAT bus route

··· Monorail route

🚊 Las Vegas monorail

🚊 Free monorail

Major sight

Highway

201

201

WEST TROPICANA AVENUE

201

SOUTH JONES BLVD

102

SOUTH DECATUR BLVD

103

104

HACIENDA AVENUE

0 kilometers   1

0 miles   1